about . . . "Barefoot in the Rubble"

"Barefoot in the Rubble . . . tells a story that needs to be heard; one of overcoming great odds, of taking risks, of reunitement with family, and of, at last, freedom."
—Barbara Kranig
National President, American Legion Auxiliary

"Barefoot in the Rubble is an articulate and engaging memoir that is candid, insightful, and a testament to the endurance of the human spirit in even the most inhumane of circumstances."
—Midwest Book Review

Comments from readers, young and old . . .

"You hold a lot of history in your memories and by publishing your new book, people will know what happened so the history is passed on."

"I liked all the stories that you told. Some were funny, some were touching, and some were scary."

"You said that people wondered why you were writing your book now, after so many years have passed since these things happened to you. You wrote it for someone like me."

"I wanted to let you know that your book has really touched my heart and has made me so much more thankful for what I have."

In memory of

My grandparents
Peter and Katharina Schüssler

My cousins
Marie Pletitsch
Anna Weipert
Elsa Schüssler

My husband's family:

His great-grandmother
Margarethe Kartje

His grandmother
Elisabeth Kartje

His grandfather
Michael Walter

His sister
Angela Walter

and all other victims of the Marshall Tito Regime.

Barefoot in the Rubble

Elizabeth B. Walter

REVISED EDITION

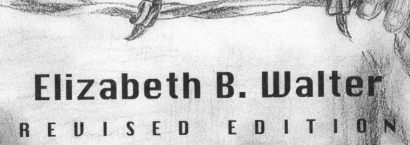

Pannonia Press
P.O. Box 1062
Palatine, Illinois 60078-1062

First Printing, 1997
©Copyright 1997 Elizabeth B. Walter
2nd Printing, 1998
Revised Paperback Edition, ©2000
All rights reserved.

Printed and Designed by Award Printing Corporation
Chicago, Illinois 60639

Illustration by E. Walter

Library of Congress Control #00 131063

ISBN 0-9657793-1-9

Printed in U.S.A.

Acknowledgment

I thank my family, and friends for their help and support to enable me to write and complete this book.

Most of all I thank my husband, Mike, who stood at my side listening, reading and encouraging me. Without him this book would never have been published.

History

I n the late seventeenth century, the Austro-Hungarian Empire re
covered its Hungarian domains by defeating the Ottoman Turks.
The Ottoman Empire had occupied the region for 150 years. Fearful that the Ottoman Turks would regain control of the area, the Austrian
Imperial Council launched a great colonization scheme to settle the recovered lands with loyal subjects. Promising land in exchange for hard
work, the Austrian Empire encouraged German-speaking people from
southwestern Germany, northeastern France and Switzerland to cultivate the region.

Since no roads linked Central Europe to Eastern Europe, the new
settlers traveled down the Danube by barge. More than 1,000 farming
communities and numerous homesteads were settled in the Danubian
Plain in what later became Hungary, Romania and Yugoslavia. The two
largest areas they settled became known as Banat and Batschka. The
German-speaking settlers became known as Danube-Swabians. (*Danube*,
because they had traveled the Danube and settled its plain, and–*Swabian*,
because their port of departure had been in Ulm, Swabia.)

The "Schwowe", as the Danube-Swabians called themselves, lived in
harmony with their Hungarian, Romanian, Serbian and Croatian neighbors.
Their hard work turned the wastelands of the former Ottoman Empire into
the breadbasket of Europe. They built their towns according to the speci-
fications of the Austro-Hungarian Monarchy, with unusually wide streets,
whitewashed houses and a Baroque-style church at the center.

Karlsdorf, the town where this story begins, was just such a town.

The Austro-Hungarian Empire became disbanded at the end of World
War I. Life for the Danube-Swabians in Karlsdorf and other parts of the newly
formed country of Yugoslavia went on much as it had before the war.

However, the end of World War II spelled disaster for Yugoslavia's
537,000 Danube-Swabians. Tito's communist government declared ethnic Germans "enemies of the state." Danube-Swabians lost all their rights
and property. Worse yet, those who did not flee Yugoslavia were forced
into concentration camps. Tens of thousands died in this, Yugoslavia's
first ethnic cleansing.

This book contains the story of one family who managed to survive.

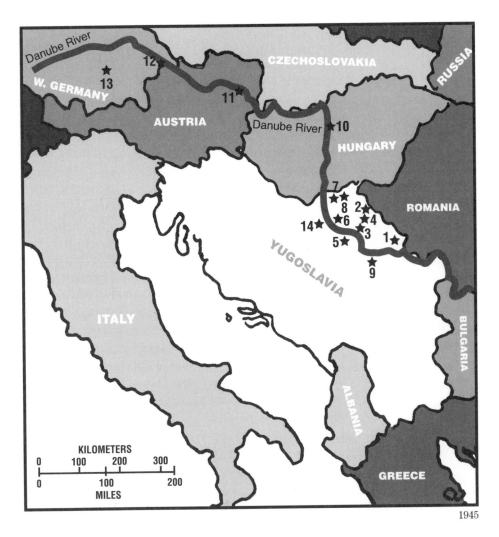

1945

1 Karlsdorf	6 Novoselo	11 Vienna
2 Ruskodorf	7 Gakowa	12 Passau
3 Rudolfsgnad	8 Kruschevlje	13 Munich
4 Molidorf	9 Belgrade	14 Vukovar
5 Mitrovitza	10 Budapest	

Foreword

Americans, like many peoples, view their history, and the history of others, through a patriotic prism. To do otherwise is to risk shame, as well as enlightenment. A good example is the popular success of yet another book celebrating the Louisiana Purchase, and the ascent and descent of the Missouri River by two white men and their entourage in 1803–1806 (Steven E. Ambrose, *Undaunted Courage: Meriwether Lewis, Thomas Jefferson, and the Opening of the American West*). The author, however, has nary a word for Toussaint L'Ouverture, the black man whose undaunted courage, coupled with brilliant generalship, destroyed the Imperial ambitions of both Britain and France for San Domingo, and forced Napoleon to sell the land that became the heart of the American Midwest. To mention the valiant Haitian would have brought up issues of slavery and racism which confound the self-image that Americans celebrate on July 4 of every year. Or perhaps Professor Ambrose was merely ignorant of the geopolitical realities of the French Revolution and its impact on the Caribbean, as well as the United States. The latter possibility is embarrassing for any historian, but far less shameful.

The same patriotic prism, which long has maligned and neglected African-Americans, has been used selectively and, often, vindictively with respect to German-Americans since our country went to war with Imperial Germany in 1917. These "Keepers of the Patriotic Flame" can be found in the classroom, the media, or in most any walk of

American life. If they have any historical or geographical knowledge, they tend to refight World War II or World War I. If the "flame keepers" lack specific knowledge, they rely on the studied ignorance that stereotypes provide. Unfortunately, there is no room in a head filled with such stereotypes for an ordinary German-speaking victim of World War II. A Jew? Certainly. A Pole? Perhaps. An Italian? If he or she were in the resistance, maybe...

With a country so successfully self-brainwashed, it is no surprise that Elizabeth Walter ran into a High School English teacher in the 1950s whose head had no room for information about Danube Swabians who ended up in Tito's concentration camps. The situation has not changed much in 40 years. There is room for an alleged "good German" like Steven Spielberg's Oskar Schindler, or even the bumbling Colonel Klink and Sergeant Schultz of "Hogan's Heroes" reruns, but these were all men cast in titular authority, not ordinary Germans. Erich Remarque's Paul Bäumer, Willi Heinrich's Corporal Steiner, and the crew of *Das Boot*, of course, were all ordinary Germans, but they were soldiers or sailors with weapons in their hands. America's patriotic prism continues to filter out any images of "Germans-as-victims," preferring only "Germans-as-perpetrators." Thus the "Ordinary Men" of Yad Vashem scholar Christopher Browning's *Reserve Police Battalion 101 and the Final Solution in Poland* become "Ordinary Germans and the Holocaust" in Harvard Professor Daniel Goldhagen's *Hitler's Willing Executioners;* and ordinary *Volksdeutsche* are labeled *Himmler's Auxiliaries* in the title of an otherwise well-balanced treatment by Valdis O. Lumans. Least publicized of all are the answers the late Cardinal Joseph Bernardin provided to his own question: "Why has anti-Semitism been part of Christian life since the earliest days of the church?" In five pastoral letters published in his "Truth in Christ" column in *The New World Commentary* from April 21–May 26, 1995 the Cardinal made it clear to me, at least, that anti-semitism was, among other things, Christianity's racism. Or to put it another way, it was more important for Hitler's anti-semitic development, that he was brought up in the Christian faith, than in the German language.

If the words of such a powerful individual as Cardinal Bernardin can scarcely dent popular stereotypes, it is well that Elizabeth Walter has set down her experiences of Tito's Concentration Camps for her own sake rather than that of public enlightenment. The situation is not completely hopeless, however. Regardless of the reasons for popular dismissal of images of ordinary Germans-as-victims during and after World War II, fair minded observers have provided compelling evidence of the suffering of ordinary Germans at the hands of the *Vertreibung*, beginning with George F. Kennan, renowned U.S. diplomat and historian:

> I...flew low, in an American plane, over the entire province (of East Prussia) shortly after Potsdam, and the sight was that of a totally ruined and deserted country...The disaster that befell this area with the entry of the Soviet forces has no parallel in modern European experience...scarcely a man, woman, or child of the indigenous population was left alive after the initial passage of Soviet forces; and one cannot believe that they all succeeded in fleeing to the West (*Memoirs, 1925–1950*, New York: Atlantic, 1967, p. 265).

Though the best scholarly accounts are found in the work of Alfred M. de Zayas, Kennan's observations have been corroborated by voluminous eyewitness testimony by victims of the *Vertreibung* from the Baltic to the Black Sea, and from Kazakhstan and Karlsdorf to Koblenz. The psychological context for lack of western sympathy is provided by George Orwell:

> Properly speaking, there is no such thing as revenge. Revenge is an act which you want to commit when you are powerless and because you are powerless: as soon as the sense of impotence is removed, the desire evaporates also...We (the British and Americans) acquiesced in crimes like the expulsion of all Germans from East Prussia...because the Germans had angered and frightened us, and therefore we were certain that when they were down we should feel no pity for them...("Revenge is Sour" *Tribune*, 9. November 1946)

In comparison to East Prussia, of course, most Germans of Banat were fortunate. And Elizabeth Walter did not suffer through a Theresien-stadt or a Birkenau. We should not have her memoir if she had. She did not suffer a Rudolfsgnad either, as she is candid enough to concede. Elizabeth Walter was saved through a combination of her own strong constitution, luck, the attentions of her family, and the idiosyncracies of the Yugoslav program for revenge on the Donauschwaben. As brutal as the treatment of many of her *Landsleute* was, the distinction between the Ethnic Cleansing of the East European Germans and the Holocaust is an important one. She does not deny this. Nor does she shrink from the conclusion that the sufferings of *Volksdeutsche*, as well as *Reichsdeutsche*, are directly linked to Hitler and the genocidal Imperialism of the Nazis.

As a survivor of Ethnic Cleansing, it is clear from her memoir that Elizabeth Walter suffered then, and long afterwards, both for herself, and her loved ones. What also comes through her account, however, are less publicized, but resonant and compelling connections between victims of that Ethnic Cleansing and victims of the Holocaust. Elizabeth Walter knew, and suffered with, a few of the two million *Volksdeutsche* who perished in the *Vertreibung*. Two million (the currently accepted number for ethnic German deaths in the Expulsion) is a hefty figure, even by World War II and Holocaust standards, and even for a people whom many in this country still imagine "had-it-coming." Elizabeth Walter also shares with Holocaust victims, and historical of slavery and oppression, the knowledge that free and secure people did not really care about her fate. Nobody cared about the Jews in 1942, or in 1943. At least not anybody with the power to help them in any significant way. In a similar sense, nobody cared about the Donauschwaben in 1944. If people thought about their situation at all, the "Schwowe" were "guilty by reason of race;" just like the Jews since the time of St. Augustine,...and the Haitians since the inception of the slave trade.

I must confess that my ignorance of the fate of the *Donauschwaben* once equalled that of Professor Ambrose concerning the Haitians. Although conversant with 20th century German History, I did not discover the fate of the Danube Swabians until I visited the *Haus der Donauschwaben* in Sindel-fingen in 1983. While my search for scholarly experts in this area was initially disappointing, I soon discovered Eve Eckert Koehler (*Seven Susannahs*), and she led me to Alfred de Zayas. In addition, were it not for the determination of Eve Koehler, and Andreas and Michael Nagelbach (*Heil and Farewell*), and several other Danube Swabians to write their personal narratives, I would not have been able to break through stereotypes drawn from a narrow focus on

Reichsdeutsche sources. With *Barefoot in the Rubble*, Elizabeth Walter thus joins a distinguished company of *Vertreibung* survivors who have refused to let the politics of memory destroy their own sense of self worth. Until more of the world's population than is now the case realize, with Orwell, that "punishing an enemy brings no satisfaction," she cannot expect a wide audience; but those of us who have read her story are in her debt.

> *Charles M. Barber*
> Professor of History
> Northeastern Illinois University

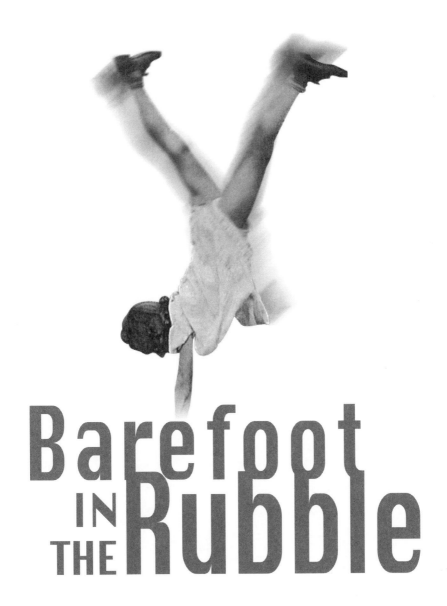

Barefoot
IN
THE Rubble

CHAPTER

1

Poppies

The thing I well remember is a large meadow filled with poppies, a sea of red flowers as far as my eyes could see. The wind danced among them, making them come alive.

I wanted to be with the poppies. I wanted to pick them and be just as free as the wind. But a barbed wire fence imprisoned me within the yard of the concentration camp. No flowers grew here. Too many people had trampled the ground. Beneath my bare feet, not even weeds had much of a chance to grow.

I remember mostly playing in the back of the yard. I stayed away from the *Partisaner* who guarded the entrance gate of the camp. Their dark eyes and mustaches frightened me. Their long bayonets stuck up from behind them, as if they grew out of their bodies. If they looked my way, I ran further back into the camp yard. I was afraid they would come and get me as they did that night when they brought us to this terrible place.

It had happened so quickly. All my life I had been surrounded with the warmth and love of my family, and within the wink of an eye my life had been turned into a nightmare. We were tossed about, churning in a sea of turmoil and upheaval. Life as my people had known it was slashed from its roots and tossed into the fire. Near the end of the war all over Yugoslavia, Schwabos – as we were called by our non-German neighbors – were rounded up by the Communist government of Marshall Tito. Let me tell you how it happened to my family.

1

I was born Elisabeth Barbara Hugery in the summer of 1940 in Karlsdorf, in Banat, Yugoslavia, a small town of 4,000 inhabitants, now known as Banatski Karlovac. My father, Johann Hugery, was a master furniture craftsman who owned a cabinet shop, also a distillery which my grandfather had started as a young man.

Like most of the three million *Volksdeutsche* – ethnic Germans – living in small towns scattered throughout Yugoslavia, Hungary, and Rumania, Karlsdorf was isolated from the rest of the western world. Our language, customs, and culture had been handed down from generation to generation for hundreds of years. My father's great-grandfather, our *Urgugandl* as we call our long ago ancestors, was the first Hugery to settle in Karlsdorf, which was established in 1802. Young, single, and adventuresome, he left his birthplace in *Elsass-Lothringen* – Alsace Lorrain – in the 1820's. He was one of the last settlers to come down the winding *Donau* River seeking freedom and a better life.

Thousands had embarked on this journey before him since the seventeen hundreds. They inaugurated their venture down the "Danube river roadway" – the only pathway to that part of the world – from Ulm, Germany on flat bottom boats nicknamed *Ulmer Schachtl* or Ulm boxes. Upon arriving in their new homestead, they dismantled the boats and used them to build their houses.

I have always regarded my ancestor with respect. To start out into the unknown all alone is a brave thing to do. What made the journey even more daring was that it was a one-way trip. There was no turning back once you set out.

Not only did my father's great grandfather venture to seek out a new lifestyle, he also had the courage to change his name. Originally our name had been Huger, a common Germanic name. A few hundred years ago it was fashionable among the elite to Latinize their last names, so Huger became Hugerius. Whether my *Urgugandl* was a nobleman or not, that fact died with him. But the rest of his offspring were just a bunch of regular people.

He "took himself a wife" and had a son, who had twenty-four children; my grandfather – my *Ota* – was the twenty-second child in the Hugery family. *Tati*, my father, has often told us how he used to ask Ota to name his brothers and sisters. And when Ota finished, Tati would ask if he was sure he hadn't forgotten anyone. At this point my grandfather usually got angry. He knew his son just wanted to annoy him. All twenty four survived birth and eighteen of them grew old enough to marry.

My ancestors on my mother's side came from the Black Forest. My mother was Elisabeth Hugery, and her family, *Familie* Schüssler, had been in Karlsdorf for a long time. *Grossvater* Schüssler grew grapes in his vineyard and farmed a small parcel of land. Although he owned both vineyard and farmland, he was not a wealthy man, for both properties were small.

We called ourselves *Schwowe* or, in high German, *Schwaben*. Because the Danube River has flown in and out of our history we are also called *Donauschwaben*, or in English, Danube Swabians. Most of us lived in the regions of Banat and Batschka, then known as the "Breadbasket of Europe". We were hardworking people who knew how to enjoy life as well as harvest the fruits of our labor. Our dialects had changed very little since our ancestors came down the Danube River. Our villages became time capsules. In many towns, people still wore the folk costumes from the regions their ancestors came from, though in Karlsdorf, which was settled from people who came from other towns in Banat, there was no dominant ethnic style, therefore people wore the styles of the time. Our town, like most of the German villages established during the 17th and 18th centuries, under the Austro-Hungarian Monarchy, had a Baroque church in the center and whitewashed houses, all similar in size and form, flanking the wide, tree-lined streets.

Another thing that distinguished Karlsdorf was the soil, which was sandy and swampy and not as fertile as in other towns; the crop that grew best was grapes. As a result, the townspeople were mostly craftsmen, not farmers, and of course we had at least four wineries.

Everyone, tradesmen as well as *Bauern* or farmers, lived in town, the *Bauer*, unlike the American farmer who lives on his land, had to travel to the fields located outside the village limits to cultivate his crops.

Many houses had a fenced in front courtyard, usually paved with cobblestones, a backyard or barnyard that housed animals, and a fenced off garden that provided the cooks of the household with the fresh vegetables and fruits needed for a well-set table in spring, summer, and fall. In the barren cold winter months the *Hausfrau* served with pride, the fruits and vegetables she had canned in summer and fall.

The townspeople took great pride in their park, located in the middle of town next to the church. A profusion of flowers grew in artistically designed flowerbeds. Ornamental shrubs and bushes, arranged beautifully to please the eye, adorned the grounds. Tall trees spread their leafy cloaks over the two wide pathways that criss-crossed in the center and ran to the four corners of the park square. In the golden, warm days of spring and summer, young and old alike strolled arm in arm down the paths or sat on the benches.

When my mother and father were young and single, the *Korso* was the place to be on Sunday afternoon in the wintertime. The *Korso* was a promenade in the middle of town where the *Hotel*, *Kino* – Cinema – and *Wirtshaus* – Inn – were located. The sidewalk was widest here, and girls walked arm in arm down the street, while boys stood around to look and make small talk.

No single girl was allowed to go on a date with a boy, nor could a boy come to visit the girl at home, unless they were engaged. The weekly ritual of *"zum Tanz gehn,"* – going to the dance – made it possible to talk to the opposite sex. On Sunday afternoons, except during Lent and Advent, dances were held in the *Wirtshaus*.

Young, single girls were always chaperoned by their mothers. At the dance, girls talked with each other and fellows did the same; only when they danced together could they talk to one another. Mothers sat on benches along the walls, gossiping and keeping an eye on their daughters. I was told about this ritual by my parents.

"I bet you hated your mother sitting there and watching you," I said to my mother one day.

"That didn't bother me," she replied. "My mother not being there would have been worse, because I would have been different from my friends."

My parents wedding, April 1935.

"How did people ever fall in love and get married?" I asked.

My father laughed and with a twinkle in his eye said; "The young always find a way."

In Karlsdorf we were generally self-sufficient. We raised all our food. In the backyard we had a cow, pigs, chickens, ducks and geese. In our orchard and garden we grew all our fruits and vegetables, as did almost everyone else in Karlsdorf. Except for electricity we had no modern conveniences, not even running water. Very few people had radios. My father can recall only three or four friends who owned one.

Mother made most of my clothing as well as the rest of our family's. We had no department stores; if you needed new clothing you'd go to the *Schneiderin or Schneider* – dressmaker or tailor, or make it yourself. If you needed a new pair of shoes, a visit to the *Schumacher* was in order. Most household items used in the home were made in town. We had basket weavers, potters, tinsmiths. We also had at least three *Ziegel Fabrik* – brick yards – at the edge of town.

As for transportation, most people walked. Not everyone had horses and wagons. We didn't. Only three families owned an *Auto:* the *Familie* Herz was one of them. They also owned the *Salami Fabrik* – salami factory. They were the richest people in town.

I was surrounded by family. Grandparents, parents, aunts, uncles, cousins and my brother Josef, nicknamed Seppi, who was four years older than I. We were a very close-knit family, living a life of hard work that was shared by everyone.

I remember a book that was half my size, dragging it across the room and struggling to lift it up on top of Grandfather's white featherbed. It was heavy, but I managed to bring it to *Ota*. I did this often. He and I kept each other company, he had been bedridden for a long time.

I liked to sit on the floor and listen as he read to me. Looking up at him, he looked as if he was on top of a mountain covered with snow.

"*Will my Madl ah Kecks?*" he asked.

"*Ja - Ja,*" I answered happily. Of course his girl wanted a cookie.

Every time, like magic, he'd pull out a box of *Kecks* from behind his featherbed with a big smile and handed me a cookie. This is all I can recall about my grandfather. Ota died before my third birthday.

I was a quiet child, readily entertained by people and things around me. Before the camp, my mother, *Mami*, and I often spent time in the kitchen. A large green table stood in the middle of the room with four chairs. I remember climbing on one of the chairs across from my mother who was standing at the table, preparing dinner. I knelt and propped both hands under my chin and studied Mami's face.

"What is Mami doing with her tongue?" I wondered. She probably had something caught in her teeth, she was putting her tongue to the inside of her cheek, making it bulge out. I found this fascinating and I too put my tongue to the side of my cheek. I copied her every action down to such minute details. If I close my eyes I still can see her face just as she looked then.

That is the first memory I have of my mother. We shared the same name, "Elisabeth."[1] I was called by the more modern nickname of *Elsa*, she was called *Lissi*.

I was always at my mother's side as she did her work: washing, gardening, canning and cooking. Sometimes on warm summer days she'd sit outside the summer kitchen door, shelling peas or beans into a *Baxsimpl*. I'd sit at her feet nestled into a tiny bowl-shaped basket just like the one she had on her lap, rocking back and forth.

Dressmaking was not only my mother's profession, but also her joy. She loved to sew and even embroider on her pedal Singer sewing machine. She had even made her own wedding gown. Her nimble fingers also made my favorite burgundy, velvet dress, *"mei Samtkleid"* or as I pronounced it *Samenskleid*. In my eyes it was Mami's masterpiece.

The earliest memory I have of my father is being rocked in the cradle that he made. It stood next to his side of the bed and served not only to quiet a newborn but also as a crib. Tati had made it wide and comfortable enough to permit each of his children to sleep in it until they were three years old.

"Tati wieg mich fescht," I remember calling.

"Tati, rock me hard," I'd call out again if his strong arm didn't reach down to the side of the cradle right away.

I also remember Tati sneaking me into the pantry. He'd lift me up on his shoulders so I could break off a piece of hard smoked *Brotwurst* for the two of us. Then we'd whisper and laugh quietly and sneak outside the house to eat our loot.

---

[1] I changed my name to the American spelling when I became a U.S. citizen.

Tati bought us a *Radio*, one of the first in Karlsdorf. The house was often crowded with people who had come to listen to the beautiful melodious sound. Music flowed out of the small box as my father danced me around on top of his shoulders. High above everyone I sat, giggling joyfully. Tati stretched out my arms, and the two of us flew as on a cloud. Sometimes we'd pass through the doorway from one room to the other, both of us ducking low, still swaying to the music.

When I was three years old I had *Trachoma*, an eye disease that was very common in Europe at the time. My father took me to the city of Pantschowa to see a specialist.

I sat on a high, narrow table in the bright white room where *"der Onkel Doktor"* was doing something to my eyelids. The doctor's soft, reassuring voice lulled me into calmness as he did the *Operation*. It didn't hurt and I was not afraid. When the doctor was finished he put a patch on my eye.

Afterwards, Tati and I went to a store with small round tables where people sat and ate *Sladolett*. I remember sitting on one of the chairs, high up with my feet dangling, as Tati and I enjoyed the ice cream. I liked its cold, sweet taste on my tongue. And I liked being in Pantschowa with Tati.

That Christmas I had my first visit from *Christkindl*, a tall figure dressed in white from head to toe. A veil covered her face. A fine voice asked me to please say my prayer like a good child, after which she handed me my present, my old doll, all clean and dressed in a new dress, and both of her arms re-attached to her body. She had been an amputee for quite some time, I had torn both of the doll's upper arms out of their sockets.

That Easter I received a pet lamb who I named *Mädie*. I loved that name. I ran back and forth, singing it over and over, *"Mädie, Mädie, Mädie."*

I did not like *Hansi*, my brother's pet lamb. Every time he saw me he'd lower his head and charge, knocking me down.

The lambs didn't stay lambs too long; they became sheep and so they were turned out to pasture with the rest of the flock.

On Easter morning, in the sun-filled garden, I found the eggs that the *Osterhas* had left in the irises next to the white lilac bush.

We had no way of knowing that this would be our last holiday together for four long years.

The sound might come at any time, night or day, with no warning. It pierced your ears and started everybody's heart racing. The shrill scream of the air raid siren would knot my stomach with fear.

Someone always grabbed my hand and ran with me, making my short legs pump so fast that they seemed not to touch the ground. We hurried to our shelter, a sloped hole dug in the back of the orchard.

Darkness encircled us as we sat huddled together in our grave-like surroundings. The cold, dank smell of the earth was always there. I clung to Mami as we listened to the droning motors of the many airplane bombers that flew over us, sometimes dropping nothing, other times raining bombs. Inside, no one spoke. Dead silence rang in our ears. Listening... what would happen this time? Would a bomb find us? No one needed to tell me how grave the situation was. I sensed my family's fear even if I didn't know what death was.

Then the siren's "All clear" screeched out, signaling that the attack was over. We'd crawl out from our dark earthen chamber and once more breathe the clean, fresh air, grateful to have survived the ordeal once again.

Once I remember sitting on the floor in the big Kindergarten room at school, surrounded by the happy sound of children laughing and playing. Suddenly the peace was once more broken by the shrieking air raid siren. I don't remember anything after the alarm until the door opened and Tati ran in. He scooped me up, raced out the door, and placed me on the handlebars of his bicycle. Speeding like the wind, we flew through the streets, to our house, into the orchard and down into the protection of the hole. I knew we'd be safe, because my father was with us.

Because I was so young, I thought this was all a normal part of life. Adults around me never explained things differently. After all, they were too busy trying to make life as bearable as possible. No one knew what the next day could bring, and preparation for the coming seasons had to be made. The work also helped people to remain sane. Fields were planted and harvested. Meat was butchered and put away for the winter. Grapes were harvested and pressed to make wine. Daily life went on as if the war were not there.

I liked to look out the bedroom window. I'd see wagons, riders, or once in a while an *"Auto."* Every day towards early evening a huge steam roller lumbered down the street and came to a halt in front of the *Familie Dolder's* house a few doors away. There it turned and moved through the large entrance door and disappeared behind the fenced-in yard.

I'd stand by my window imitating the droning sound of the big rolling drum. I'd repeat over and over, "Dolder... Dolder ... Dolder" until the steamroller was out of sight. I thought the roller was saying its owner's name. That's what it sounded like to me.

We lived *"in der Hauptgass,"* or Main Street, which was built high on an embankment; it was also the only cobblestone paved street in town. In the morning, the cows, pigs and geese were gathered from all the houses and driven out to pasture by their herders. Returning evenings, every animal knew its home and would simply step out of the herd and walk to its owner's house.

Most people kept their *G'fliegl,* or poultry, in their back yards. But I can remember the strange wrinkly necked birds that I had to pass on my way to school. They strutted back and forth in front of their building and as soon as one of them saw me approaching it started to garble its unusual greeting. All then joined in unison: *Bockl - Bockl - Bockl,* sounding to me as if they were repeating their name over and over fast to make sure I heard it. For that is what they were, a flock of *"Bockl."*

I'd then chant *"Roti - Roti - Rotznas,"* as I had heard other children do. I continued to walk around them keeping a good distance. They were almost as tall as I was. The birds kept up the racket, with blinking eyes and throaty gobbles, making the red skin hanging from their beaks sway back and forth; hence it appeared even more as if they had a runny nose. That's why we children chanted, "red - red - snot-nose." Still chanting, I kept walking around the turkeys until we parted ways.

Turkeys were considered a special and rare poultry. Very few people owned them; they were certainly not as common as ducks and geese. That's probably the reason I can recall them so clearly, or was it because they were weird looking?

The street was wide, and the houses were set far back from the road with at least one tree in front of each. Not one blade of grass grew from the road to the cobblestone sidewalk. The packed down ground, as well as the sidewalk, were swept daily by the *Hausfrau* as part of her good housekeeping.

All the houses were *g'weisselt* – whitewashed – yearly. My mother and her *Schwester Kati* – sister Kati – joined forces to do the chore; they also worked together in their families' vineyards.

I stood in silence as I watched Mami and my aunt, kerchiefs tied Gypsy-style around their heads, dunking the long-handled brush into the bucket of white paint, then moving the brush slowly up and down until the whole wall was a bright white again.

I called my aunt *"Basl"* instead of *"Tant,"* which most children used to address their aunts. I don't remember why my brother and I called my mother's sister in this manner. *Basl* and *Vetter* is what children called all adult ladies and men in the ethnic German towns instead of the formal *"Frau* and *Herr."*

This was so long ago that I have to concentrate hard to bring my aunt's face to mind; our families parted in 1949. Her dark eyes had a sad look about them, and yet her lips had a constant curved smile. Although she was only four years older than my mother, she looked a lot older than her thirty four years. Mother and Basl did not look at all related. My aunt was dark-complexioned like my grandmother Mayer's side of the family, and my mother had a light complexion with rosy cheeks and blue eyes, like my grandfather Schüssler's side of the family.

They were also different when it came to dress and hairstyles. Basl was more or less old fashioned. She always wore her long, dark hair in a bun, as this was the custom for many years in all of the Swabian towns.

Mami's hair was cut in a modern style of the forties. She used an electric curling iron on her thick, blond hair.

Mother told me one of the reasons she became a seamstress was because Basl used to make her clothes. Being not as style-conscious as mother, Basl sewed the dresses the way she liked them, not to mother's taste. Therefore, at the age of fourteen, my mother became an apprentice seamstress and from then on sewed her own wardrobe in the latest styles of the day.

Despite their differences they were best friends who not only loved each other, but also each other's children as if they were their own.

My aunt had two children, Marie and Andres. Andres was born the first day of January, 1936 and my brother Seppi was born in March. Although they were just a few months apart, Seppi looked much younger. He was small and thin where Andres was large-boned and muscular.

Marie, seven years older than I, had dark eyes that danced with a smile. She was pretty and also my favorite cousin. Being the oldest, she took it upon herself to mother the rest of us. Of course this was not always possible with the boys. But I liked it just fine. Marie watched over me from the time I was born. She happily played with me and patiently showed me how to do things. She taught me dancing, braiding, and even

My father and his workers in front of the cabinet shop.
My brother (center) standing on the bench, 1939.

the ABC's, trivial things that seem unimportant sometimes but are very important when you're small and don't know how to do them.

In front of the house stood a wooden bench where we sat and visited with friends and neighbors in the evenings, as most people did. Young people often sat together summer evenings and harmonized. Music was a very important part of life; it was the main form of entertainment. Someone in the group usually played an instrument, even if it was only a harmonica.

The courtyard was where we lived most of the day. People entered daily through the large door in the high fence. They came on foot or with wagons to do business with my family in our cabinet shop and distillery. My father designed and made furniture in his busy woodwork shop and was widely known for his craftsmanship.

He loved gadgets. His shop was the first in town to use electric machinery to build large pieces of furniture and finish the job in half the time it took by hand.

During the day electric power was rationed, no electricity surged through the wires into the shop until night time. So from eleven o'clock till four in the morning, Tati and Mami worked side by side, cutting out the wood patterns needed for the next day's work. I'm sure sometimes the day was very long for both of my parents. War or not, the daily housework and woodworking had to continue.

My father made all kinds of furniture, from chairs to large wardrobes to fancy window frames with shutters. He sometimes made toys such as wagons, table top bowling alleys and even skis. There was nothing Tati couldn't build. He had a display room that faced the street.

Not only townspeople but people from our neighboring town of Nikolenz, populated by ethnic Rumanians, came to do business with us regularly. Everyone knew everyone. Even at such a young age, I loved to be surrounded by people. Like all children, I addressed the adults as *Vetter* and *Basl*. All the adults in town knew to whom you belonged. If the older children misbehaved and their parents weren't around, whichever adult was there was the disciplinarian. And if you went home to complain, you got it again.

We lived with my father's parents. The house was built parallel to the street, with four rooms facing the front – my father's showroom, my grandparents bedroom, kitchen, and our bedroom.

Mami, Tati, Seppi and I all shared one bedroom, as most families did. Facing the courtyard, towards the back, was my family's kitchen, next to which was a storage room with an attic where the grain was kept. Then came the mill and my father's cabinet shop. My grandfather was a miller by trade; he ran the mill until he became ill in the late thirties. The mill was then dismantled and became a storeroom with a wine cellar underneath.

Near the kitchen was a large shade tree, its trunk so big I don't think even a grown man's arms could reach around its great girth. I know I couldn't, but that never stopped me from trying.

From left, my aunt "Tant," my cousin Hans, Mutter,
Ota, my mother and father, 1935.

A brick well with a roof stood on the left side of the courtyard. Because we had no refrigeration, we used it to keep things cool. In the summertime, we'd lower a watermelon down the well early in the day and retrieve it when evening came. We could hardly wait as we watched the bucket emerge from the water with its treasure. We usually tasted the sweetness of this summer treat under the rustling leaves of our shade tree; often we ate lunch there, which was the main meal of the day, with our family and my father's workers.

Next to the well was a small flower garden with a grape arbor that stretched along our neighbor's wall. Located in back was the brandy distillery. Townspeople came and paid a fee or bartered to have their fermented grapes distilled into schnaps. Next to the still was the summer kitchen where my mother and grandmother did their cooking and canning so that our living quarters stayed cool. The pig butchering was also done in this part of the courtyard.

Like most people in town we did our own butchering. Poultry and pork were "home grown". Only beef, veal, and sometimes lamb came from the butcher shop.

After butchering, the sausages: *Brotwurst, Schwartlma, Leberwurst* and *Blutwurst* were smoked along with the *Speck* – bacon – and *Schunge* – ham. To keep the other meat from spoiling, it was salted down in a large *Mulder*, a long wooden tub. This meat had to be boiled, roasted or fried within six week's time. Whatever meat was left over after that also had to be smoked.

The fat was cut up, rendered, and made into *Kraml und Schmalz*. The *Schmalz* – lard – was used for cooking and frying and had to last from one butchering to the next. *Kraml*, the small bits and pieces of meat and fat left from rendering the fat, was a treat. Cracklin was only available at butchering time.

A fence between the summer kitchen and furniture shop separated the courtyard and the barnyard. Located in the middle of the yard was the *Kloset*. Every day someone had to accompany me to the outhouse because there lived a monster behind the gate. The monster was a foot high with shimmering green, blue and brown feathers and a red spike on top of its head. Frightening spurs grew out of its fast moving legs. Two beady eyes and a sharp yellow beak stretched out to grab you as it came charging. I was its only victim. The rooster left everyone else alone.

Many animals reigned in the backyard. Ducks and geese strutted around as if they owned the place. Pigs enjoyed a full life by eating all that was set before them. Our barn housed not only a cow but also white rabbits by the dozen, all descended from one pair brought home by my father. Some people considered rabbit flesh a delicacy, but the Hugery household did not. So the rabbits did what comes naturally to the species: they begat more and more of their kind.

Tati loved the unusual – including poultry of a different feather. Besides the ordinary variety of chickens, we had chickens with colorful feathers and fancy top knots, looking as if they just came from the hairdresser. White ones with long feathers growing, bloomer-fashion, down their short legs. We even had some that laid speckled or brown eggs.

The pigeons soared above all, the sky their domain. They were housed all around the two story *Hambar* – corn bin – in the pigeon lofts, where they came and went as they pleased.

In the wooden corn bin within the confines of its slatted walls, filled to the rafters with the summer harvest, lived hundreds of small, unwelcome guests who dined and grew fat on the kernels of maize. As the winter months passed and the livestock consumed most of the golden feed, the bin's contents dwindled down to just a small pile far back in the corner. The gray little mice cowered closer and closer together in the now sparse heap of corn in hopes that the cats or the broom wouldn't make their lives come to an abrupt end.

Behind the summer kitchen was a huge stack of *Trewe*, – grape skins from the distillery – that were used as fertilizer. The animals liked to dine there. We had a cow that loved to climb on top of the grape skin pile, grazing as if she were on a mountain. Sometimes the chickens got a little high on their lunch, and we had live *coq au vin* running around our yard.

We had *Hehndlfleisch* on days like *Namenstag* – name's day, birthdays, Sundays, or more often if there were additional chickens running around because of a good year. Mami would chase the desired upcoming meal around the barnyard until she caught it.

Whenever we ran out of *Saaf*, my grandmother, whom I called *Mutter* – mother, instead of Oma, because everyone in our family did – set up her soap making kettle behind my father's cabinet shop. She'd stir the liquid ingredients in the enormous round, black metal *Kessl*, stopping sometimes to add more wood to the crackling fire under the pot.

"Geh jez weg vum Kessl mei Kind!" Mutter told me sternly.

I quickly moved further away from the kettle as I was told. Slowly stirring the ingredient called *Lau* into the hot mixture, Mutter explained to me that it was very important not to get any of the lye on one's hands or face, it could make a person's skin burn or make them blind.

At the time I didn't quite understand this kind of burning. Would my skin or eyes be flaming like the fire in front of me?

My grandmother had good reason to respect this chemical. A few years before, my father was working with lye when he accidentally splashed some in his eye. Luckily for him, my mother was quick to administer the correct antidote, washing his eye out with water, thus diluting the lye and making it harmless. If this had not been done, my father would have been blinded, he had been born with sight in only one eye.

A pathway of large, flat stones led from the backyard gate to the outhouse. The rest of the backyard was a field of mud during the spring thaw or when it rained. To venture out into that muddy domain, every household had a few pairs of *Klumbe* – wooden shoes stuffed with straw. The adults wore them to do the daily chores in the backyard.

I recall trying out the big, heavy shoes one damp, dreary day. I could hardly lift my small feet inside the large, wet, straw-filled shoes. I managed only a few steps into the backyard before I was stuck deep in the muck. Unable to go on, I stepped out of the shoes and into the mud and walked back into the courtyard with mud up to my ankles.

At the back of the yard by the orchard fence were my father's bees, his hobby. Our house was very popular with the neighborhood children at *"Honigschleidre Zeit"* when the honey was extracted. All came running to "help clean up." They licked the pots and utensils so clean that not one drop of honey remained in them.

A few yards away from the bees was a huge haystack where hundreds of sparrows took refuge during the cooler times of the year. Since almost all of the houses in town had haystacks, boys made sport by putting a basket up to the side of a haystack, hitting the hay with a stick and capturing the birds as they flew out.

A white picket fence separated the backyard from the orchard and garden. The garden was divided in half, one side for our family and the other for my grandparents. Patches of color were neatly laid out with nature's bounty.

But in the midst of all this beauty was the gaping black hole, the makeshift *Bunker*, a constant reminder of the ugly war that hung over us.

When small specks appeared in the sky, and grew bigger and bolder, and their sound got louder and louder until it became a thundering, droning roar that shook the earth, we'd run to our bunker.

The large monster soon hung over the town, a dragon made up of hundreds of propellers, wings and bellies – bellies that dropped fire out of their bowels. I'd cling to my mother in our bunker as bombs dropped by the hundreds. Slowly the explosions subsided and the droning became farther and farther away, until all was still.

The fear of the giant stayed with me throughout my childhood and up to the present. Every time I hear a plane flying low overhead, my heart pounds madly. I know that nothing is going to happen, yet deep within me the fear is still there.

But despite mankind's effort to destroy one another, the Creator continued to go about His business, as He had done since the beginning of time. One season led to another, winter, spring, summer and fall. Flowers bloomed from early March to late October and sprinkled the ground with fragrance and color. I can especially remember a large patch of violets that filled the air with their scent.

Our garden contained many different fruit trees; cherry, peach, apple, plum, apricot, even figs and quince. I always walked carefully next to Mutter or Mami as soon as we passed through the garden gate. Everyone knew that the *Garteweiwl* lived among the fruit trees and vegetable patches. The little old "Garden-witch" stood guard day and night protecting the garden from children who picked the flowers and ate the carrots or fruit without permission.

Once, when I was with Mutter, I saw her, a small figure dressed in white from head to toe. She raised her white billowing arms above her veiled head and began to moan as if she were in pain.

"Schau Elsa! Es Garteweiwl!" Mutter shouted.

I stood frozen, and before I could cry out in fear, she had disappeared.

Many years later I learned that my grandmother's good friend, Sonleitner's Resbasl, had played the part of the *Garteweiwl*. My imaginative grandmother had planned this episode with her.

Now you might be saying to yourself, "What a mean trick to play on small children." But the family depended on the summer harvest to get through the winter.

I sat on the floor beneath the bedroom window. The bedroom, one of my favorite rooms in our house, was full of interesting things to play with. Sometimes I'd crawl into the large wardrobe where Mami kept her high heeled shoes. I'd put them on and walk around the room like a grown up lady. I especially liked her fox fur piece, complete with feet, tail, head, glass eyes and snout. I'd pretend that it was alive, dragging it on the floor, opening and closing the clip under its snout and making funny noises.

But what was that noise coming from the street? I jumped up to look outside, where a group of odd-looking vehicles were rolling down the street, crawling like caterpillars. They had many wheels with a wide chain wrapped around them. A long round pipe stuck out from the top. Behind the caterpillars were rows upon rows of soldiers as far as the eye could see. I had never seen so many people. They kept coming and coming, an endless stream of soldiers. I watched the strange parade for a long time.

The march, which occurred in the fall of 1944, continued for days. This was my introduction to the many strange and painful events to come. The Red Army, with their tanks and soldiers, had arrived.

CHAPTER

2

Under The Red Star

By now, I was used to looking out the window and seeing soldiers marching down our street.

But what was this? A large group of women came marching. Soldiers with guns were guarding them in front and back. The women carried shovels, rakes, brooms and other long-handled tools, army fashion. They wore ordinary summer work dresses with kerchiefs tied behind their heads, covering the head and forehead. I watched from the window until they passed down the road.

What I had witnessed was the road gang which repaired the damage in the road caused by the Communist tanks. Women from our town would be forced to fill the potholes and repair the road.

These women had now, along with the rest of us, become non-citizens of Yugoslavia. In the early fall of 1944, the Russians took over Karlsdorf and all other ethnic German towns. The Russian troops advanced in on one end of Main Street and the German troops retreated out the other end. When I asked my father: "Why can't I recall any fighting?"

"Because you were not there during the shooting" he told me.

All of the residents on Main Street had to evacuate their homes and hide with friends or relatives who lived on the side streets. People stayed shut up in their houses as the shooting went on. My family stayed hidden with Franz Onkel Schüssler's family, all of us huddled together next door in their neighbor's basement.

My mother's cousin's wife, Katherina Schüssler, and her three children were in hiding in the cellar of the winery next door to them, which had been used as a bunker during the war, when a bullet from the attack found its way into the basement, hitting twelve year old Elsa in the head, killing her instantly. Her sister Katilie, brother Peter and mother were unharmed.

My father told me how the fighting went on for days. After the fighting ended, a band of riffraff followed behind the Russian army. Along Main Street the mob pillaged the houses. Doors and windows were broken and the rooms were emptied out into the yards and streets. The mob carried off furniture, bedding and clothing by the armful. Some looked comical as they walked through the streets with four or five hats piled one on top of the other; they drank wine, danced and sang in the street.

"How do you know what went on if you were hiding?" I asked.

"I snuck back into our house".

"Why did you do such a foolish thing? You could have been killed".

"I never gave that a thought", he said. Then he told me this story.

"I was standing in front of our house, waiting for the mob to come. As I stood there, a man in a Russian uniform came out of the house across the street. He was astonished to see me. He crossed the street and called to me in Russian, 'What in God's name are you doing here?' Quickly he pushed me inside the courtyard.

" 'This is my house and I don't want anyone to steal my belongings', I answered.

"I then invited the Russian inside the kitchen and gave him a drink. The soldier spotted a toy on the kitchen floor and asked me about my family. I led him into the bedroom and showed him our pictures. He then told me not to worry about the mob. 'I won't let them in here,' he said.

"The boisterous horde could be heard coming closer and closer. Soon they came to our house and started to push open the gate of the courtyard. Taking his gun in hand, the Russian yelled to them to be off and not touch this house.

"So it was that our house was not looted," Tati told me.

"You sure have a great *Schutzengl,*" I commented. "Your guardian angel has been working overtime all of your life".

My father stayed at home till the end of the siege. No one came near our house, and within a week the residents of Main Street returned to their homes. My father's brother Franz and his wife, whom we called

Onkel und Tant, also lived on Main Street, and when Tant returned home, not one piece of furniture remained; all the rooms were stripped bare by the looters.

The Communists were now in authority. Fear was the ruler in our town as well as in all German towns. Partisaner knocked on doors and took people away – never to be seen again.

"Every day I'd fear that they'd come and knock on my door," my father told me. "Afraid I'd be next."

Beatings, rapes, and killings took place everywhere. Blood flowed freely. All over Yugoslavia, the new Communist government gave permission for citizens to do whatever they wanted to the ethnic Germans. In towns of mixed citizenry the blood flowed the most.

In Ruskodorf – now Ruskoselo – where my husband's family lived, the population was a mixture of Germans, Hungarians and Serbians. My mother-in-law has told us how she had to go with a group of women to clean up the bloody room where men and women had been tortured by cutting off parts of their bodies. Piece by piece they dismembered their victims, pulling off fingernails, then fingers, hands, arms, feet, legs until they bled to death. They rounded up people at random and beat them. Her cousin was one of them. After the beating she was left for dead.

Women were not safe on the street. It made no difference what age a female was. My husband's great-grandmother and grandmother were riding in the family wagon when a group of Russian soldiers attacked them. They tossed his ninety-five-year old great-grandmother out of the wagon and raped his seventy-four-year old grandmother. Both died a few months later.

Many women, because of the fear of being raped, killed themselves. One old neighbor was so afraid for herself and her small granddaughter that she tried to drown herself and the child in her well. She dropped the girl down into the water and then jumped in after her. A neighbor witnessed the old woman's action and quickly ran to get help. They pulled the grandmother from the narrow hole, but the child didn't have a chance: her grandmother's layers of skirts billowed like an umbrella, pinning the small child under water.

In Werschetz, which also had a mixed population, women and children where tied onto wagons and dragged through town. Hundreds of men and women were gathered together daily and taken to a large mass grave site, where they were shot and buried on the spot.

In some places they came to the house, knocked on the door, and without a word the people were taken outside of town, forced to dig holes, then shot and thrown into the graves they had just dug. The victims were selected for various reasons: perhaps some had worked or been forced to work for the German army, which had just occupied the towns; or they had been reported as "enemies of the state" by people who disliked them. Or they had said something against the communists. No proof was needed.

Many died just for the sport of it or because someone didn't like their looks. As long as the victim was a German, he had committed a crime.

Like everyone of German ancestry in Yugoslavia, the members of my family became prisoners of the State and we lost all our property rights as well as our citizenship.

Men and women were made to work for the communists. Everyone who was able had to report to work camps every day. In the late fall, men ages 16 to 60 were taken daily to work in different towns, returning home every night. This went on for a while until one day, instead of returning home as usual, they were rounded up and confined inside the barb wire fenced-in airplane hangars just outside of town. The men slaved during the day and late into the evening. At nightfall Partisaner marched into the hangar and called out prisoners names. Those chosen were taken outside and the nightly ritual of merciless beatings began.

Then one day, without a warning, the prisoners were loaded onto wagons, taken out of Karlsdorf, and shipped off to Russia in cattle cars to become slave laborers in coal mines: they were never even able to say good-bye to their families.

This was to be my father's fate. My mother had no knowledge of his whereabouts or even if he was alive from the fall of 1944 until November 1947.

My father was not there for that butchering of November 1944. But since no one knew what was to come, the job of *Schwein schlachte* still had to be done with or without my father's help.

The noise was terrible. I held my hands tightly to my ears and squeezed my eyes shut as my brother Seppi and I stood in the kitchen, behind the closed door. I could still hear the squealing pig even with my hands over my ears. I was too short to see out the door window. Seppi was much taller than I and he had a good view. Curiosity got the better of me. Somehow I got onto a chair to see what was going on.

It was a dark and dreary morning outside. Across the courtyard by the summer kitchen, the adults were rushing back and forth. What were they doing? I only heard the squealing pig; I didn't see what they were doing to the animal. My brother started to imitate the squeal of the pig. He wet his finger, then rubbed up and down on the glass pane, making it screech. "Show me, show me how you do that," I begged. So the two of us amused ourselves and drowned out the noise from outside until we were allowed to go into the yard and help after the gruesome part of the butchering was finished.

Outside by the summer kitchen stood a large cast-iron stew pot with fire underneath it. A delicious aroma rose from it. Mutter was busy cooking the *Kesselfleisch*, a stew made from bits and pieces of meat from the butchering. I walked over to her and asked her for a taste. She told me it was not ready, so I had to wait.

Someone handed me a balloon-shaped, grayish-pink object that bounced like a ball, which my brother and I proceeded to play with. This object was considered the best part of the pig by most children ... it was the bladder.

Livestock, which was now government owned, was distributed throughout our town, so fewer people were needed to tend them. The caretakers were mostly older people or young mothers with small children. Mutter was assigned one such animal, a large brown cow that she milked and fed every day.

One day my mother, who was not quite 30 years old, had to report to the village hall, along with all other young single or married women ages 16 to 30. It was rumored that just like the men before them, they were to be shipped off to Russia.

I could see only the heads of the women in the large, crowded room. Mami held me close to her as if I were a baby, my legs tucked in the right side of her large cardigan sweater. She told me not to say a word. It was very important to keep quiet. The man in charge had to believe I was too young to talk. I was very frightened. I pressed my body to my mother's, trying to make myself smaller. I had no idea of what was going on. A long time passed. "Elisabetha Hugery," the man called out from the front of the room. The next thing I remember is marching down the street, still in Mami's arms, in the middle of the solemn faced women. Where were we going?

Soldiers with guns were walking with us. Townspeople stood on both sides of the street. I listened with bewilderment as I heard people crying. I did not dare say anything.

"Lissi, Lissi," someone called to my mother. From the right side of the street I saw Basl step out from behind the crowd. Quickly she rushed up to us. Mami handed me to my aunt and said, "Take Elsa home."

Looking over my Basl's shoulders, I saw a glimpse of Mami before we rushed past everyone and went home to Oma and Ota Schüssler, my mother's parents.

It did not matter if they had children or not; the only mothers that age able to stay were those still breast feeding. This is why my mother had taken me with her to the village hall, trying to pass me off as a young child not yet weaned – I was very small for a four year-old. She knew if she did not succeed, my brother and I would be left behind as so many other children were ... all alone.

My mother was taken with the rest of the women to the airfield where two large airplane hangars were surrounded by a high barbed wire fence. She stayed the night and then, as I had understood it, had been simply released and told to go home.

Whenever my mother talked about this event, she said only that the Russians let her go. Thus I took it to mean our little sham worked. She astounded me when she told me otherwise, after I read to her what I'd thought was the correct account of what had happened. I was showing it to her to make sure I had the facts straight. That's when she told me the whole painful story of what had gone on between the time she and the other women came to the airplane hangar and the time she was set free. This is her account of the event:

"All hope of convincing the Partisaner that you were still not weaned came to an end when I was marched out of the village hall with the rest of the women. I then knew my fate was to be the same as your father's. So, when I heard your aunt call to me, I called back and told her to come and take you home.

"As the daylight gave way to darkness we were sitting or lying on the bare ground, huddled together, talking and wondering what was to become of us in the morning. Conversation ceased as everyone started to settle in for the night, and soon all was still in the dark, cavernous airplane hanger.

"But the silence was quickly broken by the thundering, explosive sound of a military motorcycle with a Partisaner perched on top. It roared into the hangar entrance, stopping abruptly, directly in front of the crowd of woman. The Partisaner bellowed out my name. My heart pounding, I naturally kept still, afraid. 'Elisabetha Hugery,' he cried out once more. Still not making myself known, I stood quietly with the rest of the women.

" *'Lissi, besser gehscht vor, oder holt er uns alli mit.* – Lissi, you better step forward, or he'll take us all', a few of the women next to me whispered. Not wanting to get others hurt, I stepped forward.

"The Partisaner got off his motorcycle and told me to walk in front of him. Gun to my back, he marched me out the hangar and out the entrance gate, not uttering one single word.

"As I kept on walking, all kinds of things came to my mind. At first I thought he'd shoot me in the back. My heart beat wildly. When was he going to pull the trigger? Was he going to kill me? However, the further we got into Karlsdorf the less evident it seemed that this was going to happen. Why was I being led back into town? Was it because I tried to trick them about your age? What did he want of me?

"As we came to the cemetery, Basl and Tant came walking toward us. They were on their way to the hangar to bring me the allotted change of clothing as all the families of the young women had been ordered to do. The three of us just stared into each others' eyes and continued walking as if we were complete strangers, afraid to acknowledge the other's presence for fear of the consequences.

"He led me past the cemetery and into town; just outside the high walled yard of our friend, Schani Batschi, he told me to stop.

"'Go directly to your home and don't you dare turn around or look back,' the Partisaner commanded.

"I practically ran home, keeping my eyes straight ahead. Never once did I alter my gaze in any other direction" my mother told me, "I'm happy to have lived through the ordeal."

When she opened the door my mother was greeted by Mutter and my grandmother's cousin, Sofie Tant. Mother told them what had happened and that she didn't understand why. My grandmother and her cousin explained to my mother what had gone on that late afternoon.

When Mutter had learned from Basl that my mother had not succeeded in convincing the Partisaner that I was not yet weaned, she was desperate to do something to keep my mother from being shipped to Russia, like my father. She knew that a high-ranking Russian officer used her cousin Sofie's house as his headquarters and living quarters and she knew the only hope was to beg this man for mercy.

When my grandmother got to Sofie Tant's house, the officer was sitting at the dinner table. She dropped down on her knees, crying and begging for compassion. She told him that my brother and I had our father taken to Russia and now they were taking our mother. My grandmother asked if he couldn't see she was old and couldn't take care of two young children, especially since her granddaughter was only four years old and was incapable of taking care of herself. With tears she pleaded and begged him to stop them from sending her daughter-in-law to the slave labor camp.

Sofie Tant, who spoke perfect Serbian, was able to translate the pain that her cousin was feeling and the urgency of this matter to this Russian officer. He told her to go home. Everything would be taken care of. He'd send someone to release my mother and she'd be sent home to her children.

Funny how things of this importance never get told to children of a family. It's been over 45 years, and all this time I had no idea what both my mother and grandmother went through to keep us safe in this so-called civilized world.

But other women weren't so lucky. They were taken away a few days after my mother was let go. Tito's government and the USSR had made a deal whereby Tito agreed to send a quota of slave laborers to Russia's coal mines. Most were young girls and women, since there were not many young men left. The Partisaner, Tito's communist guerilla fighters, were in charge of gathering up the slave laborers to hand over to the Russian government.

The warm rays of the sun were streaming through the bedroom window onto the floor where I was sitting, playing contentedly with a thin gold chain, shaping hearts and circles. I remember being fascinated by how the small links could form all kinds of designs so easily, just by my fingertips pushing and pulling the chain in different directions.

Suddenly the quiet was broken. Yelling and screaming came from the street outside. I jumped up and looked out the window, where I saw a group of rolling wagons full of women. Mothers reaching over the sides and back of the wagon, crying children with outstretched hands grabbing onto their mothers' hands, soldiers yelling and hitting the children and mothers with the butts of their guns – over and over again and again until they let go of each other.

Why were the soldiers hitting them? I wondered. What if the Partisaner came to get me?

Those were the same women who days before had been to the village hall with my mother and me. Some were teenagers who had never in their lives been more than a few miles out of Karlsdorf; others were young mothers who had to leave small children behind, many never to see each other again. One or the other or both would perish.

The wagons took them to the train where they were put into freight cars, just like my father and the others before them.

CHAPTER

3

Enslavement and Removal to Russia

In October of 1944, after the Russians had occupied Karlsdorf for a month, an order was issued stating that all men and boys ages 16 to 60 must report to the *Feuerdepot*. My father, being thirty three years old, was among the two hundred and seventy young boys and men standing in groups of four in front of the fire station house one morning; they were all that was left of the entire young male population in our village of 4,000. Many had been drafted into the occupying German army, most unwillingly. Others had fled or been rounded up and killed by the Communists. Now, those who remained stood at attention and waited to see what was to happen next.

One of the commanders shouted an order in Serbian: "Right face." The men turned and faced the Village Hall next to the station.

The doors opened and out streamed a large group of Partisaner carrying machine guns. Pointing the guns at the boys and men, the Partisaner took over the command from the Russian soldiers, encircling the group of males and marching them towards the cemetery.

Now it is our turn, my father thought. We're going to be shot. Just as the others before us.

They passed the cemetery and stopped in front of the airplane hangars.

"The first ten men step forward," came the command from the Partisaner in charge. No one moved. They were afraid that the time had come to be executed. Again the order was shouted; still no one moved. The Partisaner then forced ten out of the line and took them into the hangar.

Eventually, all the men were marched inside, searched and stripped. Everything was taken: watches, pocket knives, belts, whatever each had with him. Then they were told to find a place on the ground to sleep.

As soon as they had settled down for the night a Partisaner came storming in and bellowed out a few names and ordered them to step forward. The men were then taken at gun point and marched into the other hangar.

"I didn't sleep that night. The screams kept up for more than an hour."

This routine of beatings was carried out nightly. If your name was called you were taken and beaten mercilessly. Some pulled through and others didn't. "I remember listening to the screams of the men every night, as I lay quietly in the dark, wondering if I would be next," my father told me.

For two weeks, the inmates kept busy constructing a kitchen by the hangars. My father, and the other cabinet makers and carpenters were put in charge. Every day they had to return to their own shops in town to fetch wood, tools and supplies. At night they had to return to the hangar.

"Rumors had started to circulate in camp that we would be shipped off to Russia." Tati told me. "One day early in November the rumor became a fact."

"We were taken to cut down trees in the forest located about twenty kilometers from Karlsdorf. But instead of going back to camp as usual, we were loaded onto wagons and driven out of Karlsdorf."

Partisaner and their machine guns accompanied the prisoners as they rolled out of town and on through our neighboring ethnic Rumanian town of Nikolenz.

The drivers of the wagons were men from Nikolenz who had been drafted to do the job. When the wagon train came to the middle of the town they were ordered to stop.

My father's wagon happened to stop right in front of the house of his good friend and customer, Kenta Bosjock. Maria, his wife, who had often been an overnight guest with her husband at our house, came running out the front door. She ran up to my father's wagon, crying out in distress, *"Meister Jani, was mache die mit enk? –* Master John, what are they doing with you?" She clasped her hands together and wept. "Where are they taking you?"

When the Partisaner saw that the driver had permitted the woman to speak to someone on his wagon, he took the butt of his gun and brought it down upon the man's body. He hit him over and over – wherever the blows fell. Insanely he continued to pound with his heavy weapon. Drenching the driver's body in blood. My father and the rest of the passengers watched in painful silence as the Partisaner persisted in all his mania, afraid to acknowledge even to themselves, what they had just witnessed.

The wagons rolled out of Nikolenz and on to the nearby city of Werschetz (population fifteen thousand). People were gathered from all of the surrounding area and transported to the city of Werschetz. A large sugar beet factory had been turned into an internment camp to collect the young men and women who were to be shipped off to Russia.

"Eventually, eight thousand souls were gathered in the basement of the enormous building." Tati told me. "That's all it contained: no furniture, bedding or straw — only human beings and a cement floor for us to sleep on.

"There we stayed for a week or two, having no idea what was going to happen to us. Then we were marched to the train station. On the way there, I recall vividly two drunks coming out of a tavern, holding up bottles.

"'Look, *Schwabos,* we're drinking your wine,'" they shouted.

"At the train station, we were loaded into cattle cars. The next stop was Pantschowa, where more prisoners were picked up. From there, for some reason or other, we were once more taken back to Werschetz. Finally, the cattle cars were barricaded from the outside and the train started on its trip to Russia.

"We still had no direct knowledge that we were finally on our way. We had been told we were going to Russia but not when.

"To reach the Romanian border, we first had to pass through Karlsdorf, but the train did not stop. The cruelty of being so close to Karlsdorf and yet unable to make contact was almost unbearable for us *Karlsdorfer's.* We shouted and cried out in hopes that we'd be heard. We looked through the slats of the car, to get a last glimpse of our home."

"I, as well as most of the townspeople heard the voices coming from the train," my mother told me. "But by the time we got to the station, the train had passed and all was silent once more."

On the cattle train it was just as if livestock was being shipped through Romania and on to Russia.

"We slept on the bare floor with nothing but a hole in the floor for a toilet," my father said. "We had to squat over the hole in front of everyone. There was no heat. No food was given to us until the twenty-first day when we got to the Russian border. We had to share what little food and drink each of us had brought with us. And as for water, only a few stops were made to take on a bucket of water from a river or lake, whatever happened to be near the tracks.

"At the border of Russia and Romania, the barricades were removed and the prisoners were ordered to get off the train. The train could go no further, since the tracks were a different width on the Russian side. Armed Russian guards and dogs surrounded us and marched us across the border, where a freight train was waiting.

"The train was as long as the eye could see. It seemed to have no end."

Tens of thousands of German women and men had been brought from all parts of Yugoslavia, Hungary and Romania that had once been Austria-Hungary.

"Each car held about sixty people. Women outnumbered us three to one. Men and women were kept in separate cars. In Rumania more prisoners had been loaded onto the cars. Some of them who I had talked to," my father told me, "had simply been kidnaped by the Yugoslavian Partisaner who had crossed over the Romanian border into German towns and snatched people off the streets.

"They had abducted young girls the same way in Werschetz, Yugoslavia. The Partisaner had gone to the German sections of the city, rounded up teenage girls and women, and took them by force into slavery.

"When everyone was aboard the new train, which had the same accommodations as the train left behind, the doors were once more nailed shut and the train rambled on to its unknown destination.

"Before the doors were sealed, we received our food supply for the trip. Our menu consisted of a raw, halved sheep carcass which was tossed into each car. No wood, stove, or container went along with our dinner.

"From the endless line of cattle cars only a handful had small wood burning stoves aboard. And as luck would have it, one of them happened to be in ours.

"One of the men had found a long railroad spike which we used to break off wood from the inside of the car to make a feeble fire. Cutting small pieces of meat off the sheep carcass, we took turns holding our portion over the flames."

The train rambled on, past Odessa and along the Black Sea; for another week until it finally stopped at Dnjeperpetrovsk, a city by the

Dnjeper River, about a thousand kilometers (600 miles) from the Romanian border.

"Everyone was finally let out of the cars for the first time and given food. The allotted portion for each carload of sixty or so people was two small buckets of salted herrings and a bucket of water. Once more we were loaded onto the cattle cars and nailed in to continue the journey."

Up until this point the weather had been mild and, around the Black Sea region, even balmy. Not knowing that they were heading for freezing conditions, the men had removed two by four's from the cattle car's walls for fuel. At the time, the open gaps left in the wall had not mattered too much. But as the freight train turned and headed northeast, towards the ice cold winter fields of the Dombas region, the cold, icy wind blew through and the frosty air reached in, grabbing at the freezing prisoners who now huddled together. My father has often told me how unbearable the cold was. Some men didn't even have overcoats and most by now were very sick from lack of food.

"Days melted into nights and nights back into days. Finally one night at around two in the morning the train stopped."

"The solders banged on the doors and yelled, 'get up and get ready to disembark.'

"We got our things together and waited. One hour, two, three: no one came to unlock the door. Soon it got lighter. Through the cracks of the cattle car all I could see was the wind whirling unending snow in all directions. The gusts blew in through the slats of the train wagon, and chilled us to the very bone. Finally at eight in the morning a group of solders came, and ordered us out.

"As I stepped off the train I was surprised to see only a few box cars standing on the tracks. Gone was the long, endless train line that had been like a large snake moving across Russia. Cars had been disconnected hundreds of miles before, a few at a time, and at different locations. Now there were only four or five left.

"We huddled together in the howling wind, holding on to our bags and luggage, waiting to see what would come next. Our group consisted mostly of young girls and women, some no more than sixteen or seventeen years old.

"We had to walk in the snow to the village of Almanzna, a hamlet consisting of nothing but clusters of mud huts. In the center of the village we were ordered to stop when we came to the *Kontora*, which is Russian for office. The building looked just like the rest of the mud huts in town. The door opened and the man in charge came out and spoke to us in Russian.

"I could understand what he was saying, Russian is very similar to Serbian. We were told to put our belongings on a pile in front of the office because our destination was up on a hill and about four kilometers (three miles) away, a truck was going to come and pick up the baggage and bring it to us.

"We put our things down as ordered, not realizing that the authorities would dip their fingers into our belongings and take out whatever pleased them. Thus when the luggage was returned, some containers were almost empty and others only half full.

"I was lucky, I had a big sack which did not open as easily as a suitcase to display all the 'goods' inside, so they left it alone.

"We were then marched out of town. The wind whistled around us, the cold numbed our bodies as we marched on through the endless white landscape. No road was to be seen anywhere.

"Later that spring when all the snow had melted I found out that there were no roads.

"Although they had no proper clothing and nothing more on their feet than silk stockings and high heels, the women who were snatched off the streets had to follow along just like the rest of us, knee deep in snow.

"We walked on until we came to railroad tracks. The guards, who were mostly Russian women, led us alongside the tracks. We marched on into the vast whiteness with nothing else before or behind us. My eyes hurt from the bright snow. The cold bit into my flesh. Never before had I felt so solidly frozen...it must have been forty below zero.

"Finally we came to a hill. A long row of electric poles led up to the top. The wind plucked at the wire, making it sing. Fighting the wind all the way, our group trudged up the hill. At last we reached the top where a square stone building stood. We sixty men, along with the two-hundred and seventy girls and women, were escorted inside. The building contained four rooms, three for the women and the fourth for us men.

"Our room was no bigger than 10 feet by 20 feet. At the longest wall, a long double decked, wooden platform, served as beds. No straw or hay was provided, only the wooden planks. If you had a blanket, fine. If not, too bad. We sixty men took turns sleeping, one shift standing up while the other lay down.

"There was no heat, water or toilet facilities. A ditch out in the open, with a long railing to sit on, was available when nature called. There sat a girl, here sat a boy; it made no difference what gender you were, for both sexes were deadened to the world.

"The last food that we had were the buckets of fish back in Dnjeperpetrovsk. Four days went by since we were brought to this place and still we had received nothing to eat.

"Finally, on the fifth day, a one horse wagon with two wheels came rolling up the hill, driven by a woman. There in back of the wagon was a large wooden barrel filled with *Borscht*. This was to be our first meal in our new home."

APRIL 18, 1945

I was fast asleep in Mami's bed. Tati was not with us anymore. Mami, Seppi and I slept in the bedroom, Mutter in the other room by herself. The shock of the bright light and men's voices startled me awake.

Quickly I sat up clinging tightly to my *Tuchet*, my feather coverlet. There by the bedroom door stood three Partisaner, their large guns with long knives on the end pointing straight at us. Dark, foreboding eyes glistened from behind black bushy brows and mustached faces. Shouting in Serbian, they started toward Mami who was standing at the foot of our bed. I watched in horror as they pulled at Mami's hand. What were they doing? They were hurting Mami. I started to cry. Their voices rose as they pulled some more on her hand. It seemed forever until they got what they wanted: Mami's wedding ring. Pointing to her ears they said something again and proceeded to take her earrings.

Seppi stood on one side of me next to the bed, not saying a word. He stood glued to the floor. My grandmother came out of her room and stood in the doorway. In shock at first, she started to cry and lament. At this point I became even more frightened. The Partisaner said something else to my Mami and Mutter, pointing their guns. I could not understand what was said or what was going on. Why were these terrible men in our house?

The next memory I have is of walking along our street. It was cold and dark. The whole street was full of people. People in front and back of us, the whole street packed all the way across.

I was on the outside left of the road, holding on to Mutter's hand, afraid and bewildered. My grandmother held on to me with one hand, in the other she carried a small bundle. Crying over and over....

"Was mache die mit uns. Mein Gott. Jessas, Maria, und Josef was mache die mit uns. – What are they going to do

with us? My God. Jesus, Mary, and Joseph, what are they going to do with us?"

I began to cry. If grown-ups didn't know what was going
on, there was good reason for my fear and horror. We kept on
walking. Every time Mutter lamented I would look up at her
pale face surrounded by the black kerchief tied on her head.
I can still see her next to me with the dark woolen
Berlinertiechl, the big woolen shawl she used like a coat
around her shoulders, holding on to me as we were driven out
of our town and into the night. They drove us past the cemetery, out to where they had taken all the young men and
women who were shipped to Russia before us. The airplane
hangars were to be our home for most of the next two years.

They came during the night. They took everything: our
right to sleep in a bed, to eat our own food, to take care of our
bodily functions in privacy.

They drove us from our homes at gunpoint, young and
old, male and female. From the just-born babe to the oldest in
their 90's, driven out the gate like our animals by their herders. But instead of loving keepers with dog and whistle, men
with rifles and bayonets herded us out of town and into the
barbed wire enclosed airplane hangars. Now we were also
considered beasts of burden. But unlike livestock, which was
cared for and protected, we were to be abolished as a people.

At the tender age of four, I was considered an enemy of
the people. A Nazi. A word that no four-year-old could even
know the meaning of or what it stood for.

The saddest part of all was that the rest of the world was
meanwhile rejoicing. Peace, peace was being shouted from
all corners of the Western world. Never again would such in-
human treatment of people be tolerated as it had been during
the war. Never.

Never except in Eastern Europe. As the world powers
cheered "Freedom," they condemned us to hell.

It is very hard for me to relate to you, now that I'm an
adult, what it was like to live for almost three years as the
property of someone else. At the time, I was not aware of what
was happening. Not until my teens did I understand a lot of

things that had gone on in my early childhood, and why. For many years, when I talked about the above incident or any other incident that had occurred in the concentration camp, I would start to shake and cry. Not until I started to write about it was I able to tell my story with my emotions somewhat under control.

We had been considered non-human and dealt with as less than animals, animals to abuse and destroy at the whim of others. At the whim of Marshall Tito's Partisaner. The guards had been told they could do with us what they wanted.

The politicians of the Western world pretended to be deaf, blind, and dumb. Truman, Churchill and DeGaul rejoiced with Stalin; rejoiced in victory. But not one of them interfered with their Communist Allies to stop what they were doing with us ethnic Germans in the eastern block. Nothing was told to the rest of the world. A population of fifteen million people were condemned for something they had no control over. More than two million ethnic Germans who had been living in Eastern Europe perished in the next few years.[2] The only crime we had committed was to be born ethnic Germans.

Neither our dead nor the camps used for slave labor and starvation were included in Yugoslavia's history of World War II. We have no pictures, newspapers, or newsreels to show the world what was done to us. No visual or written records of our internment were made public, and after more than 50 years, the facts have still not been acknowledged or made known.

One-half million people have simply been written out of Yugoslavia's history, as well as fifteen million out of the rest of Eastern Europe. It is hard when one loses everything he owns, but unbearable when one loses one's identity and history.

---

[2]From the book "Nemesis at Potsdam" by Alfred M. deZayas. London. Routledge & Kegan Paul. 1979. pp. xxi-xxv.

CHAPTER

4

In the Airplane Hangars Spring and Summer 1945

I t was always dark. Even when the sun shone outside, it remained cold and dark inside. I could not understand why the Partisaner had brought us to this place. I can't recall ever asking or being told "why." It was cold and damp sleeping on the packed dirt floor of this cavernous building. All we had was the bedding that Mami had carried with her. I did not like sleeping on the hard ground. My bed is what I wanted. People were all around us, all the people from the whole town under one roof. So many people. At night everyone slept on the bare ground, with no bed or cot, not even straw. Groups of people slept huddled together, encircling their few remaining possessions as if around a camp fire. Mami, Seppi, Basl, and my cousins, Marie and Andres, were on the outside of our group and I, the youngest, was in the middle. We slept near the entrance of the airplane hangar. At night, I'd fall asleep surrounded by my family.

When I awoke that first morning, my eyes would not open. I tried again and again, but nothing happened. Crying and screaming, I touched my fingers to my eyes and felt a hard crust on my lashes. My eyelids were stuck together!

Mami drew me onto her lap, holding me still, trying to wash my eyes with water. She embraced me tighter, talking and coaxing, and finally my eyelids opened. I was able to see once more. This occurred many mornings and made me afraid to go to sleep at night.

I had come down with a bad eye infection. Every night, pus would ooze from under my eyelids and harden. Because of the unclean conditions around us, we were exposed to minor and major infections.

I have often thought since then how hard it must have been on my mother and all the other mothers, how helpless they must have felt, not to be able to tend to their children's most ordinary needs. They could not summon the doctor – there was none. Nor was there medicine. We were lucky if we had soap.

Outside, way back by the side of the hangar, was the most degrading place in all of camp, a ditch that served as our toilet. Afraid of falling in, I did not want to use it, but I had no choice. No outhouse, no walls, no choice. When nature called, anyone could see. There was no privacy, anywhere.

Except for the church, the two connected airplane hangars were the highest structures for miles around. Corrugated sheet metal made up the walls. The unpainted tin ceilings and criss-crossing steel beams made the inside dark and dreary. Small windows, located high above, almost touched the arched ceiling and let in only a small amount of daylight. At night a group of bare bulbs dangling from electric cords produced a faint glow.

A constant buzz of voices echoed within the walls. Besides all of the remaining Karlsdorfers, ethnic Germans from neighboring towns had been brought to this *Karlsdorfer Lager* – camp; more than four thousand people, old and young, resided there.

You could hear voices in all tones and degrees of despair, especially the first few weeks. Old Otas and Omas lamented their anguish and sadness, some louder than others. Soft cries of helplessness from women, old and young; everyone had lost family members, their way of life, and all their worldly goods. Children cried and wailed; at the same time others played, sending up peals of laughter. Mothers reprimanded them. Life still went on. Order and manners still had to be taught. Life had to be lived from minute to minute, hour by hour, day to day with hope for a better tomorrow, or you would not be able to remain sane.

Invisible walls went up around each family. A plot of ground was claimed as their own space. Unmarked, no lines drawn, but each member knew that the area, no larger than a few yards, was his home base. No words had to be spoken or agreements drawn up; the human need of "home" is instinctive.

There was no heat in the building. Since all were huddled together when they were sleeping at night, breathing in the cold air and exhaling the warm moist air, a strange thing occurred every morning. During the night, the warm air rose to the ceiling from the thousands of sleeping people. Towards morning, as the air slowly cooled, the moist air became heavy and turned into droplets of water which dripped down and rained on us.

During the day, my brother Seppi, cousin Andres, and I were left behind with all the other young children and old people. I waited daily for Mami to come back from her assigned job.

Often I'd daydream about scampering under the wire to be on the other side of the fence. I'd wander over to the right corner fence post in back of the yard where the hole was. This is where Mami slipped under in the evening and snuck out. I would stand in front of the fence and stare at the place on the ground in awe. If you looked close, you could see the slight downward slope of the earth that made it possible to crawl under the fence.

The first time Mami snuck out we had only been in the airplane hangar one day. The night before when we had been driven out, Mutter, panic-stricken and disorganized, had brought nothing along to sleep on. My poor grandmother had to sleep on the bare ground. So the next day, my mother crept under the fence, went back home and got a few things so Mutter could rest more comfortably at night.

If she had been caught, who knows what would have happened. Mami was a gutsy lady. If you met her now for the first time, you would never guess the things that she did to keep her family alive.

Towards the end of the day I would move closer to the entrance gate, as close to the Partisaner guard as I dared. Not until I saw the women marching towards the camp entrance did I run up to the gate itself to greet Mami and Basl. Holding on to Mami's hand, I skipped back to the building with her. I always hoped Mami had managed to smuggle something to eat inside the camp for us. Oh, I liked it much better when Mami was back. I was always hungry.

At the beginning of our internment, all the women were marched out daily into Karlsdorf to empty our houses. Each house was stripped of its furniture, clothing, food and tools, and the animals were taken away. Then these objects were brought to designated houses to be removed eventually. One house was filled with clothing, another with food, another with furniture, and so on, until all houses had no more traces of their former German owners.

This was repeated all over Yugoslavia. In some towns, not only houses were emptied but people had to remove their good shoes and throw them on a large pile. Then they were marched to another pile of worn and tattered shoes in exchange for their old shoes. Too bad if there wasn't a pair in your size.

What had taken our people many generations to establish, Marshall Tito and his men wiped out in only a few weeks. Our birth, baptism, marriage and death certificates were destroyed. Inside our churches, soldiers used our Crucifixes and Madonnas for target practice, and their bayonets chopped off the heads of our statues of saints. Some even used the altar to relieve themselves.

By late winter, when the whole town was empty, Serbian people were brought in from the faraway mountain region. These people had no permanent houses, since they moved from place to place with their grazing animals.

"Each was assigned one of our houses", my mother told me. "They were told that the Schwabos abandoned the houses. But eventually the new residents figured out who the people behind the barbed wire fence were, for some of them stopped us during our labor in town and expressed regret that they had taken over our homes".

These nomads did not know the ways of running our property and continued to live as they were accustomed. Preferring a dirt floor, they tore up the wooden floors for fire wood. They tied up their animals with electrical wires. Some of the poor beasts chewed them and accidentally electricuted themselves.

The town was a shambles even before these people came in, and it has never been restored to the clean, orderly state of which the *Karlsdorfers* had been so proud.

One warm, sunny day, we had to line up in front of the entrance gate, as if in a parade. Everyone had to march – all four thousand of us – young and old, willing or not. We stepped out past the guard post, then turned and marched around the fence through the tall grass. My mother's brother Franz Onkel led the way, playing his trumpet. I liked the way he played. The notes made me want to dance. Mami held on to my hand as we marched near the front of the long snake of people being led out of the gates. I had a hard time keeping up with everyone, since my short legs had to step high. I was almost up to my hips in grass.

We marched around the side and back of the hangar, past the back fence. The parade continued all around the fence and back to the gate, with the music playing and the thousands of voices still singing old folk songs. It was so good to be outside.

On one side of the gate was a small hill of dirt. Franz Onkel marched to the top of the hill, and a small group of people gathered in back of him as if they were the choir and he the director. He then turned toward us and proceeded to play his trumpet, accompanying the voices behind him. They sang for quite some time. All the people around me became quiet and listened. I thought that it was beautiful.

Little did I know then that this was meant to be a punishment. On May 9, 1945 we were "celebrating" the surrender of the German Government and the end of the war in Europe. Ironically, though the people of Germany were then free, we, who had been snared into this war through circumstances beyond our control, now had to continue to pay for Nazi Germany's action. No freedom was in our future for another three and a half years, not until the end of 1948. We were still considered enemies of the state by the Communists and had to be punished accordingly. I wonder what logic was used to justify this action. Certainly they were not afraid of what we would do to the country in retaliation. All that was left of our people were women, children and old men.

"How did you feel as you held on to our hands, singing the old folk songs that day," I asked my mother.

"It was one of the darkest moments in my life," she told me. "All hope of being set free was dashed from my grasp. But I knew I had to go on because of you and your brother. That's what gave me strength to continue."

Every morning, all able-bodied residents of our camp reported for duty. Standing at attention, squinting at the sun, they listened to the camp commander's propaganda speech and had to shout, "*Schivio Tito* – Long live Tito," and pound the air with their fists before they were assigned to certain work groups. Some were sold for the day to the people standing at the entrance gate, as if they were property.

Groups of women were taken out of camp to work as road gangs or cleanup crews or for field work, or wherever large numbers of people were needed. And as the groups were marched to and from their destinations, they'd sing to help them forget their misery.

One time my mother was on duty with such a group when one of the women began to sing. All joined in, singing some of the old folk songs. Lilting tunes from happier days sprang from their throats in unison. At first the Partisaner did not mind. But with time, this began to irritate them. So to make them stop, they worked the women harder. But the harder the women worked the more they sang, for the singing made the work go a little better. Then the guards ordered them to stop.

Seeing that the singing disturbed their captors, one of the younger women said; "We *Schwabos* have to sing to be able to work happily and hard". "If that is the case then continue to sing," the man in charge grumbled.

They sang the rest of the day and continued their warbling on the march back to camp, more so than most days. Nothing more was said by the guards.

The triumphant workers marched in through the front gate as if they had been the victors. But they were wrong. The Partisaner did not let them "fall out" of line as usual.

"Attention," the captain yelled. "Since singing made your *Schwabo* hearts glad, I want you to sing until you are ecstatic with happiness. I will tell you when you achieve this."

The women had to stand at attention and sing, continuing in the moonlight until past eleven o'clock when some of the women fainted. They were then finally dismissed, and the camp commander told them he hoped the singing had brought them much happiness.

Outside, in back of the hangar, is where I spent most of my day. With nothing to play with, I spent my time gazing out of the fence, past the barbed wire, out into the red sea of flowers or up to the white puffs of clouds in the sky. I let my imagination run free. As I watched the clouds form all kinds of shapes, incredible beings and fairy tales were painted in my mind.

Sometimes my cousin Marie would amuse me in the big yard of the concentration camp. Marie was about seven years older than I. And I loved her. She was the one person who made my young life bearable. She was my big sister and protector. When she was around, life was not so lonely because she always had time for me. When I think of Marie, I think of sunshine, laughter, dancing and her smiling face.

My first memory of my cousin is the warm, bright afternoon when she showed me how to dance. Marie and my second cousin Katilie gathered two or three of us little ones together to play *Ringereie* – ring-around-the-rosie.

A boy in his early teens played the harmonica, and as he played we started to dance, hopping and skipping in circles. Then the big girls showed us how to waltz. Marie took both of my hands in hers and showed me how to do the steps the right way. I kept on looking down at our feet, watching very carefully, so I would do it correctly. My little legs learned the waltz steps quickly. Marie and I were suspended in the air as we swayed to the lilting tune of the harmonica playing in three quarter time. We flew as if we had wings. Marie's long, brown, sun streaked hair swung in time with the music, surrounding her face like a cloud with the sun shining through. Her smiling face, with those dark eyes and rosy cheeks, beamed down happily into mine and I into hers. Yes, Marie made my young life a lot happier. I wanted to be just like her.

Most of the time girls and boys Marie's age were made to work in the fields and woods from morning until night. Sometimes they had to carry heavy bundles of firewood from more than 15 miles away. Or they had to help plant or harvest in the fields. Armed Partisaner marched with them, making sure they worked hard. I'm sure that after all this she was often tired, but Marie always had time for me and never sent me away.

I was always hungry. The bluish *Grauplsupp* and rock-hard *Mallei* – corn bread – were hard to swallow. Sometimes it just stuck in my throat. Why was the *Mallei* so hard? It wasn't hard when we had eaten it at home, but instead had smelled so good. Its coarse moistness melted in your mouth when you bit into the warm golden slice. But this was so dry you couldn't even bite a piece off without soaking it in the soup first. The soup tasted awful. It was slimy. The few kernels of barley that floated in the bluish liquid were not enough to fill a spoon. After eating everything I was still hungry.

Why did we get so little to eat? I could have eaten a whole loaf of bread that Mami used to make back home, the big round loaves that were the size of a *Baxsimpl* – small basket. She used to bring them to the baker at the corner down our street. Sometimes I would go with her to watch. He placed the bread on a long flat wooden paddle that looked like a boat oar, slid it back into the big deep oven, lining the loaves up in rows, and then closed the heavy iron door with a clank. Later in the day, Mami and I would go back to pick up our bread. Oh, how good it smelled. I could hardly wait to get home to eat a slice. Before Mami cut the bread, she took the loaf and held it sideways to her chest with her left arm. Holding the knife in her right hand, she'd make the sign of the cross with the point, three times on the bottom of the loaf, and said the blessing. Then she would finally cut a thick slice for me. The crust was so crisp and tasty. And the warm, white, soft middle would almost melt in your mouth.

The only time I got to eat real bread in camp is when Mami smuggled a small piece in for me. She managed to bring something for Seppi and me every day. An apple, pear or whatever fruit she could find, or a raw potato was good. Anything that she brought helped ease the hunger. As evening drew near I could hardly wait for Mami to come back to see what or if she had managed to bring something to eat.

Hunger and malnutrition were always a problem. It was almost impossible to stay well or even alive with just the meager food rations allotted daily, and I always got *Spatze Ecke* – literally, sparrow corners. My mouth looked like a baby sparrow's with yellow on each side of the beak. I felt the hurt the minute I woke up. It always took so long for the pussy sores to heal. Every time I opened my mouth the crusted corners cracked open and oozed, making it hurt all over again. Malnutrition caused many painful conditions.

My mother did anything she could to keep us fed and alive. She had sewn pockets in her clothing and undergarments where she would hide things daily. If she worked in the fields, she'd tie the legs of her underwear together and put whatever she was harvesting in her drawers. Or if she worked in houses, or saw food on the way, she'd beg or steal whenever she could.

Sometimes mother would sneak out of camp, go back home, and get something out of hiding from our house.

A few months before we were driven out of our house, she had seen how bad things were getting and decided to hide all kinds of small articles that she thought could be worth something someday, things like nails, screws and small tools from my father's shop.

These objects are what Mami retrieved when she went back. She used them to barter for food. She had her sources, whether in Karlsdorf or the neighboring town of Nikolenz, or even with some of the Partisaner.

It took courage to do what my mother did. If she had approached the wrong guard or been caught she could have been beaten or given some other severe punishment.

But God must have watched over her. She almost always got away without harm. If she had not been so daring we might have died of starvation. Many children died because they had no parent or grandparent to take such risks. I was lucky, since I had not just my mother with me but also my aunt, Basl.

And what can I tell you of Basl? Of all three of my mother's siblings, Basl – or Kati, as she was called – was the one that Mami was closest to. They leaned on each other for strength during the dark days in camp.

Next to my mother, Basl is the adult female member of my family I remember best from my childhood. She and her two children, Marie and Andres, and Mami, Seppi and I, stuck together. Together the six of us feared, hungered, cried, laughed, begged for food, shared what we had, and eventually we escaped to freedom together.

Sometimes, if my mother wasn't around, Basl was my mother. She loved and disciplined. But to tell you the truth, I don't ever recall that she spanked me. I know that I hated to be deloused and Basl was the only one who was able to make me hold still long enough to finish the job.

My head itched all the time. The first time Mami found out that we had lice she was upset. Trying to get rid of the lice became almost impossible. This of course did not stop Mami and Basl. Just because everyone else had lice, did not mean that the war against the tiny little insect was to cease; certainly not. In fact, one of my mothers greatest triumphs was that she won the war of delousing by sheer perseverance. In fall of 1947 we had no more lice.

Armed with a *Lauskambl* – a fine-tooth comb, Mami or Basl deloused my brother, cousins and me weekly. For the boys it was no big deal, for they had short hair. But for me it was pure torture. Wedged between two knees, I was unable to go anywhere.

"Basl, net rop mei Haar." I pleaded. "Don't pull my hair".

"Muscht scheen halle dann tuts net weh," Basl told me. "Hold still then it won't hurt."

She would hold my head over a white paper in front of us on the ground, then slowly comb through my hair repeatedly, stroke after stroke, dislocating the nits and making them fall onto the paper. Once on the paper, the nits would be popped, so to speak, by clicking them between one's two thumb nails and destroying them.

When my mother deloused me I gave her a much harder time. But for Basl I would hold still. Even if the comb didn't always pull smoothly through my tangled hair, I let Basl do the job with not too much complaining.

I must admit I was very stubborn sometimes if I set my sails to make things go my way. But Basl knew how to handle me better than anyone. She'd be a little more patient, and I'd be a little less stubborn.

"Net immer glei wahne mei Kind," Basl would say to me. "Don't always cry right away, my child; smiles are better."

She was more or less a soft spoken person, but also a determined lady, and knowing this, I usually gave in and did what she wanted. Now my mother was not so patient – she had a much shorter fuse than her sister.

Hella was our neighbor who had lived a few houses down from us on our street. Since she was Hungarian and not German, she was not considered an enemy of the people and could live a normal life, or as near normal a life as could be expected under the Communists. Nothing was taken from her family.

Hella and my parents were good friends and neighbors. Before everything was taken from us, my mother had given Hella all of our money, our good clothing and some small electrical appliances to keep. In return, Hella helped us out as much as possible. She used the money that my mother had given to her to buy my mother out of camp once a week. My mother managed to take me along a few times. She sometimes talked the guard into letting me go along. He'd look the other way when we went out past his post.

Hella's husband had died during the war and now she and her son Jani lived alone in their house. I watched Mami iron Hella's clothes in the small bright kitchen. I liked to be here. It reminded me of our kitchen when we were still neighbors with Hella. The sun shone through the window, making the white cabinet with its glass door gleam behind Mami as she moved the silvery iron back and forth on the ironing board. The iron my mother used was originally hers. It was one of the items she'd given to her good friend. I have asked my mother why she hadn't used the electric iron when we were still at home. She told me that because of the electrical rationing during the war, she had to use her old charcoal iron, there was no power during the day.

Jani, Hella's son, was about my age. That first summer we played together. To cool off in the hot summer afternoons we splashed in a *Mulder* that was set up in the courtyard. The water almost reached up to our shoulders as we sat in the wooden wash tub. By the time we were through, more water was on the ground than in the tub.

Late that fall, a typhoid epidemic broke out in camp and many people died. Because barb wire does not stop disease, poor Jani's life was not spared. The illness came to claim him like so many others. Now his mother was all alone.

Being a child was not easy. Sometimes it was hard to understand why things were the way they were. One day in particular stands out more than any other.

Mami handed me one of my patent leather shoes. Oh, it was so shiny. Onkel, my father's brother Franz, had made them for me. I wanted to wear the shoes, but Mami said they were too small. Sadly I handed them back to her. We were in Hella's *Summerkuchel*. The summer kitchen is where she kept all our things hidden. All our good clothes were hung on a long pole and covered up with a blanket. Mami had asked if I wanted to see some of my dresses. The one I wanted to see most was my *Samtkleid* – my velvet dress. I watched with anticipation as she reached up high and took down my dress, the most beautiful thing that I had. *Mei Samenskleid* as I called it, was as soft as a baby chick, I remembered how when I wore it I'd run my hand over the sleeves or the wide skirt. Or I'd pick up the skirt, just to feel its softness.

The material was a burgundy color. It had long sleeves with white lace at the wrists, a white round lace-edged collar with a thin bow and a high waist. A row of tiny embroidered flowers encircled the hemline. I touched the flowers and stroked the soft nap with my hand. I recalled how I felt like a princess each time I wore it.

"Mami, Bitte, Bitte hol mrs mit." I begged. "Please, please let's take it along."

"Mir kenne net," Mami told me sadly.

"But why can't we?" I persisted. Mami, ignoring my pleas, took the dress and hung it back with the other clothing.

Later that day Mami and I walked from Hella's backyard through the other backyards of our neighbor's emptied houses. No one as of yet occupied them.

When we entered our own deserted backyard, its empty silence hung all around us. No bellowing, cackling, squawking or sudden feather flying, dust billowing commotion – gone were the animals.

When we opened the door to the courtyard its strangeness was even more overwhelming. Our *Hof* looked so different. Weeds now grew through the cobblestones and debris was scattered all about. A few flowers bloomed among the weeds in the garden by the summer kitchen.

"Wait here!" Mami said as she entered the doorway that led into our former home. All the rooms in the house were empty, as well as the other buildings. Everything was so quiet.

I walked over to the forsaken patch of blossoms, bent down and picked a small yellow flower. *Maulauf*, I uttered to myself as I squeezed the flower. Slowly the mouth-like petals opened "That's why you're called *Maulauf*, you can open your mouth," I stated to the snapdragon flower between my fingers.

Still holding the flower in my hand I spied something from the corner of my eye. My brother's old toy wagon. A REAL TOY. I was overjoyed. I held the wagon in my hands, and for a moment all was as it had been. I played with it as I had done so many times before, pulling it back and forth on the bumpy cobblestones, back and forth.

When Mami came from the house with some of the objects that she had retrieved from their hiding place in the attic (and which she would later use to barter for food), she told me:

"Put the wagon down and come along, we have to go now."

"No, Mami, no," I begged. "Please let me keep it."

Mami bent down and gently took the wagon from my hands and said, "You can't keep it. It has to stay here, just like the dress, for the guard will only take it away."

She then laid the toy wagon on the cobblestones, took me by the hand, and led me through the backyard gate.

CHAPTER
5

In Franz Onkel's House
Late Summer to Early Winter 1945

That Summer, after all the houses in our village had been emptied, we were taken from the airplane hangars and moved back into some of the now-empty houses in Karlsdorf. A few streets were blocked off and guards were posted at either end. Part of the village now was our prison.

As many families as possible were jammed into a small section of the town in houses that had only two or three rooms.

By coincidence, most of the members of my mother's family were assigned to Franz Onkel's former house, including the former owner himself. Franz Onkel was my mother's brother, seventeen years older than Mami. She has often said that because of their age difference, she can't even remember him before he was married. She always connects Franz with his wife Ritzi.

Franz and Ritzi had two children, a son, who died before his first birthday, and a daughter, Anna, who was only nine years younger than my mother. Anna's daughter, Inge, was only a few years younger than I.

Franz Onkel, a bricklayer by trade, had worked for the local Hertz *Salamifabrik*. Before the war, Hertz Salami had started to make a name for itself all over the world. The sausage was exported to other European countries and had even found its way across the ocean to America. For many years Franz Onkel repaired and maintained the company buildings. When the new government took over, the men who had been employed by Hertz Salami factory were not shipped to Russia but were kept back to continue to work and operate the now government-owned sausage factory.

It was much more comfortable sleeping in this small room in my Franz Onkel's house than on the packed-down ground in the hangar. Along either side of the wall, foot-high boards were nailed to the floor from corner to corner. Loose straw was spread between the wall and the board, creating a bed that slept ten or more people lined up in one long row. Mami, Seppi and I slept on the right side of the room, and Mami's cousin Kathi Schüssler and her two children Peter and Katilie slept on the other side by the window. More than fifty people were crowded together in the three-room house and attached buildings on my Franz Onkel's former property. Our room alone was occupied by twenty or more people. The only place one could be alone was the outhouse.

Although so many people surrounded me, I often felt lonely. Mami was usually gone for the day when I woke in the morning. Still warm and a little sleepy in my straw "nest," and not yet ready to get up, I would take a corner of my thick feather coverlet with the crook of my elbow to form a head with a peaked cap; I had my pretend friend come and join me in my straw bed. Sometimes it was my baby. I cooed to it and made it speak back to me. We had heart-to-heart talks, telling each other how lonely we were, or we'd share a little secret, then put our heads together and hug. When I felt its cool smoothness on my warm cheek, I'd feel better.

Our room was the largest room in the house. Before you entered our room you had to pass through a much smaller chamber. Among the ten souls who lived there was Heini, who made life miserable for any girl that came near him. The only way out of the house from our room was through this room. I'd always stick my head through our door and check to make sure the bully wasn't there, because sometimes he was lying in wait, ready to pounce. The room was almost always overflowing with people, so Heini was not easy to spot. On this particular day, I carefully left my room, keeping a lookout for the enemy. Since I did not see him, I started to pass through the door, still casting my eyes around the room. As I took a few steps into the room, Heini suddenly stood in front of me with his arm raised. I froze in my tracks. Before I had a chance to retreat, Heini aimed and fired. The missile found its target. The sharp object struck me on the forehead, missing my eye by a few inches. Blood streamed down, making the injury appear much worse than it actually was.

Everyone in the room came to my rescue. They nabbed Heini just as he was running out the door and justice was delivered on the spot, quickly and thoroughly, when the mother who caught him saw what he had done to me, my injury hurt less after that.

They tended my wound and tied a clean rag around my head: they found the missile, a large nail, he could have blinded me! After that, Heini was under surveillance by every adult in our house. To this day the "Mark of Heini" is still branded on the right side of my forehead.

One of the woman in our house had a daughter my age; Siska was an only child, with waist long, honey-colored hair. Her locks were her crowning glory. Both mother and daughter were very proud of them.

The woman had some sort of connections, for she was always the one that received a little extra from the people in charge. One day an order went out that all children's heads were to be shaved, regardless of their gender.

Since there were so many children in camp the job was not completed in one day. Our house was on the next day's list. That morning, before my mother went to work, she gave Siska's mother a warning: If she returned and found me bald and Siska's hair untouched, she would personally take the scissors to Siska's hair.

Upon her return that evening, my mother found Siska and me to be the only two children in camp with hair on their heads.

I was always easy prey for my brother and cousin Andres, who were both 9 years old.

Andres was dark with brown eyes and shaggy, dark hair that stood up like a brush. Seppi had a light complexion, with hazel eyes and light brown hair that always hung in his face. But both boys had the same piercing look when they were angry, and both loved to joke around and play tricks.

"He Elsa, kumm rauf," Andres called to me one day as I walked by the ladder that led up to the corn crib.

"Come up," my brother echoed. "We've got something to show you."

I climbed the ladder, but when I got to the top, all I could see was the big empty storage room with the sunlight streaming through the slats of its walls.

"What do you want me to see?" I asked, happy that they wanted to share something with me.

"Look at this magic chair we found," they said.

They stepped aside, revealing a small round stool covered with an old dirty rag.

"I don't see any thing magic about that stool."

"You've got to sit on it to make it work," they explained.

I turned around, expecting the surface to be a normal chair. But as I sat down – the rag disappeared, and I sank into the water-filled bucket underneath, soaking my behind.

A few evenings later the three of us were sitting on the straw talking when Andres asked, "Can you speak Serbian?" "Of course," I said.

"Well, how do you say *'Waschschissel'?*"

"Washbowl, that's easy," I answered back and made up some silly name like, Baschel, because I knew he was kidding. We laughed and continued our little game. They asked me some more and I obliged by giving another silly name. Then Seppi asked "How do you say *'Kraml'?*"

"Crackling," I quickly replied, "is *Krampa.*"

"*Krampa* – that's funny! You know what? You're a *Krampa,*" both sang out in unison to aggravate me. Of course, I got angry and when I got angry I cried, just as they hoped I would.

This was fuel for the fire. They started to call me *"Grillse-Grauns-Krampa,"* over and over. And I started to hit, just missing with each try. Mami came to my rescue; this was a mistake. Now they were sure to call me that just because an adult didn't like it.

So I became "Grillse-Grauns-Krampa," a name that was to stick every time one of them wanted to get me mad.

My Franz Onkel, Ritzi Tant, my cousin Anna, and her daughter Inge slept in the kitchen, the only room in the house that had furniture: a small table and chairs that stood in the middle of the room.

In addition, there was a summer kitchen attached to the main house and a barn in the backyard, both of which were used for housing. Among the inhabitants who slept in the barn was my great aunt Mayer's Resbasl. I liked Resbasl a lot. Thick salt and pepper hair framed her cheerful face. She had a merry outlook on life and a little rebel in her heart.

During the day, she kept us little ones entertained; she gathered us around her at the end of our long bed and taught us to sing. I enjoyed these lessons and so did the other children. Every day when Mami came home I showed her how well I had learned my songs.

One day Resbasl decided we were ready for bigger things than children's songs and she taught us this:

Meine Oma fährt Motorrad,
Ohne Bremse, ohne Licht.
Und der Schutzmann an der Ecke,
Sieht das alte Luder nicht.

It translates:

My Granny rides a Motorbike,
Without brakes or lights.
And the policeman at the corner,
Doesn't see the old hussy.

As soon as Mami came home that evening I sang my best for her. At first she seemed pleased, but as the song went on, her smile soon disappeared.

"Wer hat Dich des g'lernt?" she asked me, upset.

"Who taught me? Why Resbasl of course," I answered. "Want to hear the other song?" She nodded yes. Once more I sang my very best. The words to this other song were easy to understand. I understood each and every one of them, and they sure were different from any of the songs we had learned before. When I got through singing, my mothers mouth flew open. She gasped and asked, *"Hat Die Resbasl ah Eich des Lied g'lernt"?*

I nodded yes. "Resbasl also taught us that song."

"Was is den loss mit dem Weib – What is the matter with that woman?" Mami muttered as she got up and left the room.

It was a crude drinking song, l didn't realize how crude until I was much older. No wonder my mother was so angry.

My Resbasl heard an earful from my mother that day, though she didn't think the songs were all that bad. "They're much livelier than children's songs," she told my mother. "And if it bothers you so much I'll promise to behave myself and not teach such songs any more".

Keeping her word, she went back to teaching ordinary *Kinder-Lieder* to all her small songbirds.

Not only was Resbasl my singing instructor, but that summer she also became my hero.

I had fallen into the *Regen Basseen* – rain cistern – in the front yard next to the kitchen, as I was rocking back and forth on its round *Holzdeckel*. The wooden cover suddenly flipped over and I slid in. I landed on my feet like a cat, but the cover flipped back over the hole and I was surrounded by total darkness. There was no way of getting out. I was swallowed up by the deep tank. Luckily it had not rained for some time, so the cistern was empty, or I would surely have drowned.

Panic set in. *"Hilfe! Hilfe!"* I cried "h-e-l-p!" The word echoed all around me. I became frantic. I was afraid no one would hear me and I'd be trapped here forever.

Finally someone lifted the cover and saw me standing at the bottom of the empty *Basseen*, crying and screaming hysterically. I stretched my arms as high as I could. The person above tried reaching down to me, but she could not get a hold of my hands. As I looked up I saw three or four people's heads looking down and calling comforting words to me. Then, out of nowhere, came the familiar take-charge voice from above.

"Ich kumm schun mei Kind, glei hab ich dich heraus." Resbasl called to me. "I'm coming, child. I'll have you up here in no time."

And there she was, leaning down the round hole from above, like an angel from heaven.

Resbasl was a strong lady, almost six feet tall and in her late fifties at the time. I can still feel the force of her strength as she plucked me from the hole and held me until I calmed down. After we left Karlsdorf, we never saw each other again.

My cousin Anna was a pretty woman, with wavy blonde hair, blue eyes and a pale complexion. She was only twenty-one when she died, leaving behind her little girl Inge, age three.

It was on a hot day in August, 1945, when Anna got sick. She and my mother were both giving Inge and me a bath. Anna turned to my mother and told her that she was so cold.

"Please finish bathing Inge, for I must lie down."

Anna never got up again. She died within a few days, a victim of the typhoid epidemic that was beginning to ravage our town. Almost all victims died, with the exception of a lucky few. My brother was one of those who survived. In the first few months in camp when people died they were buried in a somewhat decent manner, like Anna.

She was *aufgebahrt* – laid out – in the middle of our room. Her blonde hair was like a frame around her face and her crossed arms rested on her breast. They told me she now was in heaven with the angels. I stood just a few feet away, sure that any moment she'd awake and open her eyes. People cried, prayed and lamented around her. She was laid out for a day and night, so we had to sleep with my cousin's body in our room. I did not want to be with Anna. I left the house and went outside. I found Mutter on the street corner, talking to someone. My grandmother was telling her friend about someone she knew who claimed to have died and come back to life: The lady was lying on her death bed when suddenly she found herself standing in a bright, white light. Then she heard people crying and calling her back, and she found herself in her bed again.

Now I became really frightened. I ran up the street to the camp boundary to be as far away from Anna as possible. For now I was afraid she too might get up because everyone was crying and calling to her.

By late fall, the dead were collected daily in a wagon that went from house to house. Then they were just thrown on top of one another and buried in mass graves.

During the first few months of our internment in the houses, all three of my grandparents were in Karlsdorf with us.

Mutter was a short woman, only about four foot ten. She suffered from ulcerated legs that were hardly ever healed, and the skin had turned black and blue. I recall watching her doctoring those legs in camp. Daily she'd wash them with water and then wrap them in clean rags. I took this to be an everyday thing that old people had to do.

Walking was hard for Mutter, but this did not stop her from doing so. And when she had a mission, like food for her small granddaughter, she marched. One day she came to me and said, "They are giving milk to small children down the street. You must come with me so you will get some too."

This did not thrill me, for I remembered the milk she made me drink still warm from the big, brown cow when we were at home. The smell and taste were terrible.

Before I had a chance to say no, Mutter took me by the hand and we headed down the street.

It was a hot summer day. The dusty street, its hard, dried dirt grooved by wagon wheels during the summer rain, felt hot and painfully sharp on my bare feet. We rushed across to the other side and joined a group of people standing in line with babies and small children. When it was finally our turn, the woman in charge took one look at me and said, "She can't have any; she's too old."

But Mutter was determined and when Mutter had something in mind, it was done. She started talking and reasoning. Back and forth it went. I stood there and waited. Finally the woman gave in and handed Mutter a small cup filled with milk. Mutter handed me the milk in triumph and watched as I drank it down. To my surprise it was delicious.

The milk was so good – I wanted more, but I knew better than to ask. I handed the cup back. *"Dank scheen,"* is all I said.

From late fall 1945 to spring of 1947 was the hardest time for all the imprisoned ethnic Germans. In camps all over Yugoslavia, malnutrition and disease took their toll. More and more people starved and got sick. Winter was near and there were fewer fruits and vegetables to beg, barter or steal. Weeds that we had picked during the growing season withered with the frost. We had used them to cook mock spinach, tea, and weed soup. Even if they were not filling, at least the weeds had plenty of vitamins and minerals. Now we had only the watery barley soup and the hard cornmeal bread.

More people died during that year than any other and we almost lost my brother. He had typhoid, just like cousin Anna. Every evening when Mami administered the enema, Seppi would cry in pain and I with him. Mami did not like to do this to him, but she hoped it might make Seppi better.

I felt so sorry for him, sometimes I'd sit next to him with my back against the wall and my knees pulled up to my chest and watch him when he was sleeping. His forehead was big and bony. His temples had sunken and made it look as if there were holes on both sides of his forehead and behind his ears as well. When he was awake, his sunken eyes with dark circles under them made him look like a little old man. His body, so thin that all his joints looked big and swollen, was nothing but skin and bone.

Slowly he got better. Sometimes he was able to sit up for a few hours. Once in a while he'd even tease me.

One day as he was taking his nap I once more sat near him, thinking how glad I was that he was much stronger and was going to get well. For I loved him a lot and didn't want him to die.

As I watched his chest slowly rising and falling like a person peacefully asleep and not struggling with each breath, something came over me. Something not very nice. "Go ahead," the small devilish voice whispered in my ear. "Do it, he'll never know, he's sleeping. This is the best opportunity you'll ever have."

Feeling powerful, I raised my small hand, aimed and slapped his cheek. Seppi woke with a start, but I was gone. I ran as fast as I could. I don't know if he knew what happened. But I did. I was sorry afterwards for doing it, but maybe not *that* sorry. After all he was better and almost well.

On Christmas that year Mami knitted a sweater for Seppi and a dress for me, using wool from old garments that she unraveled. She sat up late at night knitting after working all day, as I'm sure most of the mothers did, to give a little something to their children on Christmas Eve. It must have been hardest on the mothers, for they had next to nothing, not even a piece of bread, to help celebrate the holiday.

Mami spread out the pullover on the bed between us and asked what I thought of it. It was pretty, especially the letters that she had stitched on the upper left hand side. J.H. for Josef Hugery. I traced them with my index finger. I had never seen letters written in clothes before. Mami told me that the sweater was for Christmas. Christmas? I didn't quite remember what that was.

Since I hardly remembered it, I didn't miss Christmas all that much. But Seppi and Andres were almost 10 and Marie was 13 years old; at this age, Christmas was already planted vividly in their minds. Surely they remembered the Christmas tree and *Christkindl* bringing presents, as well as the wonderful smells: *Brotwurst* cooking on Christmas Eve, fresh grated horseradish, thick slices of crisp, just-baked bread. There were plenty of Christmas cookies, fruits and nuts. After Mass on Christmas Day came the big dinner of roast goose and all the trimmings.

Many of our friends and relatives would come and share in the joy and laughter of the season. Then came the *zweite Weihnachtstag* – the second day of celebration. Christmas was too important a holiday to be celebrated for just one day, so on the second day of Christmas the fun continued.

New Year's Day had been a big day for children. We went to the relatives and neighbors and wished them *"Viel Glück im NeueJahr, lang leewe und g'sund bleiwe. –* Happy New Year, and a long and healthy life." Then the adults usually reached into their pockets and gave you some *Wünschgeld* or Wishing Money. Money for wishing good luck in the New Year. If you memorized a New Year poem and did a good job reciting it, they'd give you a little more money. Christmas was officially over on January 6th. After *Drei König* – Three Kings or Epiphany.

Mami started to sing *"Ihr Kinderlein Kommet"* and asked me to learn the words so that I could sing it with everyone. I listened. I recalled having heard the words vaguely, in back of my mind, like a dream that was long ago.

("Oh, Come Little Children," was one of the first songs I taught my own children to sing and the words are still heard in our house every Advent and Christmas season.)

I can't remember the dress my mother gave me. She told me that she also made me a rag doll. I asked her if she could think of a reason why I wouldn't remember ever having a doll. She said it was probably because the rags were so worn and old that the toy fell apart after only a few days.

RUDOLFSGNAD

It was the fall of 1945 when all old people and children who had no one to care for them were gathered together and shipped off to *Rudolfsgnad*, a name which ironically translates as Rudolf's Mercy.

That summer was to be the last one that I would ever spend with my mother's parents, Oma and Ota Schüssler.

My grandmother Schüssler was tall and thin, at least from where I stood. I recall playing on a rug made of braided rags just a few feet from where she was cooking in her kitchen, before the Partisaner came and put us in camp. I remember that she was a soft-spoken woman. I'm also told that she loved to make and eat popcorn, a taste she surely must have passed on to me. I've passed up many meals for just a large bowl of white, crunchy, exploded kernels of corn.

My Grandfather Schüssler, a short, bald, stocky man was a *Wächtr* or town crier who used to stand on the corner with a drum, calling all of Karlsdorf's citizens together to announce the local and world news.

Of course all this had ceased after Fall of 1944, and he was just one of the useless old men in camp.

I remember running to the gate when I saw Ota walking toward me. He was crying. I had never seen him cry before.

"*Elsa mei Kind!*" he sighed. "Oma, Mutter and I have to leave, along with the rest of the old people. We're being sent far away".

"I want to go with you, Ota," I said sadly.

He bent down and gave me a long hug. He said I had to stay here with Mami and Seppi.

"Why do you have to go, Ota?" I cried, "I want all of us to be together".

"*Sei brav mei Madl.*" Ota said. "Be a good girl and don't cry." He turned and walked away. I watched him go. He was all bent as he slowly turned and waved once more to me. I stood at the garden gate for a long time. I don't remember saying good-bye to Mutter or Oma Schüssler at all. I never saw my Oma and Ota Schüssler again.

Rudolfsgnad was a death camp, a camp for old people and young children whose parents had been shipped off to Russia or had died. The old could not work and the orphans had no one to care for them; therefore, both were considered a burden and needed to be disposed of. They solved the problem of the useless old and young, my grandparents among them, by starving them to death.

Before 1945 the population of the village of Rudolfsgnad was around three thousand. After it became a camp, the population swelled to more than 20,000. Most houses filled from wall to wall, fifteen to twenty people jammed into a room. The camp would have been almost empty because of deaths, but the dead were replaced with new inmates from other camps. When Mutter and Oma and Ota Schüssler arrived in the camp, it was the end of October and the weather was beginning to turn cold. They ripped up the wooden floors and woodwork for cooking fires and heat.

The Kommandant at Rudolfsgnad was Jewish and he had been in the Nazi camps. He vowed that the *Schwabos* would die a worse death than his own people. They got food only once a day, a handful of raw cracked corn. Sometimes they did not get food for days, and if anyone was caught with food, other then what was rationed, they were beaten.

Nothing grew in town. Not a blade of grass or weed survived. People were so hungry that they ate anything that grew, either raw or cooked. No dogs, cats or even birds, were left in the town. All had been eaten. The only living creatures besides people were rats. They came out at night looking for food, for hunger also gnawed at their bellies like the imprisoned people.

The rats ate anything, even human waste. A friend of mine, Liesl Söhn, was ten years old when she was an inmate in Rudolfsgnad. She told me how scared she was of the rats. So many people slept in the room that it was impossible to leave the room at night without stepping on someone. If nature called you had to use a tin washtub placed in the middle of the room.

One morning, Liesl got up and on the way out the door, she passed the tub. Out of the corner of her eye she saw a gray object floating in the container.

"The sight and smell of that moment will remain with me as long as I live." She told me. "It was a large dead rat which had fallen in during the night and drowned in the urine." If people died at night, the long-tailed rodents started to devour the corpses. They were even bold enough to attack the sick as they slept. People's biggest fear was that they might start to chew on them during the night.

There were fruit trees in the town, but to prevent the children and the old people from taking the fruit or picking it up off the ground, one or two Partisaner were stationed under them with guns. This literally *was* forbidden fruit.

Disease ran rampant as hunger whittled the people down to skin and bones. If malnutrition didn't do them in, illness did. Men, women and children died daily by the hundreds. Sometimes there were so many bodies that they had to be picked up twice a day.

People became heartless, looking only out for their own. Mutter told me of two sisters in Rudolfsgnad. Each sister had a grandchild whose mother and father had been taken to Russia. When the old people were sent to Rudolfsgnad, the two children went along with their grandmothers.

Food was so scarce and the winter so cold, each grand-mother gave most of her food to her grandchild. One of the women became very ill and a few days before she died she made her sister promise to take care of her grandchild as if it were her own. This the other promised to do and did her best to keep that promise for a while. But as time went on and malnutrition took its toll, she started to give her own grand-child more food than her sister's.

Managing somehow to steal out at night, she discovered a potato field. Though the field had been harvested, a few small potatoes were still to be found. Every night she came back with two or three, which she cooked and gave her grandchild. Her sister's grandchild begged for just a small potato, but the grandmother had become so hard and so determined to help her own grandchild survive that the plea fell on deaf ears. Her sister's grandchild was slowly starving. One day death took her and finally released her from Rudolfsgnad.

I asked my grandmother how she knew all this. She told me that the woman lived in the same house with her. I asked her how could she do such a thing and Mutter said that some-times people become this way to protect their own. At age thirteen I couldn't understand what Mutter meant; surely she could see as I did that the grandmother had been heartless. But now that I'm over 50, I'm not so quick to judge.

My grandfather died in Rudolfsgnad. Mutter often related to me how he begged for salt.

"The last words that he spoke to us were *'Bitte gib mir Salz, ich brauch Salz!'* over and over again 'Please give me salt, I need salt!' But there was no salt to be had," my grand-mother told me. "We couldn't give him his final wish. We wrapped him in a blanket and waited for the death wagon to come, hoping that his body would stay wrapped and be bur-ied with a little dignity."

But the driver unwrapped Ota's body, just as he had done with the others, and tossed him onto the wagon with the rest of the naked dead. When the wagon was full it rolled on to deliver my grandfather as well as the other "freed" souls to their final resting place. A mass grave was waiting for them outside of town. Hundreds of his fellow *Landsleit* had come before him and hundreds more of his countrymen followed, from babies to old men and women. No one was there to say a last word or give them a final blessing to send them home, the home where there was no more hunger, thirst or pain. Their remains still rest beneath the covered ground with no marker to tell the world that they ever existed, or who they were, or what terrible things were done to them.

Both Mutter and Oma Schüssler were released late in 1948 from Rudolfsgnad. My Oma Schüssler died a few weeks later; the camp had taken its toll. Mutter hung on, though, and eventually joined us in America in 1951 and it was she who told me of the terrible conditions in Rudolfsgnad.

Mutter's stories about that place affected me a lot as a teenager. As I got older I learned that this was not the only death camp in Tito's extermination plan. A few others like Mitrowitza, Kruschiwel, Jarek, Gagowa and Molidorf were just as evil. In Mitrowitza which had more than 4,000 inmates, only a handful survived that first year.

My husband Michael was a child of eleven when he and his thirteen year old brother Anton, his sisters Angela, fifteen, and Anna, nine, were taken to Molidorf, a camp just as bad as Rudolfsgnad. Their mother was put in a work camp a few towns away. All the children in Molidorf were separated and grouped with children of the same sex and age in individual houses.

My husband has often told of the time the boys in their house caught a *Katz*. The boys killed the cat, skinned, butchered and cooked it. No birds or other animals, except for rats, lived among them.

"We snared any animal we could to fill our belly. Once we even tried to get a rat," he told me.

As time passed, almost all the children developed *Scorbut* including my husband, his sister and brother. A toddler had such a severe case of scurvy that he had a hole in his cheek. In order for him to eat and drink, someone had to hold his mouth closed, spoon the food or drink into the hole, then cover it with a cloth so he could swallow

Many children died in Molidorf, including my husband's older sister. Angela died all alone in this God-forsaken place. She died of malnutrition, no mother or father at her side, and is buried with the others in one of the mass graves. Only God knows its location.

CHAPTER

6

Moved Back and Forth
Winter to Spring 1946

e were moved back and forth like pieces on a checkerboard, in the winter to the hangars, in the summer back to the houses. In the beginning of 1946 we found ourselves once more in the airplane hangars.

We did not have to sleep on the bare ground as we did the spring before. We slept on crude wooden platforms filled with straw which had been built during the summer months of the previous year, double decker structure that stretched across the hangar from wall to wall with aisles in between. I was glad that we were not on the bottom row. All you could see there were the people in front of you and those next to you.

We climbed up a make-shift ladder nailed to the scaffolding that held the upper platform. I loved to climb up and down. I don't know how Mami liked it up there. I thought it was great – like a huge tree house!

The platforms in the center of the hangar were a little lower than ours. From my perch I could watch the woman in the bunk in front of ours make flowers out of crepe paper. Her quick hands stretched one side of the red crepe ribbon, making it flare out. Next she rolled the straight side of the ribbon around the top part of a wire, shaping it into a rose. To me it was a lovely thing to behold.

On very cold days, I sat on our straw bed with the covers wrapped around me and pretended to be smoking, as my breath turned into steam. I tried to "puff" out smoke rings, but failed to produce a single one.

The two story platforms created a lot more room. The Communists brought in more women and children from neighboring towns, Werschetz, Alibunar, and Weisskirchen.[3] They filled the two hangars from top to bottom. Even with all our old Omas and Otas gone we had over four thousand inhabitants under those roofs.

I always suffered from some form of malady. My whole body itched constantly. I had what we called *Beissiches*, a constant unbearable itching, and the worst place was my back. I could not scratch there. I had lice and bed bugs but they were nothing like this constant itching. I remember waking up in the middle of the night unable to sleep because of it. We had all kinds of sores on our body. Mami, Seppi, I, and everyone else had boils filled with pus. As soon as they would heal, a few days later new ones reappeared. My *Gschwer* was always at my waist. The cloth of my underwear rubbed the boils open, letting the pus ooze out, then it dried and stuck to my underwear. Every day my mother had to peel it off carefully so it wouldn't hurt.

I thought this was all normal, that life was like that. I had no idea that this was not happening to most of the little children in the rest of the world.

I also had whooping cough. I was very ill and Mami had nothing to give me to ease the terribly deep coughing spells. Once she called in several of the women to examine the soft bump beneath my belly. Some said it looked like I had a *Bruch*. I guess my mother agreed with them.

"What's a 'Hernia'?" I asked. She said that she didn't know exactly how to explain it for me to understand. I wanted the pain and the bump to go away.

My left ear hurt all day. That bitter cold winter, Mami had a hard time keeping us warm. We all had many colds and I was prone to ear infections. Mami had some medicine extracted from a plant that grew like a

---

[3]From the town of Weisskirchen there was a young girl named Grete, age ten; her little sister, Inge, age four; and her mother, Frieda Gutjahr. We lived in the same hangar in Karlsdorf. In 1947 when some of us were taken to other camps far away from Karlsdorf, Grete and her family went to the same place we did. The strange thing is, we did not get to know each other until 1961, when I met her at my future sister-in-law's bridal shower. Our paths had become very similar – both of us moved to Chicago with our families, and ended up with the last name, "Walter," because we married brothers! She married Tony and I married Mike, and we both have daughters named Heidi.

weed and was said to help cure ear infections. I could hardly wait until Mami came back from work. She would surely help me. But when I saw her hold the big spoon with the clear liquid in it over a match, I wasn't so sure. I started to cry. Basl had to help Mami hold my head right side down so Mami could pour the *Medizin* into my left ear. Both said it would make it better.

But as soon as the warm fluid hit the inside of my ear, fire surged through my head. I screamed. Mami and Basl both spoke sympathetically and stroked my hair.

"Shhh, shhh, mei Kind, es wert schun besser were. Mori is'alles v'rbei," Mami said over and over.

"Shhh, shhh, my child it will be all better, tomorrow it will be all over." But the pain raged on. I had a lot of ear infections that winter. Every time I had one, the big spoon came out to help make me better and I screamed when I saw it.

One thing I find strange, and I have often thought about this, is that I cannot remember any snow during those two whole winters in camp.

We had a lot of snow when my father was still with us. I remember Tati opened the kitchen door and, lo and behold, there was a wall of snow blocking the doorway. I had never seen such a sight. Even the kitchen windows were snowed in, so that we could not see out.

On a sleigh ride, I sat between Mami and Tati, a blanket of fur skin covering our laps, all the way down to our toes. Three other people sat across from us. We were whisked over the snow as the horses' hooves trotted soundlessly down the street. All the houses and trees seemed to fly as they rushed past and out of sight. We felt the wind on our faces as we *schussed* down the road, the sound of our happy laughter breaking the quiet whiteness surrounding us.

Because of these memories of snow in previous years, I know it must have snowed in the winters of 1945 and 1946. My mother told me there had been a lot of snow, but maybe because we were all confined to one area and so many feet trampled it down, the snow almost always disappeared as soon as it fell.

One early March evening, Andres decided to make himself a whistle from one of the reeds on the thatched kitchen roof. As soon as he broke one off, someone yelled in Serbian, "Halt, what are you doing?"

Andres froze as the guard grabbed him by the neck. "You're under arrest!" the Partisaner bellowed and dragged my frightened cousin out the gate of the camp yard, where another guard held two older boys at gunpoint.

The two Partisaner marched the three young prisoners to town and locked them up. The prison was nothing but a large dark cellar in a big house, the same place my mother was to occupy later.

With only the thin clothing on their backs, the boys found a spot to bed down on the dirt floor against the dank wall. In my cousin's own words, *"Es war sau kalt."* This, loosely translated, means: It was cold as the devil. Andres broke down and cried. Both of the older boys were sympathetic and consoled him, told him not to be afraid. Everything was going to be all right. Hearing these comforting words of the "older and wiser boys," Andres fell asleep with his young protectors' arms for a pillow.

Early the next morning the young boys were taken out into the back yard. The morning was wet and dreary, the yard muddy. Each of the boys was given a bucket and told to go to one corner of the yard, fill the bucket with mud, carry it to the opposite corner and dump it out. Feet and clothing soaking wet, the boys trudged back and forth, cold to the bone in the drizzling March rain.

All of a sudden a drunken voice came from out of nowhere. "All line up, you're going to be shot." The boys lined up, and the drunken Partisaner aimed their rifles. My cousin, the youngest, wet his pants out of sheer fright. The guards started to laugh and poke at them until the game became tiresome; then they marched the prisoners back into the so-called dungeon. They were locked up for two more days and nights.

Things of this nature took place not only in our camp, but also in the other camps. Some didn't end as just a game, but with bullets finding a human target and ending someone's life.

Gray winter days turned into bright, spring days. The red poppies in the field blazed with color again and the green hills met the blue sky in the distance. My yearning returned to be outside the barbed wire, to pick flowers to my heart's content, and to feel the cool grass on the soles of my naked feet. One day my wish came true.

The very young children were gathered and led out the gate to a big patch of *Kamille* flowers growing outside the fence. I had seen this large patch of small, white-petaled flowers with their yellow centers from behind the barbed wire, and now I stood ankle deep in them. The little flowers were a velvety carpet beneath my feet. We were instructed to pick every flower, but only the buds, not the stems. I held my skirt like a basket and dropped into it the white and golden fragrant blossoms. At first I enjoyed the assigned task, but as time went by, it became tedious and the strong fragrance of our harvest engulfed me like a perfume too powerful for my nose. I wanted to stop and play. Unfortunately we had to continue until all the flowers were gathered; then we had to march back into our empty, plantless confines once more. I remember walking with our flowers out of the greenness, back into the gray yard, my nose full of that strong fragrance. I have disliked the odor of chamomile ever since.

One evening I met Marie as she came through the entrance gate with the other teenagers returning from their labor detail. She looked tired as she took my hand and walked toward the hangar with me, I was chattering away the whole time. I remember looking into her eyes to make sure she heard every word I spoke. Her long braids had been undone and her wavy hair hung down her back. I told her I liked her hair that way and that she looked nice.

That night I came down the ladder from our bunk and found Marie sitting on her straw bed below, braiding her long, wet hair. She was so fast that in no time she had completed four or five braids before I could ask my first question.

"Why are you braiding all those thin braids, Marie?" I asked. "I like you much better with just two." She laughed and replied: "I'm not going to keep them in braids. When my hair is completely dry, I will undo all of my braids and then I will have nice wavy hair all over my head."

Now this I would have also liked for myself. So I begged her to show me how to braid my hair. She said that it was not going to be easy, but she'd show me how it was done. This took some doing on her part and mine. But after many tries I got the hang of it. Since my hair was much shorter than Marie's, it was also much harder to braid. I can remember practicing many times by myself, perched in my upper bunk. I knew one thing: learning to waltz was much easier than learning to braid my hair.

Marie showed me how to play *Abholle*, which is called cats cradle in English. The two of us sitting on the straw bunk for a long time making all kinds of designs. My fingers were not long, and sometimes the string slipped and we had to start all over. This didn't discourage me; I didn't want to stop. I'm sure Marie was long tired of this game, but I wasn't.

From then on I'd pester all the members of my family to play with me. Mami was one of my loyal players. Many an evening we'd play with the long string until it was bedtime.

Another toy I played with for hours was a *Triller*, a button threaded on a string loop. It spun so quickly, first forward then back, twisting the string as if it were a rubber band. All one had to do was pull on the twisted loop to make the button dance. My husband who was a full fledged red blooded *Schwowebuh* – Swabian boy – informed me that this toy was not called a *Triller*. It was called a *Brusch*. The correct method of making it was from the small bone of a pig's foot that you drilled two holes into to make it spin right and make the proper brooshing sound. When I asked him how many pig's feet he got a hold of in concentration camp to make this instrument properly he had to admit it was never in camp, but only in the good old days when such things were obtained during hog butchering time.

We children ran in and out of the hangars constantly during the day. The buildings had only two entrances, one just a few yards from the entrance gate of the camp where the guards were stationed. I avoided this exit as much as possible because I feared the Partisaner. The other exit led into the back of the yard. I didn't want to use that door either because that's where the old man lived. The bigger children said he might put a hex on anyone who came close to him. But since I had to choose one door or the other, I took my chances with the back entrance.

Although I was afraid of him I also felt sorry for the old man. Why was he not in the main building like the rest of us? Why was he all by himself in the entrance hallway? He never spoke a word to me or anyone else. He didn't even look my way. It was as if he could not see or hear. Like a rag doll.

His drab and baggy clothing hung from his lifeless form. His eyes stared into nothingness. I wondered who this old man was. But I never dared speak one word to him as I passed him going in or out the tunnel-shaped hallway. I always walked around him, as far away from him as physically possible, pressing my body to the opposite wall, until I came to the doorway. Then quickly I'd run, in or out as fast as I could. One morning he was gone. Gone to a happier place than this painfully lonely patch of earth in the hangar entrance way. He had finally escaped from this purgatory, as so many of his fellow inmates – through death.

CHAPTER
7

Weckerle

That summer we were sent to a place just outside of Karlsdorf called Weckerle. With its rolling hills and sandy soil, Weckerle was best suited for growing grapes. We were brought to work in *"Die Weingärter"*.

Most of us lived in the small huts built long ago by the owners of the *Weingarten* to use as living quarters during the summer and fall, when most of the work was done in the vineyard. Ironically, the same people who had built the huts and owned the vineyard now worked in those same fields as slaves, including my family, which also had owned a vineyard in Weckerle.

One bright night, the moon was shining into our windows. We were all fast asleep on the straw when the rhythmic chirping of the crickets was drowned out by Andres' loud scream. His frightful screaming and thrashing around woke us all.

"Sie kumme, sie kumme m'r nohch," he screamed over and over. "They're coming, they're coming after me."

Before Basl could catch him, Andres was up and running out the door, still screaming that they were going to get him. I remember standing by the door watching his dark eerie figure run across the field in the moonlight with Basl and Mami right behind. They brought him inside and calmed him down. He was still crying as he went back to his straw "bed". Mami said that Andres had a bad dream and everything would be all right. We all went back to our sleeping areas and in a little while the crickets' chirping returned once more.

Mami and Basl had to report like soldiers every morning with the rest of the women, just as they had in town and in the hangar. They were taken to work in the vineyards, men with guns always watching over them. Marie and the rest of the teenagers also had to report for work detail daily.

No trees grew around the one room house. It sat in the middle of nowhere with sand all around. I recall the hot sand on my bare feet. It was so hot sometimes that you had to walk in the sparsely growing weeds on the side of the road to keep your feet from scorching.

Andres thought it was so hot that you'd be able to fry an egg in the road. I found this very interesting and wondered how that could be done. I was getting a little smarter by now and didn't always trust what they would say to me. I just wished I could get an egg somehow and try it out. But I knew that wouldn't be likely to happen. Even if I had an egg, I sure wouldn't have wasted it by frying it on the dirty sand. I was always much too hungry to do that.

The one thing that I liked about Weckerle was that I was not fenced in and I could roam free. I could pick flowers to my heart's content. I also picked *Unkraut* for cooking. Mami showed me which weed made the best mock spinach, the one that looked just like rabbit ears – hence the name *Hase Ohre*. Whenever I saw a patch of it, I'd pick the choicest leaves and bring them home.

Even today in America, in this land of plenty, my eyes still spot the weed whenever I'm outdoors in summer or fall. Often I make a mental note if the quality is good enough to make a tasty spinach.

Sometimes I'd play in the vineyards near by. I'd sit between the vines in the sand and collect snails and play with them. They were my living toys. I'd pick them up, touch their two long feelers, and watch as they retracted into their pretty shells. Soon they came out of their *Haus* and I'd let them crawl over my toes. They felt cool as their wet bodies slithered over my skin.

In Weckerle, rain came out of nowhere. One minute the sun was shining, and the next rain poured down. Just as quickly, the rain stopped and the sun came back to dry off the land. After the rain, there was always a huge puddle in front of our hut. Seppi and Andres with their long legs quickly headed for it, and as usual, I was right behind them.

They waded into the large puddle. I watched to see if it was shallow enough for me to venture in.

"Kum rein Elsa," they called to me.

"Come on in, see, it only reaches up to our calves."

I wasn't so sure that I should. That day, instead of wearing just my underwear as I usually did, I had on my dress. I had to be careful when I wore it, if I ruined it there was nothing to replace it. But the puddle was just too inviting. I tucked the hem of the dress into my underpants and carefully waded in. The closer I got to Seppi and Andres the shorter my legs seemed to be. But this was fun. Soon the water was past my knees and then halfway up my thighs. Before I knew what happened, my feet slipped out from under me, plopping me on my behind. There I sat in the middle of the puddle with only my head sticking out of the dirty water.

I recall having to walk daily to the *Kuchel.* I'd turn left on the road in front of our hut that led down the center of a potato field. After passing through the field, the road curved to the right and continued up a hill until it ended in front of a large, white, two-story house. This is where the community kitchen was located and where everyone had to go for their daily ration of food.

It was a short walk from our place to the house on the hill, but I always took a long time to get there. On the bottom of the hill by the bend of the road grew a clump of tall thin trees, and all kinds of grasses and weeds. I'd usually stop to look for *Kettlgrass.* This was a small low growing weed with round leaves the size of a silver dollar. I never passed without first searching under the leaves for the small, green, edible, loaf-shaped seed pods for *Brot.* Having found and eaten all the "bread", I'd continue on my way. Sometimes I amused myself by picking a fistful of the leaves to make a *Kettl* and a *Krone.* I'd wear the chain around my neck and the crown in my hair as if they were made of emeralds.

Once Mami and I were walking along this same spot in the road. As we strolled up the road, holding hands and talking, Mami spotted something in the grass. She bent down and picked a small yellow *Butterblum.* Holding the dandelion under my chin she said: *"Loss mich sehe ob du Butter gern esst.* – Let me see if you like to eat butter."

"Oh, Mami, Mami, sag mir, ess ich Butter gern?" I begged. "Tell me, do I like to eat butter?"

"You sure do," she told me laughing. "Your chin is all yellow." I was glad to hear that I liked butter.

"Mami, was is Butter?" I asked her.

Taken aback, my mother knelt down in front of me.

"You don't remember what butter is?"

I shook my head "No".

For a few seconds Mami peered sadly into my eyes, then she got up, took my hand and we continued to walk up the road.

I don't recall her answer; all I can remember is the look in her eyes.

At night we slept on the straw-covered floor. Mami, Seppi, and I slept on the wall opposite the door, and Basl, Andres and Marie on the adjacent wall.

Suddenly Andres again let out a piercing scream in his sleep.

"Sie Kumme – Sie Kumme mich holle." He yelled. Thrashing about with all his might, my cousin was running from his nightly nightmare. Once more Andres was confronted by his pursuers in his sleep, as he had been so often these last few weeks. Most of the time, Basl grabbed him before he got to the door, but this time he was off and running out the door before she got to him. She caught him just a few yards from the hut and woke him up. Reassuring him, my aunt brought him back inside and calmed him down. Quiet settled in and we all went back to our places. In my young mind I knew a terrible thing was happening to Andres. Who was going to come and get him?

Years later, my brother told me what had gone on in Weckerle that summer. Every day a group of Partisaner came and took my brother and cousin as well as a number of boys approximately the same age, and used them for target practice.

They made the boys line up in a row, stood in front of them like a firing squad, and told them that today they were going to die. They then shot at the ground in front of their feet as well as over the tops of their heads, deliberately missing. Then they would tell them the next round was to kill. After a while the boys were let go. The next day the whole thing would start all over again. The soldiers played with them the way a cat toys with a mouse before he devours it.

My brother came to the point where he was so afraid that he wished the bullet would find him and release him from this agony. And Andres was running away from the Partisaner in his dreams as he relived the nightmare that he faced during the day.

I'm sure many things of this nature happened during our two and one half years of living in concentration camp, but because of my young age I did not exactly understand what was going on.

My brother, being older, saw and heard more cruel and hateful things. Things that would be difficult enough for an adult to watch, but for a ten or eleven year old boy it must have been unendurable. Very seldom has my brother talked about life in camp since we left Yugoslavia.

CHAPTER

8

Fall 1946

ate that summer of 1946, Mami, Seppi, and I had to leave
Weckerle and return once more to my Franz Onkel's house.
Basl and my cousins had to stay behind in Weckerle through
that fall.

Over a year had passed since our imprisonment and the food was
still insufficient and getting more repulsive. One meal in particular stands
out from all the rest. I remember sitting on my straw bed, with the small
bowl of *Erbsesupp* on my lap. Although hunger gnawed my stomach I
just could not bring myself to lift my spoon and put the pea soup into my
mouth; it looked and smelled particularly unsavory that day.

I hated it, but that's all there was to eat. The *Erbsesupp* was worse
than the *Krauplsupp* because it had bugs in it. Finally my hungry stomach
overruled all my other senses. I disregarded the revolting food on my spoon
and shoved it in my mouth. When I bit into the peas, the bugs crunched like
half-popped kernels of corn, but they certainly didn't taste like corn.

After I had eaten the pea soup, my stomach felt funny. I felt as if I had
to throw up and I promptly did. I threw up almost all night. I recall that
night very clearly. The taste, crunch and smell of the pea soup remains
very sharp in my mind.

In front of my Franz Onkel's house was a huge *Maulbierebahm*, whose
branches spread across the whole house. When the big, juicy, ripe mul-
berries fell to the ground, they made whatever they came in contact with

purple, especially your fingers, mouth, and teeth. They fell as if from heaven. That was the only food I can remember ever being able to eat enough of during those years in camp.

One day during the purple season, someone had used the mulberry "ink"" to write over the white wall of my uncle's house. As I looked at the purple on the white wall, I decided it looked nice. Even though I was told that the words were nasty.

Franz Onkel was still working at the *Salamifabrik* and was able to bring home *Wurscht*. Evenings I'd look in through the open kitchen door and watch as he cut into the sausage and took a bite. Oh, it looked so good. If only I had a piece; I could just taste it. I stood in the doorway, hoping they'd notice me and give me a piece. I was always hungry.

Ritzi Tant put a piece of sausage in her mouth. She looked up from her food and gazed at me. I swallowed hard and looked her straight in eye; But she turned away and continued to eat. I kept on standing in the doorway – no one gave me anything. All three, Ritzi Tant, Franz Onkel and Inge, just went on eating.

I became very bitter toward my aunt and uncle. How could they keep on eating and not offer me even one small piece of sausage? I was so small, my eyes hungered for just one bite. I'm sure they saw how much I wanted a piece, but they ignored me and kept on eating. Why?

This question always came up in my mind whenever I recalled the incident. Even when I was an adult and in my thirties, I still was bitter. When we went to Germany in 1977 we went to see them both. My Franz Onkel was a sick, old man. He was almost 80 and did not quite understand who I was. He kept on calling me Lissi, thinking I was my mother, his sister. She was about my age when he had seen her last. I felt sorry for him. And my Ritzi Tant was just as I had remembered her in camp. She had not changed much. She still complained about what a bad life she had. Not one good thing came out of her mouth. I saw she was to be pitied. All she could see in life was the bad.

When her only surviving child Anna died of typhoid, she became hateful. She had asked my mother, "why couldn't my Anna live instead of your Seppi?" I guess that's the reason they could be so cruel.

I didn't like my second cousin Inge. Just because she was two years younger than me, she got away with everything. Ritzi Tant, Inge's grandmother, spoiled her.

I did not pull down the wash; I saw her granddaughter do it. I watched her from the side of the house. She ran off and I went over to investigate. As I bent down to pick up a piece of clothing, Ritzi Tant came running and scolding. I tried to tell her that I didn't do it, but she didn't even listen; she yelled at me and when I told her that Inge did it, she hit me. I squirmed out of her grip and ran away. I didn't like Inge: she was a brat.[4]

Because the weather was still warm I played outside most of the time. Being a bouncy six year old; I was too busy to sit still. I never walked if I was able to run, never ran if I could skip or jump. Because of this, I was always stumbling or falling and always had some sort of sore or bruise somewhere on my body.

Since the earth was warmed by the autumn sun I ran around *blosfussich* all day. Running around barefoot had its drawbacks – it was so easy to trip and injure a toe. I injured mine three times that year and lost a toenail every time. The third time Mami had to doctor my toe she was not as sympathetic as the first two times. The daily routine of soaking my foot in water and wrapping the injured toe with a rag to protect it from dirt and infection was not her favorite job. It took weeks for a new nail to grow in and the routine of cleaning and bandaging had to continue until then.

The simplest object can become a plaything in a small child's hands. I was no exception. One hot sunny day I found a glob of *Terr*. I liked its smell and how it pulled apart, forming a long thin string from one piece to the other. But it became the most fun when I formed the tar into a ball, stuck a feather in it and threw it up into the air. It swirled down, dancing and twirling – turning round and round – free as a bird until it landed on the ground.

Apricot pits were also good to have, they made a great *Pfeifl*. I became an expert whistle-maker. Too bad that it produced only one shrill note.

---

[4] This is one of the sharpest memories I have of Inge in camp. We met again as adults in 1977. By this time we both were married, had children and were in our thirties. She was still blond and blue eyed, like her mother, just as I had remembered her. She was very warm and friendly. Too bad we now live so far apart. I think we'd be friends.

I also liked to play with *Kuckrutz Hohr,* weaving the corn silk into pretty yellow braids. The golden, satiny strands looked and felt like real hair and I'd pretend that they were attached to a beautiful doll's head.

I also enjoyed making long ropes of braiding *Kukrutz Liesche.* I was so proud of myself for being able to braid the corn-husk all by myself just like many of the bigger children and women.

Some of the women made corn husk shoes. They became expert shoe-makers. If one had the ability to make things from material that was readily found, like corn husks for shoes or scraps of fabric for dolls, the finished products were easily used to barter with. One could trade the objects with the new occupants of Karlsdorf for food, soap or even a little money.

That year Hella was still able to buy Mami out of camp to work for her. Sometimes I was able to go with her. I remember one time clearly.

Mami and I were walking past the guard at the end of our street.[5] I was excited. We were going outside of our area of confinement. I looked all around, being sure to see everything of interest as we passed by. I looked at all the houses, doorways, and brick walled-in court yards with their large entrance gates. Everything looked different and yet the same. We saw strange people dressed in bright colors who talked as if their mouths moved faster than my ears could listen. I didn't understand one word as we passed them.

"Why do they look and talk so strangely?" I asked. Mami told me that they came from the mountains, far away, where people dress, speak, and live differently from us.

As we walked up the street, I saw an old woman sitting on a stool next to an entrance way. She was throwing an object in the air. It looked like a large spool of wool and had a strand attached to a fuzzy looking material on her lap. She caught the spool with one hand and twisted the strand with the other. I found this interesting and asked Mami what the old Oma was doing. Mami told me that she was spinning wool with a spindle, just as on a spinning wheel.

The farther we went, the more people we saw. I kept staring at their shoes. I can still picture the feet walking past us. They all looked the

---

[5] The bought prisoner received a slip of paper showing who bought them and at what address. This paper allowed the prisoner to leave camp and go to their master for that day.

same. The dark, honey-colored woven strips of leather came to a long point and curled over the big toe. The tops of the shoes above the arches were decorated with red designs. I was so busy looking at the feet of these strangers that I cannot for the life of me recall what mode of dress they wore. Just a blur of color comes to mind and I remember they looked very different from what I was used to seeing.

We went on, past the schoolhouse and church, and came to the market place. Mami and I entered under the large shade trees. Sounds of voices crying out their products and wares for sale came from all sections of the market. It was filled with people both selling and buying. My eyes couldn't believe what was in front of them. There was so much food that my mind was not capable of absorbing all the different fruits and vegetables in front of me. I recall just one kind. Melons, sweet juicy melons ... a small mountain of watermelons and cantaloupes. In all my life I had only seen one or, at the most, two melons at one time. Now right there before my feet were hills of them, some higher than I was.

It was like a dream. Then I heard Mami say something in Serbian to the man in front of us who was selling the melons. She bent down and thumped on one of the watermelons with her knuckles, then another and one more. In disbelief I thought to myself; Was she going to buy one? As if she could read my thoughts Mami turned to me and asked;

"Wilscht ah Zuckermilaun oder ah Wassermilaun?"

"A watermelon", I quickly replied. Cantaloupes were good but *Wassermilaun* was the best food in the world. My heart thumped with joy as Mami picked up the small watermelon and paid the man. Hand in hand we walked away from the marketplace with our melon tucked under Mami's arm.

How many times had my mother been down this street before when she was still free? She has often told me the story of when our neighbor died in the summer of 1944. As was the custom, all the friends and neighbors gathered in the deceased's home where the body was laid out. From there, they accompanied the black *Todewage* – hearse – to the cemetery.

My mother was among the group waiting when the pastor arrived with the altar boys to lead the way. Up front was Seppi, carrying the cross, dressed in white starched vestments. Mami smiled when she saw her eight year old son. Then she looked down at his feet. She couldn't believe her eyes; he was bare footed. His grimy feet stuck out from the long white robe for all to see. What were her friends and neighbors thinking?

But there was nothing she could do about it. My mother, who regards *Reinlichkeit* – cleanliness –above all else, had to march on with the rest of the mourners, hoping that no one would see her son's dirt covered toes. She said it was the longest procession she had ever been in.

Now, as we walked down the same street, I'm sure she would have given anything to bring back those days. For what was so terrible then was nothing compared to the dirt in which she now had to raise her children.

Aside from a half-year of *Kindergarten* – preschool – when I was four, I had no schooling. Now we sat in a row on the ground, four or five of us. Marie stood in front of us. She was the teacher and we her pupils. This had been her idea, not mine. I didn't want to go to school. I didn't like going when we still lived happily in our house, I remembered how I'd haltingly walked up the street every day, looking back longingly. I wanted to stay at home with Mami and Mutter. I kept looking back as Mutter stood in front of our house, watching me. Sometimes I'd start to turn around and head back home, but Mutter didn't let that happen; she'd quickly call to me; *"Kumm mr netzuruck. Nur scheen in die Schul gehn."*

I'd reluctantly turn my footsteps back to their original path. I didn't want her to yell again not to come back home and to keep heading towards school. I was embarrassed and didn't want the whole town to know that I didn't want to go to Kindergarten.[6]

So when my cousin Marie decided that it was time I learned to write, I didn't agree with her. But all my arguments fell on deaf ears. My older and wiser cousin had made up her mind that I was going to learn, willing or not.

She collected a few more students and brought the school to me. We had no desks, paper, slate or pencil. But we did have nice strong sticks that scratched the packed-down dirt so we'd be able to write. This was good enough for me and my fellow students, since most of us didn't know what real supplies looked like.

Marie began with the ABC's. First she scratched the letters in the earth and then we had to copy them. I was not too impressed. I'd have rather just drawn pictures.

---

[6] I guess I was also afraid of the air raids. I felt safer at home with my family in our bunker than far away at school.

She did her best to keep our attention. But soon her pupils became as disinterested in learning their letters as her small cousin. The class stopped listening to the teacher and did more laughing and giggling than writing – so the teacher had no choice but to dismiss her class.

Besides that one day lesson with Marie, I didn't see or hear anything about the ABC's again until January, 1948.

What excitement! A small package arrived from America, a box not bigger than one foot by one foot. I don't even remember what was in it besides the *Kaugummi*. I had never seen or heard of *Kaugummi*. Even its name was strange. Chew rubber. It was only to be chewed and not swallowed. How could that be? I took the piece in my hand. It looked like a small pillow. I felt the hard smooth surface. I popped it in my mouth and bit into the shell and felt a sweetness going down my throat. The more I chewed it, the softer it got. I liked this "gum." But soon all the sweetness was gone.

One of the children showed me how to make a long string by pulling part of the gum out of my mouth. I did this for many hours. I saved the gum from day to day.

But all things come to an end. So did the gum. This did not stop me. I invented my own gum. I'd take a string or thread, pretend it was gum, chew on it and pull it out of my mouth. It didn't quite make the grade as gum, but it served its purpose.

When Tito took over the country with his Partisaner, he put those same guerilla fighters in charge of our concentration camps. Their feelings of vengeance and hatred toward us was great. Although we were mostly women, children and old people, all they could see were their hated German enemies.

But by the late fall of 1946, boys were drafted from our own areas to replace some of the old guards in camp. Since they knew who we *Schwabos* were, they felt more sympathetic towards us than Tito's guerilla fighters. I recall one young soldier who stood guard at the end of the block.

I hung around at his post almost every day. I wasn't afraid of him. He always smiled at me and didn't stand at attention, with his rifle sticking from his back like the other Partisaner did. He usually just propped it against his leg or leaned it next to the tree.

He must have been able to speak a few words in German, for how else could he converse with me? He'd joke around and look down at me with his friendly blue eyes. I recall they were blue because I was deathly afraid of the dark eyes of the others. He even took his cap off sometimes when it was warm, letting his straight blond hair hang down his forehead. His red-cheeked grin had not one trace of whiskers or mustache like the others. He looked more like a big brother than a Partisaner.

One night Mami sneaked out to go back to our house and get a small barrel of wine which she had hidden on our property. She had no problem getting out of camp, but before she had a chance to retrieve the wine, they caught her and locked her up in a cellar. They kept her there for three days giving her nothing to eat or drink. The prison, where Andres had been the March before, was located away from our camp in one of the houses not far from church. Basl and I went to visit her. A set of small stairs led down to the dank, windowless cellar. Mami's bed was the dirt floor, without blanket or straw. She had rats and mice for company. It was so dark down in the cellar where Mami was. Although the sun shone brightly outside, down here there was barely any light. I didn't like it here. I think I even saw a rat.

"*Ball kumm ich raus mei Kind.* Mami told me as she kissed me good-bye. "Soon I'll be out, my child."

On the way back I heard singing, which got louder the closer Basl and I got to our camp. And as we turned the corner, about five or six bigger children sat on the ground a few yards away singing a silly song. It went like this:

"*Drei Chineser mit dem Kontra Bass.*
Die sassen auf der Strasse und erzählten sich was.
Da kam die Polizei, sagt was ist denn das?
Drei Chineser mit dem Kontra Bass."
Translated.....
"Three Chinese with a Base Viola
Sat on the street and talked about this and that.
Then came the police and asked what is this?
Three Chinese with a Base Viola."

We stopped and listened. They sang the song again, but this time they changed all the vowel sounds of the words to O's, making it sound as if they were singing in a foreign language. As I caught on to what they were doing, I started to sing with them. We changed the vowel each time until we used them all, then we started all over again. This was fun.

The little singing lesson is vivid in my memory, but I had almost totally forgotten my trip to visit Mami in her cellar prison. Years later my mother retold the story of what it was like in that cellar. When she finished I knew exactly what that place looked like and I made the remark that I thought this was a strange thing for me to know. "No it isn't," she said, "you came to see me there, that's why you know." After Mami was let go from prison, she waited a week or so and went back once more to get that small barrel of wine. She succeeded this time and exchanged it for food, making life a little easier for us all.

The next day I walked up to the corner to share my happiness with my friend. I stood in front of him and looked up into his eyes.

"Des mol hawe sie mei Mami net g'fang. – This time they didn't catch my Mami," I proudly told him. "Isn't it grand that they didn't catch her and put her in jail like before." I smiled from ear to ear. "This time Mami got the barrel of wine and swapped it for food".

I prattled on about how brave and clever my Mami was and wasn't it great that all went so well. He looked at me with a quizzical look in his eyes. He started to laugh heartily and I with him, thinking he was as happy for my brave Mami as I was.

He probably had no idea what I was talking about. Or he was a kindhearted young man who chose to ignore my childish chatter and pretend not to know. I didn't realize what danger I was putting my mother in. If I had, I'm sure I'd have kept my lips sealed.

CHAPTER
9
Hangar 1946 - 1947

For the third time we were in the large airplane hangars. This was our second and final winter there. My family was assigned to the smaller hangar this time. The same one we had occupied in spring of 1945, Basl, Marie and Andres were in the larger building that all of us had been in last winter. The hangars were attached, forming an L shape. Only a narrow door connected the smaller building to the larger one. I went back and forth all the time.

Every night, I'd sit on our top bunk and observe the young lady on the straw-covered bunk across from me. She'd glide a comb through her long hair, making it come down the side of her face like strands of brown silk. She looked like a princess, but she was not a princess: she came from one of the poorest families in our town. But one need not be rich to be regal. In fact, all of the inhabitants of the hangars were now equally wealthy; it made no difference how much wealth anyone had had, all were now poor as church mice... poorer than church mice, for the mice had more to eat and could come and go as they pleased.

Ever since I could remember, Mami had a beautiful, multicolored sweater with vertical stripes of purple, navy, cornflower blue and light blue. Now it was mine. Mami altered the sweater for me to wear on cold days. Every time I wore it, I couldn't stop admiring it. I liked the way the stripes bent when I bent my arm. And the small-stitched surface felt so soft and smooth under my fingertips.

I loved the colors, the deepest shade of blue and purple under the sun. Next to the red poppies, these colors were my favorites – the hue of the sky at different times of the day.

I wore that sweater for more than three years. Besides my *Samptkleid,* it's the only garment that I can picture clearly in my mind from my early childhood.

I write this small, happy reminiscence on Mothers Day, 1991. I have my mother to thank for this sweet memory as well as most of the few moments of joy in concentration camp. My mother helped me retain as much of my childhood as was possible in a world of hunger and hardship.

I don't remember anything about Christmas 1946. I recently spoke with a friend of ours, Nikolaus (Klosi) Wiegert, who is two years older than I and lived in the same camp. He told me what he remembered.

Dr. Miatowich was one of the kindest persons in town. He had been the town doctor for over twelve years, and all people respected and loved him. Because he was Serbian, he and his family were among the few free *Karlsdorfer* citizens left.

The good doctor wanted to do something to make Christmas a little happier for the children housed in the hangar whom he had loved and cared for most of their lives.

He went to the *Strazniza* or camp commander and asked for permission to put up a Christmas tree outside the entrance gate of the camp. At first the request was denied. But the doctor was persistent, and finally, to rid himself of the determined doctor, the *Strazniza* gave his approval. This is how, on Christmas 1946, Dr Miatowich brought the *Christkindl* to all the children behind the fence.

The beautiful tree, with candles aglow in the night, stood on a small mound of dirt just outside the gate in all its shimmering glory. Klosi recalls how he and all the other hundreds of children pressed against the entrance gate and fence to get a better look, and how he went back every chance he had during the rest of the season, to feast his eyes on the sight just outside the barbed wire.

I listened to the grown man tell of that special Christmas tree. Tears came to his eyes, for the pain was still there, more than fifty years later. He mourns the years that were stolen from him and the other children, years that can never be returned and were never acknowledged by the thieves.

There was a kitchen and a laundry building, both so small that only a few people at a time fit in them. Considering that there were four thousand people in camp, that was almost as good as nothing. The kitchen and laundry had no running water, only a few wooden tubs for washing clothes.

Many an argument broke out among the women about whose turn it was to use the facilities. Needless to say, some people, just as today, didn't wait their turn, so loud discussions took place over who was next.

I was fascinated by the toilets. No more using the ditch. I could actually walk into a building and use one of the toilets without being afraid to fall in. The ditch was still there. It flowed out from under the outhouse. But that was okay. I was used to it being there. The bigger kids used to jump over it as a game. I didn't because my legs were too short.

Sometimes I'd go into the outhouse just to sit on one of the seats and look at the new raw wood. This was the first new anything I remember seeing in my young life. It was like having a whole big room all to yourself. Since the building was perched on short stilts to raise it over the ditch, you had to go up three or four steps. On one side of the room was a long bench with ten seat-like holes, no walls or doors separating them. On the other side were two or three windows, nothing else. If there were people inside, I wouldn't stay long.

Marie was our shoe maker – instead of leather she fashioned them out of wool. Her nimble fingers clicked knitting needles in and out of the wool loops so quickly that in no time a long strand became a slipper. On a warm sunny morning in spring, Marie presented me with a brand new *pair*. I loved them. They were so colorful; blue, red, yellow, purple, pink – just like a rainbow. She had made shoes for me many times before, but I thought this pair was the most beautiful. I danced in little circles when I put them on. I knew they looked especially nice on my feet.

I ran outside the hangar to show them off. Mami called me back. "Be very careful and don't mess them up. They are to last for a while. Wool is hard to get," she reminded me. I promised I'd be very careful and skipped out the door.

The sunny sky smiled down on the camp yard and all the children were outside on this fine spring day. I guess it was Sunday, Mami and a lot of other mothers were in camp. I liked it when there were so many people outside. I spotted Seppi and Andres by the ditch with a bunch of other kids. I ran over to them and watched as each one took a running start and jumped across. They were having so much fun. I thought to myself, "maybe I might be able to do the same. Maybe my legs had grown a little longer over this winter."

"Hey Elsa," someone called. "Why don't you try?"

Why not? I moved back, took a running start and ran as fast as I could, stretching my leg as far as it went when I came to the ditch. I flew up into the air like a bird and came straight down – with both feet – in the middle of the ditch. I was up to my thighs in human excrement. Someone took my arms and pulled me out of the foul-smelling ditch that had held me as if I was in quicksand.

When I was on dry land again I looked down and saw that my shoes had been swallowed up by the muck in the ditch. My shoes, my beautiful shoes. I ran into the hangar just as I was. I cried and tried to tell Mami how bad I felt. But she didn't listen. When she saw that my shoes were missing she just yelled at me and started to spank me. I tried to tell her I was sorry, but she just kept on hitting me. Mami didn't stop, and the smell from my legs and clothing finally became too much... and I threw up.

Never before or after had my mother spanked me that hard. I was angry with her for a long time, I held that day against her. But as I grew older and became a little wiser, I understood. We had so little and now I wasted the little that we had. Losing those shoes was the last straw.

It was bedtime. The hangar was dark and voices were dying down for the night. We had said our prayers out loud, and as usual we asked God to watch over Tati, wherever he was tonight. I crossed myself at the end of our prayers and said, *"Mami, wer is' der Tati?"*

She didn't answer right away.

"Mami, who is this Tati?" I asked again.

Mami embraced me and let out a soft sigh,

"You don't remember your father do you?"

I could feel that this question had shocked my mother and that it had distressed her greatly.

This is the last thing I can recall from the Karlsdorfer Lager. In the late spring of 1947, we were taken to several different camps, from which we made the first of our escapes.

CHAPTER
10

My First Taste of Freedom

Everyone traveled light. *A Bingl, a Sack, un a Dorba* held all of my family's worldly possessions. The bundle contained our bedding: the cloth sack and bag contained the rest. We were transferred from one camp to another during the spring of 1947 until we came to Novoselo.

On the way to Novoselo my recollections are like flashbacks in brief sequences, as if the beginning and end of a film and parts of the middle have been cut out, leaving only some of the highlights of our journey from one camp to the other.

Throughout our ordeal I usually felt safe – unless the adults around me panicked. Then, I too became afraid. No one needed to tell me if we were safe or not, I could always sense what our situation was.

We were moved from camp to camp, we stayed from a few days to a few weeks. One camp stands out quite clearly. It rained all the time. The roadway was full of deep, water-filled ruts, making it look like a collection of small rivers; mud was everywhere. Gigantic, light brown animals with large horns pulled wagons up and down the street. At first I thought they were big cows, but I had never seen cows with such huge horns before. Their feet plodded, deep in the mud, massive heads bent as they pulled the heavy load. A yoke connected the two animals, making it look as if they had one shoulder with two heads. Their bodies were so wide and their heads so tall, they seemed to reach all the way into the dark clouds. I kept my gaze on them until the *Ochse* were out of sight.

Basl, though not a tall or strong woman, had been assigned as an oxen driver. She had a hard time handling those big animals. Luckily it was only for a few weeks. Then we were moved to another camp.

Sometimes we were driven like a herd of animals from camp to camp, other times we had the luxury of riding on wagons, and one time we got to ride on a train.

We came to a place that looked like a big open yard criss-crossed with railroad tracks. No trains were on the tracks, except for the one long line of cattle cars. It was early in the morning when we arrived. At first there were just a few of us. Later, when the sun came out, more and more people came.

The Partisaner guarding us started shouting orders and moving us towards the cattle cars. I don't recall getting in the cattle car. I just remember sitting on the floor of the car in front of Mami with people sitting very close, surrounding me. All I could see was the top of the big sliding cattle car door.

The train started to roll. Since we were packed so close and I could hardly move, I stared out at the sky of the open car door. And as I watched I saw the electric wires outside slowly move from pole to pole. As the train picked up speed, the lines came alive. They looked as if they were running from the top of one pole to the next. Dipping up and down, jumping up to the tops of the poles, rolling down on the other side and jumping up once more. The lines ran faster and faster, repeating the same route over and over, putting me in a trance.

This train ride and the traveling overhead wires are the clearest memory I have of our journey to Novoselo, the camp where we spent most of the summer in 1947.

The summer we spent in Batsch Novoselo was to be our last one in Yugoslavia. Unlike Karlsdorf with its more than 4000 inmates confined behind barb wire or barricaded streets, here in Novoselo we stayed in houses in the middle of town; no guards were posted during the day although we were guarded at night when all the grown-ups were back in camp.

Early in the morning, the Partisaner came and got all able-bodied workers, including teenage boys and girls, and marched them out of town to work in the fields. At sundown they returned. We children were left to roam as we pleased. The Partisaner knew we wouldn't go far, they had our mothers.

During the day I went exploring. For the first time in years I was free; there were no fences or guards. I saw a lady walking on the other side of the street, draped in black from head to toe. I could see the outline of her legs beneath the many layers of her long, flowing gown. Behind the square fabric covering her face I could see the profile of her nose. I wondered why her face was covered. Maybe she had something wrong with her mouth.

What if she had no mouth? But that couldn't be. Still thinking, I watched her walk up the street until she came to the doorway of a house. She stopped, opened the door, and disappeared.

This was my first encounter with our neighbors across the street. I was to see her or women like her daily. Muslims from another part of Yugoslavia had been brought to Novoselo and given property that had belonged to our people. In fact, the whole town was populated with new-comers from all over Yugoslavia. It was a diverse group: Muslims, mountain nomads, Gypsies and Serbians, all different from the German population which had built this town.

A short distance up the street from the Muslims was a mill of some sort. A team of white oxen hitched to a long bar toiled endlessly turning a flat millstone round and around. I crossed the street, paused to examine the animals, then moved on.

I came to a large fenced-in garden a few houses up the street. I stopped at the gate to look at the garden. A large tree grew in the middle of the garden and looking up into its leafy branches, I saw pears, lots and lots of pears. I put my hand on the gate.

"Maybe if I was really quick I might find a pear on the ground before anyone saw me in the yard," I thought to myself.

My eyes did not leave the door to the house when suddenly it opened and a woman came out. She called to me, *"Mala Seco,"* I didn't understand.

"Mala Seco, Mala Seco," she repeated.

Not knowing what to say, I blurted out, *"Molim Leba,"* the only words I knew in Serbian. The woman came up to the gate and opened it to let me in. She took me by the hand and walked over to the pear tree, picked a nice big one and gave it to me while still talking softly in Serbian. Again the words *Mala Seco*, stood out from all the other words she said. I took the pear and said *Dankscheen*. We walked up to her house. She went in and came out with a piece of bread. Again I thanked her and walked towards the gate with my treasure in both hands. She called something and waved to me when I got to the gate. I waved back and went out the gate and home to eat my sweet pear and soft white bread.

When Mami came back from the fields that evening, I asked what *Mala Seco* meant. Mami told me it meant *Kleines Fräulein*. I was happy to know that the lady thought I was a "little lady."

From that time on I went to see the lady often. And she always had something good for me to eat. Even if we didn't understand each other's words we knew that we shared feelings of friendship.

The words *Molim Leba* mean "Please some bread." These were the words that my brother taught me. He was gone most of the days in Novoselo, out begging for food. Some days he came back with lots of food and others with nothing. Thanks to my brother, I often had a full stomach.

As I write this little story about the kind lady who only saw a hungry little girl and not some no good *Schwabo*, my heart goes out to her. For she is the one that let me see that not all Serbian people were like the Partisaner. Just like Germans, most were good and some were bad. That is how it is with all nationalities.

We arrived in Novoselo in June to harvest wheat. After the wheat fields were harvested the work crew was taken to different places to gather whatever vegetables or fruit were ripe. Mami and the rest of the mothers smuggled as much food in at night as their underwear and their hidden pockets could hold. To make this possible, one or two of the women who were fluent in Serbian would try to chat with the guards to distracte them, making it possible for the others to conceal on their person whatever food they were harvesting. We children would be waiting anxiously for our mothers to come home so we'd get something good to eat.

We still received the same horrible ration for the day as we had in Karlsdorf. Especially the pea soup – we got more of that than anything else. It smelled and tasted just as bad here as it did in Karlsdorf. And just as many little wormy bugs, if not more, swam on top of the bowl. We picked out as many as possible, but plenty were left. Many times I'd go hungry and wait until mother returned. Anything that she brought back would be better then this soup.

I recall such an evening quite clearly, I was so hungry that I ran out to meet her. But all she had for me that day was one very large white onion. I took it and went out to my spot on the veranda and started to peel it. I sat and looked at my dinner for a time before I finally took a small bite.

What a surprise! It didn't taste like an onion at all. It was sweet. I took a bigger bite. It was still sweet. I ate it like an apple. I remember looking up into the evening sky, happily filling my stomach. Now I was glad that the onion was so big, for I didn't have to go to sleep hungry.

Because the *Donaufluss* flowed just outside of Novoselo, Seppi and Andres became Danube River fishermen. All they needed was a long stick, string, wire for a hook, and worms. Sometimes they were lucky, many times not.

"Schau was mr gfangt hawe," Seppi yelled as he came running.

"Look what we caught," Andres echoed, as he raced past my brother.

"We caught fish – catfish."

"Loss mich schaue," I begged. "Let me see."

Andres stuck the dark grey seven inch fish in front of my face, squeezed its mouth and growled, *"Er werd dich fresse. –* He's gonna eat you up."

Its glassy eyes stared at me, two long, shiny, meaty whiskers hung down on both sides of its big wide mouth. It was the ugliest fish I had ever seen.

"Ugh, get that thing away from me!" I shrieked as Andres continued poking the fish in my face.

Despite their ugliness, catfish were good to eat. I ran ahead of the boys to tell about their great catch. As soon as I saw Basl I called out the great news. *"Basl, Basl mir hawe Fisch!"* I hopped and skipped around my aunt singing over and over; *"Mir hawe Fisch! — Mir hawe Fisch!"*

The boys proudly handed over their prize. Basl held the fish up and said; *"Heint were mr gut esse. Des gibt a feines Fischpaprikasch. –* Today we're going to eat well. These fish will make a fine fish stew."

I had never eaten fish until we came to Novoselo, for in Karlsdorf there was no place where one could go fishing. I was happy that we'd have this delicacy once more.

Anything was better than the regular camp's cuisine of the day, the pea soup with bugs. Before coming to America I don't recall ever being completely full and being able to say, "I can't eat one more bite." Even in Novoselo, where Mami could smuggle in food from the harvest and Seppi begged, hunger was always on our menu. The fish from the Danube is the only memory I have of eating "meat" in any camp.

Life was so free. It was a long time since I experienced just walking in any direction without a fence, or an armed guard to stop me at some point along the way.

One day, as I was exploring a street that I had never been on before, I came to a high fenced yard with the entrance gate wide open. I stopped and went in.

This was an unusual place. The wide dusty yard with its packed down earth had not one blade of grass growing out of it. Instead, colorful broken pieces of stones were scattered all over; yellow, blue, white, green. Like dusty flower petals of all shapes, they looked up at the sky.

Way in back of the yard was a drab brick building, the same color as the dust in front of it. The only opening in the structure was a large doorway that almost reached to the top of its roof. The sun shone brightly, making the dark entrance to the building look like a tunnel. On one side was a high stack of brightly colored, shiny bricks.

I picked up a light green chip that felt warm in my hand and wiped the dust off. It sparkled green in the sun's bright light. I ran my fingertips over it; it felt like glass. It was beautiful. Even today I still can "see" that shiny mint green piece of brick. I now know that what I had seen was a brick yard where they made *Kachel* – glazed tile bricks – for *Kachelofen*, the tile stoves used to heat bedrooms or sitting rooms.

What was this? I stopped playing in front of our house when I heard something that I had never heard in Novoselo before, a faint trumpet sound coming from the center of town. The last time I heard a trumpet was in Karlsdorf when my Franz Onkel played that day we marched around the airplane hangars.

Soon there were more sounds of other musical instruments. They were coming closer. In the distance I heard a drum and more horns. My eyes and ears remained fixed on the end of the street and finally I saw a small group of men come marching toward me. The evening sun was sending its last rays down upon their shiny instruments, making them sparkle. They became bigger and bigger and the music louder and louder. The sound made my heart leap. The trumpets and trombones glowed a rosy gold as they marched past. People who heard the music came out of their houses to see what was going on; they lined the street, waving happily as the six-man band marched by.

I had never heard anything so lovely before. Music to me was something that came from a small harmonica or people singing. I recalled music from our radio, long ago, but that I had almost forgotten. Soon the men were far up the street and the sound that they made became fainter and fainter. Finally, they were gone, though I kept on looking and listening, hoping to hear and see a little longer.

I have no idea why that little parade came down our street. I have asked my mother and brother if they remembered the musicians, but they couldn't. I will never forget it. It was one of the happy memories in my young life.

The sun was out on the tenth day of July, my seventh birthday. I played by myself in front of the house, bouncing a ball Seppi had made from rags. He and Andres made many such balls. They went from house to house to sell them, sometimes for a *Dinar* but mostly for food.

"Seppi," I called, as he came whistling down the street. "Do you know what day it is today?"

"No," he replied.

"It's my *Geburtstag,*" I told him proudly, expecting him to be as happy as I was.

"So what? *Grilsegrauns-Krampa* has a birthday today." He mimicked my high voice, and ran into the house.

"Why was he so nasty to me sometimes?" I wondered to myself.

One morning late that summer, a group of older boys were out in front of our gate. I played nearby, bouncing my rag ball off the front wall of the house. Their voices got louder and louder, and children came out of the courtyard to see what was going on. I walked over to see why some children were yelling for the boys to stop what they were doing.

Some of the boys had sharp sticks, and they were poking at something on the ground, laughing each time they jabbed at the object in front of them. When I saw what it was, my stomach turned. They were poking at an *Igel.* The poor creature was trying to protect itself by curling up into a prickly ball. But this did not stop the heartless boys from further attacking the poor hedgehog. Turning it on its back they kept on jabbing at the small, now bloody and mud smeared animal.

I turned and ran back into the courtyard. I tried to get the event out of my mind, but I kept on seeing the sticks striking the helpless animal again and again. I felt sick once more.

I'm glad that my brother and cousin were not among those boys. I don't think that they would ever have done anything like that. Both are much too soft hearted to hurt even a mouse.

Late one afternoon, I saw Seppi in the distance outside of town as I was going to the river to play. He had been gone all day as usual, begging for food. When he saw me he started to run and call happily.

"Elsa, ich hab was gutes! Ich hab a Wassermilaun! – Elsa, I have something good! I have a watermelon!" We ran towards each other. When he stopped in front of me he held out the melon for me to touch. It was a little smaller than a soccer ball. Its dark green skin felt smooth under my finger tips. My brother smiled from ear to ear, proud of what he had brought home.

Seppi lifted the melon over his head, still admiring it. Suddenly it slipped out of his hand, dashed to the ground, and broke into pieces in front of our feet. My heart sank as I looked down and saw the wet green and red pieces of fruit, shattered and covered with sand. My brother sat down right there in the path, picked up a piece of the fruit, and started to eat, paying no attention to the sand on the melon. He motioned me to come and eat. I sat down and joined my brother. The sweet, warm juice felt like honey on my tongue. It ran down the sides of my chin, dripping all over my hands and chest. I hardly tasted the tiny kernels of sand on the piece of melon. I was happy to be able to still my hunger there by my brother's side. I knew then that he cared very much for his little sister; he could have eaten the melon where he got it, but he came back to share his treasure with me. I also knew I loved him as much as he did me.

For many years I believed that my brother had accidentally dropped the small melon. Just recently I asked him if he remembered how we ate the watermelon, sand and all, and wasn't it a shame that he accidentally dropped it.

"I didn't drop it," he said, "I threw it. How do you think we'd have been able to eat the melon without a knife? I had to break it somehow."

Leave it to an eleven-year old boy to think of a quick way to solve a problem. Besides, a little sand never hurt anyone.

The house we now occupied probably had belonged to a wealthy German family, who, if they were still alive, went through the same ordeal as we did, possibly even worse. All the towns that now housed concentration camps had had an almost all German population.

I thought ours was a grand house to be in. I had never lived in a house with steps or a great, white-pillared veranda. I liked to stay in the shade of the veranda which ran along one side of the house by the courtyard. Its red, slate-covered roof was supported by columns resting on a short, wide wall. I'd sit on the wall next to one of the five pillars and watch the children play in the courtyard below. This was a lofty place to be.

Once when I was on top of the wall daydreaming, loud screams jolted me back to the present.

"Der Bicko is' heraus. Alli rein. – The bull is loose. Everyone inside." Somehow the bull got loose from its pen in back of the courtyard.

Children ran screaming everywhere, scrambling to get inside. The big black animal was charging, head down, through the courtyard. Quickly I ran into the house with everyone else and watched him from the window as he ran up the steps, onto the veranda and down again. Luckily, everyone had managed to escape the sharp horns of the bull.

When Marie did not work in the fields she was my caretaker. Because Mami and Basl worked long hours, sometimes they didn't come home until dark, and my cousin became my stand-in mother. One of her chores was to delouse her ward.

We usually sat on the warm cobblestone courtyard, with the sun shining down on us, I detested every stroke of her *Lauskambl.*

"Des is lang genuch. Her auf, her auf. Ich will nimmer. – That's long enough. Stop, stop. I don't want to anymore." I squirmed and complained. Anchoring me with her legs, Marie continued with her comb – determined to carry out her task. Sometimes I'd wiggled free and run. Marie ran after me and finished what she started. Most of the time she was the winner. But sometimes, she gave up and let me get away.

Taking care of me was not an easy job. Although my older cousin was very patient, I'm sure at times she was not happy with me. Like the time I discovered that spinning my body around very fast turned the entire world into one big blurred, colorful streak.

"Elsa, her auf, du werscht noch breche!" Marie yelled from the veranda.

Ignoring my cousin's plea for me to stop, I continued whirling. "Stop it or you're going to vomit," she shouted once more. I heard her scream, but I continued.

All of a sudden two hands grabbed me by the shoulders and my body came to an abrupt halt, but not my stomach. I retched, and the foul smelling vomit splattered over the ground as well as over my cousin. I had never before or after seen her so mad. She didn't say one word, but her eyes said it all, as she cleaned us up.

Another incident comes to mind about Marie that summer in Novoselo. One hot, sunny afternoon a rainstorm came out of nowhere, turning day into night. I stood in the yard and let the rain surround me. It felt warm as it soaked my clothing, down to my skin.

Suddenly big, hard, balls of ice fell from the sky – *Hagl.* Hail the size of small eggs bombarded the earth, bouncing off the ground like white ping pong balls. I stood frozen to the cobblestones as I watched in amazement. *"Elsa, kumm rein. Kumm rein!"* Marie yelled frantically. "Come in, come in out of the storm!"

As in a dream I stood fast, in a daze, oblivious to her call. I had never seen anything like this before. Soon I felt Marie pulling me by the arm onto the veranda. From there we watched as the yard was quickly covered with the white, icy hail, like snow in January. Since that day, I think of Marie whenever hail falls from the sky. I loved her very much and she loved me.

Our sleeping area was, just as in all the other houses and in all the other camps, nothing more than straw spread out along the walls of the room. Except this room was big enough for four rows of people along the walls instead of two. More than thirty people slept here nightly. Basl, Andres, Marie, Mami, Seppi and I all lay next to each other; this was not always the case in some of the camps. Sometimes we had been separated.

One evening, as the sun's last rays streamed through the windows and everyone was back for the night, I had just come in the door and saw Basl get up from her straw bed and start to walk across the floor. She stopped abruptly, all of a sudden blood started to squirt from her leg like a fountain. In just a few seconds a pool of blood was on the floor around her.

"Ich blut! Hilfe!" she screamed, "I'm bleeding! Help!"

The whole roomful of people came to her aid, trying to stop the flow of blood. I watched Basl disappear behind the curtain of people. Then a man in the room told everyone to move back so he could help her. I watched everyone move aside and saw the man tie a rope around her upper leg.

A hush came over the room as all eyes were on Basl, sitting in the pool of blood, and the older man working over her, until he finally stopped the bleeding. I had never seen so much blood before.

I didn't know why my aunt was bleeding. But I knew at the time that what had happened was a threat to Basl's life.

My cousin Andres told me that the older man who stopped the bleeding was experienced in first aid. It was lucky for Basl that he happened to be housed under our roof. One of the arteries in her leg had burst and if he had not acted quickly she'd have bled to death in a short time.

I thought my brother knew everything. I asked him about almost anything that came into my mind. I can recall asking him in Novoselo why horses had tails. His answer was because they don't have hands to swat flies with, dummy. That made sense to me. Seppi was smart. After all he was four years older than I.

That summer, Seppi and Andres even let me join them in some of their games. *Gatschgonjei* was one of them. I had no idea what the name meant, it must have been a Hungarian game. It was similar to baseball but much more dangerous – a boy's game – girls very seldom got to participate. Instead of a ball, a wooden stake, pointed at both ends, was used. The stake was laid across a hole, flipped up into the air with a stick and batted as hard as possible towards the player in the outfield, who had to catch it. My effort only landed the stake a few yards from my feet, but that was okay. I got to play with Seppi and Andres. Sometimes my brother asked me to play a game with him that only *"Die grossi Buwe"* – the big boys played.

A rectangular outline was drawn in the dirt, divided in half by a line drawn down the middle. The object of the game was to carve a piece off your opponent's space and add on to your space by tossing a knife across to his side and making it stick in the ground. If it stuck you claimed that section from your opponent's space. The game continued until the knife-point failed to impale the earth. Then it was the other person's turn. Again I lost, just like when we played *Gatschgonjei* but I was happy because Seppi let me use his prize possession, his pocket knife.

The small knife was of great value to my brother. It was probably the only thing that belonged only to him. He used it for many things. He was an expert *Pfeiffelmacher.* His knife whittled the best whistles in camp.

After a heavy rain, when the dusty street turned in to mud, we played *"Pitsch, patsch, pollerloch."* Everyone scooped up a glob of mud, formed a ball, then a bowl-shaped mud pie and spit in the center. Chanting *"Pitsch, patsch, pollerloch,"* we threw it as hard as we could on the cobblestones. With a loud pop, our mud missile exploded.

Simple objects were great toys. White wax berries were good for crushing and squirting at things, a sturdy twig and a piece of string became a *Peitsch* or whip that cracked to make my make-believe horses race like the wind. After I got tired of that, the string and twig was fashioned into a *Fitschipfeil.* Stretching my arrow carefully across my bow, I'd try to make it fly straight into the air.

Some evenings I'd become a *Grotte Jäger* – the world's greatest toad hunter that never caught one.

Paper was a scarce commodity in camp. Whenever I received a sheet it was a great treasure. Cutting paper or anything else with a scissor was out of the question. Mami's *Scher* was off limits. Her *Nodl und Zwirn* belonged to the same category. I can't ever remember using any of my mothers sewing notions – they were for her use only. Scissors, needle, thread and pins were carefully tied into a piece of cloth and safely tucked away with the rest of our few priceless possessions. Without them we'd have been in rags, and my mother was much too proud to let that happen. In fact, about fifteen years ago my mother and I were interviewed by the Barrington Courier-Review, our town newspaper, and the reporter suggested that because of our circumstances, we must have been dressed in rags. My mother got very upset and stated that her children were never dressed in rags. She always patched and mended any rip or hole in our clothes.

I became an expert at tearing paper, but before a piece of paper was ever torn, I'd have folded it into different shapes. It became a small hat first, then a boat which sailed on small puddles for a few days, getting wet and dry many times.

Then I'd unfold my paper boat and smooth it as well as I could back to a sheet of paper. I'd fold it into a square by creasing and tearing until I turned it into four identical pyramids that opened up sideways and front ways. I'd turn it into a large mouth puppet. Sometimes it was a bird with a big beak, other times just a friend to have a conversation with. Other times I played a game called *Himmel und Hell* – Heaven and Hell.

If I was lucky and had a pin, I'd make a *Windmiehl*. I'd crease and tear my paper carefully to get four sharp points. If the points weren't even, your pinwheel didn't twirl well. I'd run, turn, blow for hours making my windmill swirl on its stick. What fun!

Unfortunately, after creating a pinwheel nothing much was left except a tattered piece of paper at the end of a stick.

I always kept the pin; pins belonged to the same category as scissors, something rare to be treasured.

A crisp, spotless piece of paper has always been a special thing for me. A sheet, still snow white and untouched by human fingers, is like a snowflake just fallen from heaven. A certain feeling comes over me when I see and handle a fresh sheet, a feeling that I also have on winter days when my eyes look upon a landscape just covered with snow, unspoiled and undisturbed. I have a reverence for things simple, yet beautiful. This is the adult me speaking to you now; the child didn't dwell on such thoughts – a new piece of paper was just pretty, that's all. Later, when I became more aware of my surroundings and became interested in creating images with paint and pencil, paper became not only a lovely object, but a friend.

I guess the artist within me was already awakening as I dreamed and played on the shores of the *Donaufluss*.

The Danube River just outside of Novoselo was the only large body of water I had ever seen in my seven years of life. The sand felt warm on my bare feet as they dug into the ditch-like footpath that led down to the shores of the *Donau*. Other paths crossed it, coming from different directions, all headed towards the river. On either side of the foot-worn ditches, tall, greenish-yellowish tipped blades of grass waved gently in the soft summer breeze.

Closer to the water the trails ended, and the ground became flat and hard under my feet; I was now walking on boulders embedded in the ground. Sparse patches of grass grew between the sand-filled crevasses until the rocks took over the entire shore line.

Where the pathway ended, a gnarly tree grew, its enormous trunk covered with thick, grooved bark. Its leafy branches reached to the sky, like a large hand with many crooked fingers. The roots were partially exposed and grew over the path, so you had to be careful not to trip over them. Sometimes I'd sit on them as if they were a bench.

A few yards from the tree, the rocky shore sloped down to meet the water. I had to be careful not to slip and fall over the slippery stones. Mami had made it clear that I was not allowed to go in the water unless someone was with me. She also let me know that I was never ever to go any deeper than up to my knees. If I did and she found out, I'd be sorry.

She didn't have to worry. I had no desire to be swallowed up by the river. I always stayed close to the shallow bank, climbing up and down on the rocks that lay there as if someone had picked up the earth and given it a good shake, scattering all the rocks into the water at the river's edge. The rocks were just right for scaling and jumping from one to the other.

Before stepping into the cool water, I made sure to tuck the hem of my dress in the bottom of my underpants. This did not always work, since I slid from wet sloping rocks into the river. By the time I reached the river's edge my bottom was usually wet. But it didn't take long for the summer heat to dry me off.

Many times I sat on the rocks and studied the other side of the river, daydreaming and wondering what was there. This part of the Danube was wide and deep and a boat was needed to get to the opposite side.

The smoothness of the water reached to the other bank. But instead of a rocky shore like the one I sat on, huge stone slabs rose from the bank forming a wall; large trees grew from its uppermost edge. Small plants poked from the cracks of the mossy slabs of stone. Rarely did the sun smile on that side of the shore; nature's walled garden was kept in the dimness of its own shadows, even on the sunniest of days. The flowing river's sunlit waves cast rays of shimmering light upon its dark boundary, turning it into an enchanted and mysterious land.

Occasionally men came as if out of nowhere from the other side, standing in their small *Tschinackl*, moving their *Ruder* quietly across the water. This sight helped inspire my fantasies. Stretched out before me was a huge painted canvas come to life. Each small colorful figure plunged his oars in and out of the water, gliding through the sunny liquid, one stroke at a time, moving the long rowboats filled with fruit and vegetables. Parting the water, the boats continued across and then disappeared behind the rocks that obscured my view of the shore downstream. I never saw the boats land or discovered where they came from. And I always wondered how they had come down from the high rocks.

I was told that on top of the high tree covered wall was a town. This puzzled me. In my childish way I thought that across this large body of water the whole land was elevated as I saw it in front of me. I wondered, how did they build a *Dorf* so high on all those rocks? I sat and imagined all kinds of marvelous things that must have gone on in a town resting on nothing but towering stone walls.

The town was called *Vukowar*. Almost fifty years later that same town would be the first to be destroyed by the Serbs. Ethnic cleansing would become a household word. Sarajevo and Bosnia-Herzegovina would become known all over the world for its hatred and bloodshed. Serbs, Croations and Muslims killing each other – each claiming the land as justly THEIRS. All the world would be shocked by the events in the nineteen nineties in Yugoslavia. But Yugoslavia's first "Ethnic Cleansing" of its half million ethnic Germans would still be hidden from the history books.

Also unknown that summer of 1947 was that one day in America I'd befriend a girl named Erna who was born in that same town high up on the other shore of the Donaufluss. Erna and I eventually became sisters-in-law, for she married my brother, though we left out the in-law and became the best of sisters. But that's another story for another time.

I knew I was being mean when I told Mami that Seppi went swimming in the Donau again. I told on him every time, as if that was my duty, and I wanted to do the job well. Sometimes I did it to get even. Seppi usually got punished for disobeying the no swimming rule. I was sorry afterwards for telling, but the next time he did it, I told again.

I enjoyed being by the river. It was so different from any place we had ever lived. Its swirling water was a source of food and fun. If Seppi and Andres were lucky enough to hook a fish or two we'd have a good meal once more.

My mother and all the other women, cleaned and washed our clothes in its rushing stream, the same stream that carried our people hundreds of years before to settle the land. They had come floating on their flat bottomed boats to a land of swamps and wilderness and worked hard to turn it into a fruitful paradise. The Danube was like an umbilical cord to our past, to the ancestors who had built our *Heimatland*. We, their children, now had been severed from that homeland and put into bondage. Children don't think of these things but surely our mothers, as they washed our garments in the *Donaufluss*, recalled our history and anguished about the future.

After the harvest was gathered that August, we were told that they were moving us to another place. I was sad to hear this, I liked it here, more than any other place we had been. We were a big group of people when armed soldiers marched us out of town one evening as the sun was going down. We walked away from the houses and into the fields, away from the town of Novoselo.

Besides the poppy field in Karlsdorf, the countryside of Batsch-Novoselo and the Danube River are all that I remember of the beauty of the open country of Yugoslavia. Sometimes, I get a longing to go back and see the land of my birth. But I know this cannot be – for it does not exist anymore.

CHAPTER
11

In Search of Freedom

Transported by wagon we came from Batch Novoselo, to the
outskirts of the town of Torschau.

Where we were now living was a lonely place. Fields surrounded us, nothing but fields. Not one tree or bush grew near the little
hut, only fields of green, low-growing, leaves, which I was told were
Zuckerruwe. Sugar beets grew to our right, for as far as the eyes could
see, and to our left grew *Kukurutz* – corn as high as small trees. If we
had come here in late spring, we could have cooked the young, tender
feed corn, but since it was late summer it was impossible to eat, it was
hard as pebbles.

We lived in a small, white cottage. There was not much to it; a door in
the middle and two windows on each side. The six of us were the only
people assigned to this little hut. During the day Mami, Basl and most of
the time, Marie were taken to work in the sugar beet fields, the sugar
beet harvest was why we were brought here. Sugar beets were the only
thing that Mami was able to smuggle home. No more onions, potatoes,
tomatoes, pears, apples or watermelons – just sugar beets.

To consume our booty we had to cook it first. With the cottage came a
big black iron kettle that was used to boil the beets over an open fire. The
first time we did this, I knew just from its smell I would not like it. The finished product was a syrupy, overly sweet, beet soup which tasted disgusting.

Although I was hungry, I could not eat the beet soup. Just to bring
the spoon to my mouth made me retch. So I went without and ate my
ration of pea soup and waited for something better.

Although hunger ravished all of us, Seppi was nothing but skin and bones. He had suffered from typhus two years before, and his body was unable to build itself up because it lacked sufficient nourishment. This was one of the reasons my brother was good at begging. He'd walk to town, which was a few miles away, and knock on doors. *Molim Leba*, he'd plead. He looked so hungry and pitiful standing there, asking "Please, give me bread." Many people gave him something to eat. Of course, my brother was also courageous: sometimes the man of the house would swear and take a stick to him and chase him off the property. Seppi's hunger overrode his feelings of embarrassment or fear. If a door was slammed in his face, he'd go to the next one until someone gave him food.

He'd eat some of it right then and there; the rest he'd put in his sack to bring home. My mother has often said, "Without Seppi's help, who knows if we would have survived our ordeal."

Since my brother was off begging most of the time, Andres was the one who got stuck watching me. On our last visit to Germany, Andres told me his worst job was making me eat the *Zuckerruwe* meals. I just wouldn't eat the beet soup. He did everything he could think of to make me, but nothing worked. And he was the one to get in trouble afterwards whenever I didn't eat.

One day he even banished me outside the cottage along with my bowl of beet soup. *"Du kumscht mer net rein bis fertich gess hascht,"* Andres bellowed as he pushed me out the door and slammed it shut.

"I don't care if you won't let me in until I finish eating," I thought to myself. I was hungry, but I was not about to eat this. I saw a cat come toward me.

"You're going to help me out," I thought. I took the dish and put it in front of the animal. It sniffed and backed off. I grabbed it by the neck and forced its nose into the dish. But the cat stood its ground, hissed and humped its back, squirmed free and ran away.[7]

---

[7]Many years later, I was making a Christmas gingerbread house for my firstborn and the recipe called for molasses. The odor was familiar as soon as it reached my nostrils. Where had I smelled that sickening, sugary smell before? I tried to remember, but it didn't come to me. Then my mother took one sniff and started to chuckle. "It's made of the sugar beets that you refused to eat in Torschau," she said. The minute she told me, I remembered the cat, and I laughed with her. That was the first and last time molasses was on my pantry shelf.

I always felt so small when walking between the huge rows of corn on our way to the kitchen in the other house for our daily ration of food. Eight foot tall *Kukurutzstengl* grew on both sides of the narrow road, so tall that sometimes I was unable to see their tassels. Back home our corn was stored in our *Hambar*. How much fun it was in the bin filled with corn. With both hands I'd scoop up the kernels and let them rain down on me: or sometimes I'd lie on top of the cool corn and let my body sink into it.

I liked it best when Marie went with me to get our meals. We'd walk quietly, hand in hand, between the corn. The late summer sun was hot, slowly turning the green corn stalks brown. Soon the corn would be harvested and stored.

As we went on our way, Marie and I would chat, or she'd tell me stories, or we'd sing songs or discuss the things around us. "Look at all this corn. Too bad we can't pop some."

"Marie, did you ever pop corn?" I asked.

"Yes, but mine didn't always pop. Many times it burned and smelled up the kitchen. *Die Oma hat der beschti Batchkukruz gmacht.*" Marie continued.

"She did?"

"She sure did. Oma made better popcorn than anyone."

"I wish we could eat some now." I told her.

"Me too," she sighed.

I liked to talk about *"Drhahm."* It helped me remember what back "home" was like. Marie's memories, as well as the rest of my family's, were of whole events. But home to me had become more or less bits and pieces of disconnected memories.

"Imagine how much work it would be to sit at a *Kukrutzripler* and remove all these corn kernels from their cobs." Marie said, spreading her arms out.

"I remember what a *Kukrutzripler* looks like," I said. "It's a small bench with a slanted, spiked board, like a wash board attached to one end." When I was little, I tried it out once. I remember how I climbed onto the work bench and straddled it, picked up an ear of corn from the basket next to it with both hands, and rubbed the *Kukrutzkolwe* – corn-cob – back and forth on the spikes. The hard kernels made a clicking sound as they came off the dry cob and rained down into the *Baximbel*, the small basket on the ground, beneath the spiked board. I felt so grown up, sitting on the bench, making feed for the animals in our barnyard.

Sometimes I helped my mother feed the chickens, who came running as soon as the corn was scattered on the ground, pecking faster than I could fling the corn, dining until they were full.

Here in Torschau we had no chickens to feed. We hardly got fed ourselves. I was never full, hunger gnawed at my insides every day.

The corn was like a forest. On every turn of the road more corn grew. It didn't end until we came into the yard of the *Bauernhof.*

In the middle of the farm yard was a large brick house surrounded by shade trees. The big leafy branches sheltered us from the hot sun – a cool island in the middle of the hot fields

Since the farm house had more rooms, many people were housed here. This is also why the kitchen was located here.

I always stayed outside underneath the shade tree by the road. I liked to eat my meager square of hard corn *Mallei* and small bowl of soup under the rustling leaves. It reminded me of our summer meals back home.

We stayed in Torschau for only a few weeks. Rumors were circulating among the women in camp that if one could get to Gakowa, a camp near the Hungarian border, it was possible to escape from there. Early one morning at the beginning of September, Mami woke me just before sunlight.

"Elsa, steh auf – zieg dich schnell an – mir gehn durch." she told me. Not entirely awake, I didn't understand at first.

"Come on, get up and dress quickly. We're going to escape! Everyone is ready to go."

Although I had no idea what was going on, I did as I was told and joined Basl, Andres, Marie, Mami and Seppi. Carrying our few belongings, we slipped out of the house.

Outside we met three other women. An older woman, Berfangers Lisbasl, her grown daughter Marie and Terri Buro, who was my mother's age. All were from Karlsdorf. Mami, Basl and the other women had pooled their meager coins and hired a Hungarian who would help us escape and transport us by wagon to the town of Sombor.

We crossed over a cut, stubbly field as the sun came up, I remember being carried piggy back, high above everyone, fully enjoying my ride. I had no idea how dangerous our outing was.

Off in the distance a man stood with a wagon and an old horse. He loaded us onto the buckboard. Slowly the horse tramped down the dirt road carting us closer to freedom.

When we got to Sombor our guide unloaded us and our belongings in the barn of a *Wirtshaus*, where we spent the night. Early in the morning our group slipped out of the barn door of the Inn and headed for Gakowa – full of hope that the camp would be our "stepping stone" to cross the border into Hungary.

When I think of Gakowa, I think of a place with no sunshine. The days were gray and depressing. Once more we lived crowded together, wall to wall. Instead of just a few streets used as a camp, the whole town was packed with imprisoned ethnic Germans. Conditions were worse here than in Karlsdorf. It was a starvation camp like Rudolfsgnad. At least fifteen thousand people were packed into this small town, compared to the four thousand in Karlsdorf, and there was less food. The town was heavily guarded day and night. Although there was no fence, armed Partisaner paced the outskirts of the village.

We arrived in Gakowa in the middle of September, 1947. Mami and Basl worked in the fields from morning till night. My mother has told me how the guards beat the women if they did not fulfill their daily quota.

"I was not as strong as the others and always lagged behind," my mother told me. "If it wouldn't have been for your aunt and the other women, I would have been severely beaten. They helped me fill my quota every day."

Although the work was exhausting and the hunger almost unbearable, my mother and aunt were happy about their decision to come here, this was surely the only way out.

Many people escaped from Gakowa including my husband's family. At the time he was thirteen years old and he remembers that it cost 500 Dinars or $1.50 per person to cross the border illegally. If you could come up with 1000 Dinars or $3.00 you were able to leave legally. At today's rate that would be about $30.00 illegally and $60.00 legally.

My mother has told me how she, Basl, Berfanger's Lisbasl, her daughter Marie, Terri Buro, Kernste Kati and Trautmanns Anna, also from Karlsdorf, made plans to escape.

"We found out about some Hungarians who'd take us across the borders for a price," my mother told me. "All of us had saved a few Dinars and sewed a few things of value into the seams of our clothing. "We pooled our assets and managed to scrape together enough to pay a guide to lead us out of town and across the Hungarian border.

"How did you find this man?" I asked.

"From other inmates. You'd be surprised how quickly a thing like that travels among desperate people."

"If we were so heavily guarded, how could so many of us get out without being noticed?" I asked.

"It was said that some Partisaner were willing to look the other way for a price. So when that particular paid-off Partisaner was on duty, he became *blind* when the guide, who slipped him the money, passed through his post at the prearranged time."

"Weren't you afraid that we all could have been killed?"

"Of course," my mother answered, "but we had no other choice. It was the only way out of this hell."

So one dark night a week or so later, the six of us walked to the edge of town, where we met Lisbasl, Marie and Terri with the two other older women. We all waited in fearful silence by a fenced-in shed.

It seemed to take forever as we waited in anticipation for our dangerous journey to start. Finally our guide arrived and with him he brought more escapees. He told us to be very quiet and keep together as close as possible. With pounding hearts our small band of women, children and grandmothers followed the man into the dark fields – our journey to freedom.

Mami, Seppi, Andres, Marie, Basl and I were at the tail end of the group. It was like playing "Follow the Leader." We walked between the tall rows of corn, the six of us always behind. All I could see was tall adults in front of me, forest-like corn on either side and the twinkling stars above.

Suddenly our party came to a halt. The people in front whispered excitedly. I knew something had happened, but what was it? "The guide is gone," were the words rippling back to the tail end of our group. He had abandoned us. Panic set in. Loud whispers moved back and forth between the adults as all moved closely together for protection.

"No need to worry," came a confident, reassuring voice from a woman in front. She raised her hand and pointed to the bright stars above and said she knew how to navigate by the stars. All we had to do was follow the *Himmelswagen* – Heaven's wagon as the Big Dipper is called in German.

Confused and puzzled, I searched the heavens for the object that was supposed to be rolling on high, but for the life of me all I could see were stars. Not even a single wagon wheel rolled across the velvet blue sky, let alone a whole wagon. I came to the conclusion that occasionally grown-ups are a little crazy, or their eyes are easier to fool.

We continued to follow our new leader for a long time. I was tired by now, very, very tired.

"Mami, ich will nimmer gehn," I whined. "No more, I don't want to walk anymore. I'm t-i-r-e-d."

"Sh – sei ruhich oder die Partisaner here Dich!" Mami commanded. I stopped complaining instantly. I surely didn't want the Partisaner to hear me.

"In a short time we'll be free and you'll be able to rest," she said. Holding me tightly by the hand, she pulled me along and we marched on. The stars in the sky began to lose their glow as daylight approached. Suddenly we stopped walking. A buzz of voices whispered in front of us. "We're back where we started from. Oh, no...we're back in Gakowa."

We had walked in a circle all night, returning to our place of departure. We were re-captured by the patrol and locked up.

CHAPTER
12

Escape

A ll my life I have feared small, dark basements, though I was unable to explain this even to myself. I learned why when my mother told me recently that after our return, the Partisaner locked us up for a week in a small cellar with no windows. More than fifty of us were down there. It was so crowded that we could not lie down without taking turns. There was nowhere to relieve oneself in the dank room.

My mother and aunt had to start planning our escape all over again. This time it was a lot harder, since we had lost all our funds. My mother and aunt sacrificed our pillows and a few other smaller items to come up with enough money to pay off a guide. A few weeks later, we started out at night into the danger zone. We marched between the cornstalks, a little wiser than before, and more fearful of being caught.

The people in front of us moved like dark shadows as we trailed behind, heading toward the border. Seppi, Andres, Marie and I were the only children. No one said a word. I kept very still, I was even more afraid than the grown ups. The dried cornhusks rustled under our feet as we walked on. We came to a clearing. "Halt, wait here," our guide ordered. "I'll go and investigate the clearing up ahead."

As the man disappeared across the empty field, we watched in silence. Our small group of women and children hid in the corn and waited. It must have occurred to every member of my family that we might be abandoned again.

Loud Serbian voices shouted out of nowhere and suddenly Partisaner with guns stood in front of us, with the captured guide in tow.

"Everyone out!" they shouted. We scrambled from our hiding place and came out into the clearing. Motioning with their pointed guns they ordered, *"Da vei! Da vei!* – Move it! Move it!" They ordered us to march across the field until we came to a white house on a small hill. In front of the house were two high poles with a long bar nailed across the top. We children were told to sit there and wait while the adults were escorted up to the house. A man came out and looked our way and then at the women in front of him. He talked to the adults in Serbian for quite some time. Although I didn't understand his words, I knew he was interrogating them. We sat in the grass, not taking our eyes off the Partisaner and the women. What would they do to us?

By this time it was morning and the autumn sun was shining brightly. We spent the day under the funny-looking post, and in the early evening we went to sleep under the same landmark. I asked Mami what this thing was. She replied abruptly that it was called a *Galje*. I had never heard this strange word before. I lay under it and looked up at the sky, with the stars shining down and Mami next to me as I fell asleep. I found out later we had been playing and sleeping under the gallows.

The border patrol had nabbed our guide out in the field and made him tell where we were hiding. But God was with us. When they led us to the border station, the officer in charge decided to let us go. He made the women promise not to tell anyone at which point we had crossed the border if we were caught.

The officer said, "It would be better if you left after midnight." He allowed us to stay the day and part of the night by the post.

I heard Mami's voice from far away. *"Elsa, weck auf.* – Wake up, its time to go." In the darkness, I didn't know where I was; then I saw the black shadow of the *Galje* against the night sky and knew. We quickly got our bundles together and joined the rest of our group at the white building.

In back of the building a ditch ran as far as one could see. Reeds grew on the side of the ditch near the house, their thin, dark stalks taller than a person.

We followed the path that led from the side of the house down toward the ditch. Hidden amongst the reeds were a few weatherbeaten boards, a makeshift bridge.

On the other side, the land sloped slightly and flattened into a wide area. Mami grabbed my hand and yanked me with her as she fled across the grass-stubbled dirt. Everything and everyone was cloaked in dark shadows. We ran in the direction we were told, always listening for shots at our back. Finally a dark wall of rustling cornstalks swallowed us up as we ran into its rows for protection.

As we got to the other side of "No Man's Land" my mother knew that we were finally in Hungary, the rows of corn were planted differently here than in Yugoslavia. This was the landmark she had been told to look for.

"Gott sei Dank! Endlich sein Mir aus dem Elend heraus!" Mami and Basl proclaimed, as they hugged and kissed us. Yes, thank God – finally we were all out of that wretched place, and free of Tito's clutches.

Although I couldn't quite understand the meaning of what we had just achieved, a feeling of happiness washed over me. Not until I was much older did I understand what danger we had faced in escaping from bondage. At last we all settled in to sleep before daylight. The towering rows of corn were our fortress. We weren't out of danger yet, we could be caught by the Hungarian government. Although the country was not communist, the Hungarian officials still might send us back to Yugoslavia for Hungary's political scene was leaning more and more towards the red.

It took us almost a month to get to the Austrian border and true freedom, making our way across the Hungarian countryside, sometimes by night or early morning. Trying to remember our journey is like rummaging around in my brain with the lights out and having just the use of a candle to illuminate my memories.

We lived in hiding. It was hard to forget about hunger. My stomach grumbled. It knotted itself up as a constant reminder that it was empty and wanted something to fill it. I was only seven years old and didn't always understand that Mami couldn't fix what was wrong. I whined a lot.

Marie was the one in charge of me. She was fourteen and understood our predicament better than I, and she helped take my mind off the hunger pangs by making up stories and games and carrying me *Bucklranse.* These piggyback rides were short, but long enough to make me happy. She even asked me to whistle. *"Pfeife, Du wilscht das ich pfeif?"* I asked in astonishment. "Are you sure you want me to whistle?"

"Yes, I'm sure," she replied.

All summer in Novoselo and Torschau I had tried and tried to whistle. I'd pucker up my lips just so, pull in my breath, puff up my cheeks, and blow. And nothing happened. Over and over I tried to make that first shrill pitch pass my lips. But all that came out was a cool, soundless breeze.

Then one day as I started to inhale, a faint sound came from my mouth. I whistled...I whistled! What jubilation. Now I was a musician as I had dreamed. I practiced in the morning, in the afternoon, at night and in between. Some days I guess I was overbearing with my talent. Even my patient cousin Marie could only stand so much of my musical efforts.

"*Elsa, Madle solle net pfeife,*" Marie told me one day.

"What, girls shouldn't whistle?" I said. "Why not?"

"*Die Mutter Gottes hat net gern wann Madle pfeife.* – The Mother of God doesn't like girls whistling," she answered.

I stared dumbfounded at my cousin for saying such a thing. Whistling was so beautiful; it was like nothing else on this earth. I decided right then and there that my cousin was wrong. I whistled softly to myself. Surely the Blessed Mother loved it as much as I did.

My mother and aunt were lucky that Marie was so mature for her age. Between Andres, my brother, and myself they had to do a lot of persuading to keep us moving toward the border.

One night we slept in a barn. I burrowed into the fresh sweet-smelling hay and let its protection warm my chilled body. It had been a long time since we had all slept under a roof, so it didn't matter that the roof was over a barn. What mattered was that we were not out in the open. I fell asleep almost instantly.

Like a barn swallow emerging from its nest, I awoke and crawled out from within the hay next to Mami. I yawned and stretched.

"*Ich hab hunger* – I'm hungry," I said. Those were always my first words.

"*Heint were mer gut esse, mei Kind,*" Mami told me as she put her arm around me. "Yes, today we're going to eat well," she repeated. She reached into her pocket and drew out my earrings, little gold oblong rings with small red rubies. I had not worn them since we were imprisoned and had forgotten that I even had earrings. My mother had sewn them between the seams of a dress, the last treasure hidden in her clothing.

"I'm going to buy us a good meal," Mami said as she got up and walked out of the barn.

In a little while she was back with the *Bauer*. The farmer walked in carrying a large platter of thick sliced white bread.

It had been years since we had seen so much food.

"Schen langsam Esse!" Mami said as she handed me a piece. "Eat slowly." On top of the bread was spread a thick, navy bean sauce. I had a hard time holding it in both of my hands as I bit into it. It had been a long time since I had tasted anything so delicious. The cold beans and bread stilled my ferocious hunger.

Once during our escape, we rode on a wagon, hitching a ride from a kind hearted farmer. We sat in the hay as the wagon slowly moved down a road. Seppi sat next to me in the rear of the wagon with Resbasl and Terri facing us. Resbasl was an older grandmotherly type. She was not as talkative as Terri. Terri was my mother's age or younger and almost always brought out the lighter side in us. She had brown, curly, chin-length hair and an almost constant smile. She is the only adult I ever addressed by a first name before coming to Munich.

I sat next to my brother and listened as Terri spoke to Seppi. As the wagon creaked down the road, she told him what was going to happen when we'd safely cross the border and reach our destinations.

"I'll save the stamps from all the letters I receive and send them to you," Terri said. "That should get you started on your *Briefmarken-sammlung.*"

"What's that? What's a *Briefmarkensammlung?*" I asked. "That's when you collect stamps and save them in a book," she explained.

"What are stamps, Terri?" I asked.

"Stamps are like little pictures that you buy and stick on a letter to send to someone."

I sat back in the hay and contemplated what these little pictures might look like. How interesting. I had never seen a stamp or a letter.

Gray, threatening rain clouds darkened the sky, as October's fickle weather displayed its menace. The wind whipped the branches of the tall trees, making them appear to reach down and try to grab me away from Mami's hand. We had been walking endlessly along this wet, tree-lined dirt road. It ran ahead and behind us for miles, like a long, never-ending ribbon, with a water-filled ditch running alongside it. The cold, raw air blew through my multi-colored striped sweater.

"Mami, ich hab so kalt," I whimpered. The wind drowned out my words as it howled and darted around us.

I put my head down and turned it away from the wind, held on tighter to my mother's hand and stumbled on. After we had walked for some time I noticed a small foot bridge crossing the ditch. All it consisted of was four wide boards laid across the three foot wide ditch. As we continued on, another bridge crossed the ditch, the same size as the one before. And a few yards down the road we passed another and then another. I found it strange that there was a bridge every ten or so yards. "I wonder what all those small bridges are for?" I thought to myself. Watching the bridges kept me occupied for a little while but not for long.

Again I whimpered to my mother. "Mami, I'm so cold." The raw wind danced around us as I walked next to my mother on the outside of our small company of escapees.

This time my mother heard me, took my hand and moved me between Basl and her. *"Zwischer der Basl und mir is Schurm, do is net so kalt.* – Between Basl and me there is protection, it's not so cold."

Schurm. I liked the sound of the new word. I repeated the word over in my mind a few times. Walking between Mami and Basl, I felt the difference almost immediately. The wild wind could not get to me as easily as before and it was much warmer.

Schurm – protection. Maybe protection is what brought my whole family together once more: protection sent down from above and our protecting each other down below.

The days varied almost as much as the color of the leaves on the trees. Some days the October sky was cold and threatening, other days warm and playful, others hot and glaring.

The early morning sun already promised a hot day when Mami aroused us from our sleep. A row of corn had been our room for the night. The wind gently rustled the long dry leaves on the cornstalk "walls" of our "accommodations" as we got ready for our daily hike. Seppi was not in a happy mood. He grumbled when Mami packed his share of the load he had carried daily since we started this journey. I don't remember carrying anything. I guess, being the youngest, I had gotten away with less responsibility than the rest.

Once more we found ourselves on a dusty, dirt road with nothing around except corn. Mami, Seppi and I were behind the group as we trudged forward. Even Basl, Marie and Andres were quite a ways ahead of us.

Mami called to my brother. *"Seppi, kum doch schun, geh schneller."* Repeatedly she told him, "Come on, move faster." Each time she did, he went slower. Mami started to yell at him, getting angrier each time.

Seppi took his bundle, placed it on the dusty road, sat on top of it. *"Ich geh nimmer weider!"* he stated angrily. "I'm not going any further."

"Oh yes you are," Mami yelled hotly back at him, pulling him by the arm.

"No I'm not!" my brother yelled back as he yanked his arm free. "I don't care anymore. I'm too tired to move. I'm staying right here."

Mami put her bundle down and grabbed him by both arms and pulled him as hard as she could. But she couldn't budge him. Seppi remained seated, his angry eyes staring at the ground in front of him.

Not knowing what to do next, my frustrated and weary mother yelled furiously; *"Dann bleib do sitze, mir gehn ohni dich.* – Then sit here, we'll go on without you." She took my hand and we walked on.

I kept looking back over my shoulder as the figure sitting on the bundle got smaller and smaller. I glanced at Mami. Would she actually leave him there?

Seppi was far down the road when we finally stopped. Mami turned back and looked towards my brother. I watched her unhappy face as she turned to me and mumbled for me to stay. She had to walk back quite a ways to the small figure down the road that was still not moving. Soon, I saw Mami coming back up the road with Seppi – a feeling of relief came over me. She walked in front of him, carrying two bundles and he behind her, empty handed.

We had to rush to catch up with the rest of our group.

Wings fluttering across the still, marbled-gray sky predicted that autumn's days were numbered. Soon winter would rule the air with its wind and cold white fury.

Birds by the hundreds perched on the telephone wires that ran along the side of the *Landstross*. Like a magician's cloak come alive, they would swoop up in unison and land right back on the long thin wire next to the road. The wires were filled with birds coming and going. Throbbing wings and loud chirping surrounded us. The black little birds were etched into the dismal sky.

"Mami, warum sein so viel Vögl am Droht?" I asked. "Why are there so many birds on the wire?"

"Because they're flying back home for the winter, to where it is warm," my mother answered. "Soon it will be too cold for them to stay here."

We kept on walking. So many birds, the air was astir with them. They were lucky, for if their feet were cold or tired they'd just pick up their wings and fly away.

We found ourselves again plodding forward on a muddy road. On this cold, damp early morning of late October 1947, we continued in our pursuit of the Austrian border.

We passed a two-story, reddish-brown brick building with a pointed slate-tiled roof that looked different from the Hungarian houses we had seen before. Shortly after, we turned and started to go down the embankment on which the road was built. When we got to the bottom, we huddled together and the adults whispered for quite some time. I stopped paying attention, since I didn't know what was being said. I was used to being ignored at times like these.

I looked out at the vastness in front of me. It was hard to see because of the weather and the early daylight hour. Nothing grew on the flat land. I couldn't even see the end of the field.

The next thing I knew someone grabbed my hand, and started to run as fast as she could with me behind her. We flew over the flat dirt field. Three shots rang out behind us. I don't remember who ran with me, I just remember the sound of the gunshots that rang out as we fled. My heart pounded wildly. At last we came to the end of the field and collapsed as if we were a heap of rags. Then, when we had gathered enough energy, we got up and rushed into the forest ahead of us.

"Mami, where are we now?" I asked as I held on tightly to her hand.

"We're in *Österreich,"* she said as she looked down smilingly into my eyes. "In Austria – where we'll be free at last."

The women walked from tree to tree and I followed.

"Look for white and red. That means we're in the American zone," Basl was saying. "We're still in the Russian zone."

Ever since we crossed over into Austria I had been looking at tree trunks. I looked at each white painted ring on the bumpy, grey grooved bark, hoping to see a clue as to why they were painted.

"This is a strange country, why would anyone paint trees?" I pondered as I followed my relatives and fellow wanderers.

After the war, Austria had been divided into four zones: English, French, Russian, and American. We definitely did not want to be in the Russian zone. The English was okay, but the American zone was the one for us. We wanted to be free.

I bent down and picked up one of the many pears lying around me. Pears were all over the ground among the weather-worn fallen leaves.

I wiped off the mud and the bits of damp, brown foliage that stuck to the small pear. Although it was a little rotten, part of the pear was still good. I bit into it. The pulp was like honey in my mouth. What luck to find such luscious fruit in the middle of nowhere. Pear trees grew on both sides of the straight road and fallen pears were all over. I ate my fill.

The wetness of the late fall weather penetrated our very being as we plodded along. The shoulder of the mud-soaked road was covered with dark, golden brown leaves which felt like a soft carpet underneath my knit woolen slippers. The leaves kept our feet a little drier than if we had to walk directly in the center of the muddy road.

We came to a mountainous area which we had to cross to get to the American side. For days we had plodded along in the cold, wet, Austrian autumn countryside. I was so tired that I could hardly pick up my feet. Now we had to climb over a mountain. I was not going to walk any further. I stopped and insisted that Marie carry me. But Marie would not hear of it. She took me by the hand and pulled me along.

"*Trag mich! Trag mich!*" I fussed and complained. Marie refused and pulled some more.

"*Ich bin zu mied,*" I whined.

"I'm not going to carry you!" she said. "I'm tired just like you." My feet were soaked. Wet snow seeped through my *Patsche* – making the slippers icy. I might as well have been barefoot. But just like the rest of our band of refugees, I had to continue, wet feet and all.

"We're almost on top," coaxed Marie, as the two of us lagged behind the rest. The partially snow-covered, rocky slope was hard to climb. Wet patches of frozen ground between the large stones were slippery. We slipped down almost as much as we climbed up.

I was cold all over and made no effort to keep quiet about my discomfort. I kept on complaining as we clambered up the mountain. Marie continued pulling me up, deaf to my pleas.

Whimpering softly, I started to cry. Marie stopped and looked down at me.

"Why don't you whistle for me?" she said.

"No, I don't want to. I don't feel happy."

At last we reached our goal. Tall, upright pine trees grew near the top and down one side of the mountain. Next to them, a wide clearing sloped to the valley below. Almost at the bottom stood a house, far away. And to my chagrin, I was told that now we had to go down to that house below. Too tired to grumble, I just stood there.

Everyone was waiting for us. I looked at the women, spotted my mother among them, and started to walk over to her. Suddenly Mami fell to the ground and cried out loud.

"Ich kann nimmer, ich kann nimmer." She sobbed as she sat amid her bundles, hugging her legs, crying over and over again, "I can't go on anymore, I can't go on anymore."

I stood still, more afraid than I had ever been in my life. I was dumbfounded. I had never seen my mother cry like this. Her whole body shook. Every one of the women surrounded her and helped her up. Still sobbing, she got to her feet and began to calm herself.

This was the only time in all those years that I had seen my mother fail to pull herself together. She was only 32 years old at the time and had experienced so much pain and worry. I've often wondered how she and the other parents and grandparents did it.

After Mami regained her composure, we started down the mountainside. Going down was not quite so hard as climbing up. I looked around, up here, everything was different from anything I had seen before. The tall, dark green pine trees seemed to meet the gray sky. They made me feel small as I looked up into their branches.

A blur caught my eye as it moved from branch to branch. It stopped just a few yards away from me and looked me straight in the eye, ears pointed up. The bushy tail swished behind its head. Not moving anything else, the animal sat on its hind legs, with two front paws holding onto the tree branches, ready for flight.

"What is that?" I cried out, all excited.

"It's an *Eichkatzl*, someone informed me. The squirrel looked almost like a small, black kitten in a tree. It looked at me as curiously as I looked at it, making me forget how hungry and cold I was.

We moved slowly down the mountain, over rocks and stones.

When we were nearly halfway down, we came to a small stream that originated right there out of the ground. It tumbled down every which way, twisting and turning in its bed of rocks, skipping over and under them.

I stopped to look at the dancing water. It was ice cold when I stuck my fingertips into its prancing path. Terri came down behind me.

"Des is a schöner Bach! – What a lovely brook!" she exclaimed. She came to stand next to me to get a better look at it.

"The *Bach* is pretty," I agreed. Once again I had learned a new word. Come to think of it, I learned many new words and saw many new things in the year 1947 because of all the places we had been.

Now we hurried down as we neared the house below. We stood in front of the dark green door and waited for someone to answer our knock. No one came.

We knocked again and waited. Suddenly a woman opened the door and yelled. *"Geht nur fort von hier, ihr Flüchtlinge. Wir haben nichts für euch,"* and slammed the door shut. I can still hear the words in my head. "Go away, you refugees, we have nothing for you."

The eleven of us stood speechless before the closed door. Now what? We had come all this way, only to have a door slammed in our face. The big warm-looking house with its clean brick walls and painted windows and door had looked friendly. But all we got was the cold shoulder.

Not knowing where to go next, we turned and searched for a different house. Leading up the mountain was a narrow footpath, which we decided to pursue. We followed the winding dirt path as it led us back to the heights that we had just descended. At the end of the path, nestled in a clump of trees, was a small, white cottage.

The weathered door opened slowly. An old woman answered our knock and invited us in. We filed into the small room where the woman introduced herself and her grown daughter. We told her our story and asked if she could please help us. The two women invited us to spend the night and share supper with them. I watched with big eyes as the "Oma" took the huge pot of boiled potatoes off the stove and said they were for us to eat. That pot looked like it was a foot and a half high! We ate as much as we could of the delicious, steaming yellow potatoes.

My stomach was finally filled and my body was warmed at last by the high, white feather bed that Seppi, Andres and I shared. This was the first bed I had slept in since April, 1945, more than two years and six months before. It was also the only bed in this one-room house; everyone else, including our hostesses, slept on the floor.

In the morning we thanked the old Oma and her daughter for their kindness and continued down the mountainside and into the small village of "Spital am Pyhrn."

CHAPTER
13

Flüchtlinge – Refugees

N ow that we had gotten over the mountain, we were in the *Amerikanische Zone* – American Zone – in Austria and *Flüchtlinge* – refugees – was our new label. We were expel- lees and as such, we had no home or identification papers, the lifeline to one's existence after the war years. Wherever a person went, his identifi- cation papers were needed. No papers meant no ration stamps, no food. Since we had none, we were really not free.

We were shuffled from one *Flüchtlingslager* – refugee camp – to the next. We stayed only a short time in each. I have no idea in what order my jumbled memories occurred.

I clearly remember sitting on the floor, surrounded with all kinds of playthings. I was fascinated by them. This is my first recollection of play- ing with real toys since the wagon in our deserted courtyard in Karlsdorf.

I remember standing behind a high fence at an open double gate, wait- ing to be loaded onto a large, canvas covered army truck. The back of the truck faced us, and I waited with anticipation to ride in it. Finally the drop gate was opened. My family, with a group of 20 or 30 more refugees were loaded aboard and the half door was shut. I got to sit behind the tail gate: I could see the landscape whiz by as we rolled down the road. This was my first ride in a motor driven vehicle, and it was wonderful.

And at a third camp, I remember being in a large room, seated alone at a long table with many chairs and eating a meal. The table reached from one end of the room to the other.

I remember playing outside between rows of barracks as soldiers walked past, without being afraid. Here they walked among the people freely, not to guard but to go about their business just like everyone else. I knew here we were not prisoners, for the gates stood open and no one guarded us with a gun.

Austria, as well as Germany, had quite a number of refugee camps. Thousands of displaced persons came streaming over the borders from the Eastern European countries daily. They came not only from Yugoslavia, Hungary and Romania, but also from Poland and Czechoslovakia. Most were ethnic Germans like us. More than fifteen million had been driven out of their homelands by the communists.

The last *Flüchtlingslager* we stayed at was not far from Linz, where my mother found her cousin Margaret Deckert. She and her husband Josef lived in a one room apartment. Margretbasl and Sepvetter, as we called them, invited us to stay with them.

You can't imagine what joy we felt when Sepvetter told us that Tati was alive. Our father was living in Munich. At this joyous news, we made plans immediately to journey to Munich, Germany, regardless of our lack of papers. This trivial hindrance did not stop my mother and aunt. If it wasn't possible to cross the border legally, we'd do it illegally.

With the money we received from our relatives, Mami and Basl bought train tickets and we rode to the end of the line at the border of Austria. From there we walked until we got to the *Donaufluss*. The Danube River was the dividing line between Austria and Germany, and somehow the six of us managed to cross over without being turned back.

"I did a lot of quick talking," my mother told me many years later. "We must have looked pitiful. Four children and two women with nothing but thin clothing on our backs and a few bundles under our arms, the wind howling all around us.

'Go on, cross over quickly!' the *Grenz Wache* ordered. "Before the border guard had the words past his lips we made a dash to the other side – which was Passau, Germany, never looking back as we continued towards the *Passauer Bahnhof*. And when we got to that train station, I thanked God for bringing us this far and asked him to please stay with us just a little longer until we're safe with your father."

In the Passauer train station, the dark, high backed seats made me feel at home. I nestled into the wooden bench with its carved backrest and armrests and fell asleep. We had been sitting here for a long time waiting for a train that would take us to Munich.

The warm and cozy waiting room was a far cry from the cold weather outside the high windows. The winds blew the falling snow past the glass panes, while inside all was muffled and still. The dark brown, wood-paneled walls matched the color of the two or three benches in the small train station.

Before I had fallen asleep, I had passed a new milestone in my life. At age seven and a half, I lost my first *Milchzahn*. I held the baby tooth up toward the light to admire it. The little pearl-like object was no bigger than the snowflakes falling outside; in fact some were twice its size.

Finally, I was not a baby anymore. Now I'd look more grown up. I had waited for this moment for a long time. Everyone my age had lost their first tooth ages ago and had big front teeth, not tiny ones like mine. I felt very happy.

We were on our way to my father. But truthfully, Tati was only a dream-like person that I had known long ago, someone that Mami talked about to me, but his face was very fuzzy in my mind. The important thing was my tooth; now I was like everyone else.

"Don't talk to anyone on the train," Mami had told me. "The less you children say the better our chances are to get to Tati." So I didn't dare say a word when the *Schaffner* walked through the door of the waiting room. The conductor, an older man, stopped and addressed my mother with a knowing smile, *"Sind Sie Weiss oder Schwarz hier angekommen? –* Did you arrive here white or black?" – Mami smiled back and answered, with a twinkle in her eyes, "Why, white of course; it's snowing outside isn't it?"

What a strange thing to ask, I thought, not knowing what the two colors had to do with us. I looked out the window at the falling snow.

She told him about my father and what we had been through to get here. He said he'd help us reach Munich. We should stay here and not move, and when the time came, he'd let us know when to get on and off the train.

Soon we were on the moving train heading for Munich. I watched in silence as the winter landscape ran past, still puzzled as to what the conductor had meant.

The six of us sat close together at the back of the car, very quietly, trying to be as inconspicuous as possible.

The conductor walked towards us, halted, looked directly at us and said something to my mother. He gave me a wink, and a smile; then he turned and walked past, and opened the connecting door that led to the next car.

And that's how we came to our new home in Germany, white, with no papers.

CHAPTER
14
Tati

The shrill train whistle echoed through the hushed countryside as the speeding locomotive carried us closer and closer to our destination. Soon the rural setting of forests, fields and farms gave way to large broken buildings.

"Bal, sein mr beim Tati," Mami said as she hugged me. "Yes, we'll soon be with Tati," I wondered what he'd be like.

We got off the train in the huge bombed out *"Hauptbahnhof,"* the main train depot in the middle of Munich. Tracks crossed and re-crossed each other from different directions, like an enormous puzzle of silver ribbons. The entire railroad yard must have once been covered with a glass ceiling, but now all that was left were black, broken steel beams and jagged pieces of sooty glass.

We walked along the boarding platform and entered the large waiting room. High above us loomed the skeletal remains of a glass domed ceiling just like the one over the tracks. Its shrapnel-scared stone walls and pillars still looked grand. Groups of people filled the depot, all in a hurry, rushing back and forth. A drone of voices and footsteps echoed throughout the place.

"You children stay here and don't move," we were told by our mothers before they disappeared into the crowd. It didn't take long before Mami and Basl came back, both very upset. "No one knows where Markomanen Strasse is," my mother said. "They told us to go to the Red Cross which is right outside the *"Bahnhof."*

We picked up our bundles and headed for the exit. Outside the depot was a wide street with rubble all around. Everything around us was tumbled down. Next to the train station stood a trailer which served as the office of the Red Cross.

We crowded into the small mobile office. The lady behind the desk looked up and greeted us and asked if she could be of help. Mami handed her a small piece of paper and asked, "How do we get to this address?" A puzzled look came over the ladies face. She looked up and said, "Marko-manen Strasse? I have never heard of such a street."

"What do you mean! You must have heard of it."

"I'm sorry I don't know where it is. Munich is a big city."

A feeling of dismay washed over us. We had come all this way, some-times even facing death, as we battled fear, hunger, wind and weather, crossing over three borders, climbing over mountains, to get to my fa-ther, and now no one knew how to find his street.

"What are we going to do now?" I thought to myself as the lady looked through other maps in hopes of finding the street. We looked on ner-vously. After a few minutes passed, she still hadn't found it.

Then a woman came in and took her place in line.

"Markomanen Strasse is nowhere on any of these maps," the lady behind the desk stated.

Basl and Mami looked at each other with sinking hearts.

"Excuse me," the woman in back of us said. "Did I hear you say you can't find Markomanen Strasse? I think I can help you. The street you're looking for is located right outside of Munich. It's very short and runs in the middle of open fields with only one high rise building standing on it."

You can't imagine what a feeling of relief we felt. The stranger told us which *Strassenbahn* to take. "Make sure you don't get off the streetcar until the end of the line," she instructed. We followed the woman's direc-tions and arrived at the three story apartment building, where my father rented a room.

I had never seen so many steps before. We climbed up and up until we reached the third floor. A thin, dark-haired, older lady answered our knock and, smiling happily, asked us to come in. She received us with open arms, as if we had been part of her family all our lives.

"And you must be Elsa," she said to me. "Why don't you call me Tante Mitzi."

The hallway had doors that led to three rooms, two bedrooms and one kitchen. She ushered us into the kitchen. The small room with its table and chairs in the middle and the cupboard against the wall looked neat and clean.

"Won't you sit down?" she asked. "You must be hungry."

The six of us watched as Tante Mitzi brought out a large loaf of rye bread. She cut thick slices and put them on the table. Mami took a piece and spread something creamy on it and handed it to me.

"This is butter that I'm spreading on your bread," Mami told me. "Remember, in Weckerle? The dandelions?" I bit into the soft, fresh bread and let the flavor linger in my mouth for a while. It was delicious.

I was sitting with my back toward a large glass door that led out to a *Balkon*. I had looked curiously through the door when we came into the room. All I saw was a cement floor, railings and the sky. I found this fascinating. I asked my mother if that was a room outside. She told me it was a balcony. How interesting, I thought. It must be fun to be standing outside like on a cloud.

Tante Mitzi told us that my father should be coming home later in the evening. By the time we finished eating, it was dark outside. I was very tired. Mami asked if she could put me to bed, she could see that I could hardly keep my eyes open.

Tante Mitzi ushered us into a bedroom. "This is your father's room," she told me. It was a small room with a bed next to the wall. The bed linens were so white, crisp, smooth and new-looking unlike the straw "beds" I was used to. Tante Mitzi looked at me and with twinkling eyes she asked, "Would you like to see what is under your father's pillow?" Before I had a chance to answer, she picked up the pillow and to my surprise, a small grey object scooted out from underneath. It was a *Maus* —a mechanical wind-up mouse.

Tante Mitzi laughed. "This is a little joke between your father and me," she said. "Every once in a while, when I change the linens, I hide the wound-up mouse under his pillow." From that moment on, Tante Mitzi and I were friends.

Mami put me to bed. The large feather bed was so soft and cool as I crawled between the sheets. Laying my head on the fluffy pillow, I ran my tongue over the empty space between my teeth one last time before I snuggled down into the fresh smelling whiteness of the clean bed and fell asleep.

From far away I heard someone calling. *"Elsa, weck auf dei Tati is do.* – Wake up, your father is here." I heard, but my body fought to sleep. Slowly I came out of my deep sleep and found myself staring into a strange man's face. I cried out and clung to Mami, who stood next to the bed.

Mami sat down on the edge of the bed and cradled me in her arms and said, *"Elsa, net wahne, des is doch dei Tati. Du brauchscht ka Angst hawe* – Don't cry, this is your Tati. You needn't be afraid." I looked into the man's face as he anxiously leaned over the bed, not saying a word or taking his eyes off me.

I looked into his eyes and I didn't know him, he was a stranger.

November, 1944, was the last time I had seen my father, and now it was three years later, a long time, almost half my lifetime. No wonder my father's face was foreign to me. All those years we had no picture of him. Maybe if we had, I would have remembered.

Later that evening, Tati helped us gather our bundles and took the six of us – Mami, Seppi, Basl, Marie, Andres and me – to our new home where we spent our first night of freedom all under one roof.

Our new home was a rebuilt two-story apartment building that had been bombed during the war. Nothing but a few walls had been standing when Tati and three of his friends began to rebuild so that their families would have a place to live. It took them six months to complete it. And on the day of our arrival they had just put on the finishing touches.

It didn't take long for Tati to win me over. He made me smile with his joking ways and his funny stories, like the time he went hunting for rabbits.

"The first thing I did was to take along a salt shaker," he said.

"I thought you need a gun or a bow and arrow to hunt anything," I interrupted. "How do you hunt with a salt shaker?"

"Why you sneak up behind the rabbit and sprinkle a little salt on his tail. I'll guarantee he'll never run away after that."

At first, I believed him, until Mami and Seppi started to laugh and Tati laughed right along with them.

"It's a joke, isn't it?" I asked. Tati gave me a wink and answered, "Could be, but maybe one day you and I will try it and find out."

Yes we had a lot of things to try out and learn about each other, we had years of catching up to do. He and I as well as Seppi and Mami. Every evening the four of us gathered in our large bed, sharing stories, filling in the spaces of time lost together as a family. This is when Tati told us about his ordeal in the Soviet slave labor camp.

During his first six months, conditions were so wretched that it's hard to imagine how anyone survived. Hard work and little nourishment were the daily routine. The prison, a small, damp stone building, stuffed to the rafters with people, stood alone on top of a hill in the Russian county of *Voroschlovgrad*, surrounded by nothing but snow and ice. Except for the small town of Almanzna out of which they had been escorted, no form of civilization was to be seen anywhere. An electric wire snaked up the hill along a row of single electric poles until it reached the very top of the hill. In each corner of the fenced yard, a pole reached toward the sky, shining bright light down on the camp.

My father and his fellow inmates, confined behind barbed wire, were lost to the rest of the world, locked away in a strange country as different from theirs as the moon. Three thousand kilometers – almost 2,000 miles – from their beloved homeland with no way of ever getting back, they hardly dared hope ever to see their loved ones again.

"The weather was so cold that my breath froze on my beard," Tati told us. "And when nature called, the urine froze before it hit the ground. Because of the terrible conditions, we got bladder infections. The gangway leading to the outside became caked with frozen urine, from those of us who couldn't make it in time to the outside ditch.

"A small spring, about half a kilometer away, was our only water supply. From morning until night, the women marched through the large prison gate, back and forth with their buckets between the spring and a large wooden barrel which held the water for all three hundred and thirty of us. We used it up as fast as it was replenished.

"For breakfast early in the morning and for dinner we ate our small ration of *Sauerkraut Borscht.* Nothing was in the soup but water and sour cabbage. During the day there was no lunch. The only solid food parceled out every day was provided at eleven o'clock each night: a small piece of black bread, which measured about four by three by two inches.

"They formed us into work crews. One crew of young girls and women did nothing but haul logs up from the town to the camp, using nothing but heavy wire. It did not matter if the person was small or large, weak or strong, male or female. All were equal, all did the same work.

"Every morning at eight, the prisoners were called to attention in the camp yard and then dispersed to work in whatever work crew they were assigned to. Most of us worked outside the camp grounds, in different places around the countryside.

"The largest group had to work in the coal mines, this was what we had been brought here to do. Enormous mounds of dirt marked the entrance to each mine. Hills of earth dotted the countryside: the deeper the mine, the higher the hill. Some hills were mountainous, and others were mere dirt mounds next to large holes in the ground, the very beginning of a coal mine shaft.

"One such crater was located just outside the camp about one hundred feet away. This was the future entrance to a new mine. The hole had been created by placing explosives in the ground and blowing up the earth. After the loosened earth was removed, more dynamite was used to deepen the hole, and the process was repeated again and again. It took many hours of hard, back-breaking work, until a tunnel started to form. The tunnel, which measured about ten feet wide and six feet high, descended at an angle, deep into the ground. Wooden frames were made to hold up the deep mine shafts and to keep the earth from caving in. The frames were made outside the mine by a group of men who did nothing else except cut, shape and nail scaffolding together. I was assigned to this crew.

"I figured the less they knew about me the better. I never let on that I was a cabinetmaker. I went about my work and did what I was told. A month went by. Soon the man in charge noticed that I was good at this job. One morning, he came to me and told me that a good man was needed to make scaffolding at a bigger mine. Because I was one of the best workers, I was to go with five young workers from the village below.

"From then on I was escorted every day out the gate and to the mine, three kilometers – 1¼ miles – away. My bodyguards were young girls who worked at the same place as I did. However there was a big difference between them and me. They got to go home at night to food and a warm bed.

"As we marched down to the work place, the cold wind whirled around, freezing our very breath as it mixed with the frigid air. By now I had a full grown beard. As I exhaled, small icicles formed on my mustache, like icing on a cake.

"Once there, I worked outside all day. The only thing we had to keep us warm were small fires placed here and there, fueled by scraps left over from the frames.

"I wonder how we could have produced anything in that icy hell of winter.

"The work in the coal mines was continuous. Three shifts worked around the clock. Each crew had a special job to perform. One man did the dynamiting. He was the only member of the team that was a government man. Then the clean-up crew came with their wooden litters. After each discharge of dynamite, they would shovel debris onto their carriers and haul out the dirt. When this work was finished, a new group came to chip away at the coals with pick axes. Sometimes the crew members had to crawl underground on their bellies, like moles.

"This work would have been difficult for strong, healthy men, but we were starved slave laborers, mostly young girls and women that hardly were given enough food for sustainence, let alone for hard labor.

"Some did not survive even the first few months, and as they died off, a fresh crop of German slave laborers, specialists in coal mining, were brought in from Upper Silesia."

"There was a young child in the camp. As a baby, he had been pushed through a missing slat into the slave train by his Oma seconds before it pulled away from the station in Werschetz. The grandmother acted out of sheer desperation, sure the baby would have a better chance of surviving with his parents, who were in the freight car, than by remaining in Yugoslavia with her. Before the guards saw what had happened, the grandmother disappeared into the crowd.

"The toddler lived in the stone building along with the rest of us. The only people he ever saw were guards and prisoners. Now the child was two and a half years old, and he was the joy of all his adopted Tantes und Onkels. He was a loving boy who chattered with every one of his three hundred and then some aunts and uncles.

"One day the woman who drove the *Borscht Wagen* brought her two small children along. When the children jumped off the wagon, the little boy happened to be outside. He walked up to the children and stared in amazement. He touched them and walked around them, not sure of what he was seeing. Then he clapped and chattered and grinned. Never before had he seen someone who was as small as he was. He was ecstatic as he babbled in his small vocabulary, trying to communicate with the young children.

"As I stood with my fellow inmates around the three children, a feeling of joy for the child swept over me. I was happy for him, yet sad because something as normal as being a child and playing with other children had been denied him all this time.

"As we looked on, my mind wandered back home to all of you. Where and how was my family? Were they safe and warm? And would we ever be together again?

"I'm sure there was not one mother or father in our group who did not have the same thoughts."

"In spring as the weather warmed up, we set up a large army tent in the camp yard. The tent, a gift from the American government, was to help ease the crowding in our stone hut. Although this tent helped, conditions were still crowded. Eventually, some of the prisoners took it upon themselves to dig holes and cover them with boards as a cave-like shelter to sleep in.

"In April, when the tent was put up, I was one of the workers assigned to help. At the onset of the work, I began to suffer from painful swollen joints. I had a hard time handling tools and walking. I tired easily and many times during my work had to lie down in the grass to get my strength. By the time the huge tent was standing upright, my walk had become a shuffle.

"My whole body slowly filled up with fluid. My eyes sank deep in my swollen head. My belly bulged and my hands, arms and the rest of me swelled. Every day I became weaker and weaker. Soon I was unable to walk, and it became hard for me even to pull myself up. It was a burden to tend to my daily needs.

"By now it was early May, and I, as well as many of my fellow prisoners, were housed in the large empty, tent we had set up. No cots or bunks had been provided, and we lay on the bare, cold spring ground. By this time, many of the inmates were very ill, like me, unable to walk, let alone work. So we were put on the 'sick list.' All this meant was that we did not have to go to work.

"The ailing patients were looked after by a nurse, who could not do much to relieve our pain. She had nothing to give, except an occasional dose of quinine powder. The sick still received the same ration of sour cabbage soup and black bread as before. Some of the patients, too weak to eat, simply died.

"One day, a four-woman team of medical personnel came to inspect the sick. Rumor had it that we were to be sent back to our homes. The women wrote down the names of the patients who qualified. I was one of them.

"After the medical group left, I began to hope that the next day I and the rest of the ill inmates would find ourselves on our way to our families. But days turned into weeks and weeks into a month and nothing happened. Hope once more turned sour, and I became sicker.

"Each night I fell asleep with one thought on my mind. Will I still be alive in the morning? Each day the nurse's toes poked at my body and called, 'Ivan[8] are you still living?' Shaken out of my sleep, I awoke to see the large woman towering above me, happy I had made it through one more night."

As the early spring sun got stronger and stronger, the sun's rays started to heat up the cold ground. The warmth beckoned and the young grass and weeds poked tufted green shoots from beneath the soil. Outside the canvas walls of my father's tent, dandelions sprang up all over the camp yard. Like these tenacious flowers, Tati's nature asserted itself. He resolved never to give up and die. He'd survive so that he could be with his family once more.

"I must fill my stomach with something else besides Borscht soup, I decided." Tati told us: "I forced myself onto my feet, then stumbling and crawling on all fours, I made my way out into the camp yard. Sprawled on the ground, I gathered enough strength to claw the green dandelions from the ground, roots and all. I laid them out on the earth to dry. Exhausted, I retreated inside and once more waited for morning to come. The next day, I crawled out and collected enough twigs and dried grasses to make a small fire. Placing the dried dandelions and water in the tin soup cup, I proceeded to boil weed tea."

My father continued his daily tea time. He drank his brew and ate his piece of black bread and no longer ate any of the sour cabbage soup. After three or four weeks of this diet, he slowly began to get better. The boiled, weak green tea and his own determination saved his life. The tea gave him the vitamins he needed to fight malnutrition, and his spirit gave him the spark he needed to go on. By summer all the bloating had dissipated from his body. He once more had the strength to stand on his two legs and walk upright.

With summer's greenery all around and the sun warming his body, Tati's life became more bearable and the work a little less harsh. Many

---

[8] "Ivan" Russian for Johann or John.

had died that winter and early spring. The ones remaining went back to work, weak but still alive. They also learned to survive as most of the citizens of the USSR had: by helping themselves to whatever they could get their hands on, inside the camp or outside. My father tells an interesting incident to illustrate this. One day a surprise inspection was held by the guards in the women's quarters. Everything from under, above, and in the bunks had to be piled in the center of the room. The inspectors watched in amazement as the pile grew higher and higher. Food of all kinds, from potatoes and squash to melons and fruit, was added to the stack. The prisoners had learned fast.

"I spent nineteen months and nineteen days as a slave laborer," Tati told us. "Throughout those months and days I carried a small packet with me wherever I went. Sometimes when there was any danger of items being confiscated, I buried the packet in a shallow hole in the camp yard. This small flat treasure contained two things: a picture of Mami, Seppi, and Elsa, which had been taken just a few months before I was shipped to Russia, and my *"Tischlermeister Papiere"* – Master Craftsman Certificate and license – the papers I earned as a young cabinetmaker.

"Whenever I held the packet in my hands it brought back hope of seeing my wife and children again. It was tangible evidence that I was not just a number in a Russian slave labor camp, but a person who had achieved the title of *Tischlermeister* – Master Cabinet Maker.

"In July 1945 a new *"Lager Kommandant"* or camp commander was assigned to the labor camp. He was a young man in his late twenties who had been a prisoner of war in Germany.

"He spoke a better German than I. Maybe because he had been a prisoner himself, the new *Kommandant* often went and mingled with the people and was very civil to us. Perhaps he had learned, as I had, that most people, regardless of nationality are alike. Some are rotten – but the majority are good.

"By this time I was up and around and almost totally recovered from my illness. I was put back to work making frames at the coal mine located just outside the fence of the camp yard. Each coal mine had a name and a crew of workers called a *Brigade,* pronounced brie-gah-de. The name of the group and mine next to the prison camp was *Brigade Bene.*

"Each mine was run like a company, with a president or *Natschalnick* and vice president in charge of the workers. They were responsible for seeing to it that the mine and workers produced their best. As an incentive, a sign was posted at the mine entrance, with the name of the brigade and the amount of coal they were to produce daily.

"Soon I was totally recovered. Fall came to an end and winter was once more upon the land. By now I had managed to barter some of the items that I had brought with me from home for food. Peasants came regularly to the fence of the camp yard and brought all kinds of food items in exchange for clothing the prisoners were willing to do without. Some came with bread, cornmeal, fruit and even baked chickens. I bought small parcels of cornmeal, and made myself a serving of *Mamaliga* or cornmeal mush, every day. So I had enough food to help maintain my health through the coming winter."

"Some of the inmates were not so lucky," Tati told us. "The first morning that the peasants came with their ware a few of the men bought a whole chicken and wolfed it down. By nightfall two of the men were dead."

"Why did they die?" I asked.

"I believe malnutrition had some how shut down their digestive system and it could not handle such a massive amount of rich food all at once," he said.

"We had all become accustomed to the cold. We were able to tolerate it and the icy wind much better than the previous year.

"By the time December came we managed to make the best of our terrible conditions, we even learned to make the evenings enjoyable. All of us would crowd together to talk, sing and sometimes even dance. Most of the young people confided in me and called me Jani Batchi.

"A few days before *Heilicherowed* we talked about celebrating Christmas Eve. Since only low growing evergreen shrubs grew around the camp they came to me and asked 'Jani Batchi could you create a *Tannenbaum* for us?'

"The next day I went to work. I whittled a tree trunk from a piece of wood with a *Spitz* on top. I carved the point to make it look like an ornament. Then I drilled holes, at an angle, into the trunk and stuck small branches all around the stem, creating a christmas tree. We decorated the tree with curled wood shavings and paper ornaments that the women made.

"On Christmas Eve, we returned from work, ate our sour Borscht supper, then gathered all around the tree and sang *Weihnachtslieder*. The guards as well as the Kommandant, came and listened to our Christmas carols. We sang with heavy hearts, tears streaming down our faces as we remembered better times and our loved ones.

"Thirteen months went by. One day I was standing in the doorway in the so-called workshop that had been set up by the prisoners in the camp yard, when the young *Kommandant* came along. 'Ivan, how are you?' he greeted me. Soon the two of us were deep in conversation. The *Kommandant* asked me where I had lived. I told him all about our small town of Karlsdorf, and about my wife and young children and how hard it was to be here and not know what was happening back home.

"The young man listened patiently and then in turn told me all about his family. During our conversation he revealed that his wife was expecting their first child.

"Eventually, I told him that I was a cabinetmaker by trade. When the *Kommandant* heard this he said, 'Ivan, I want you to make a cradle for my child.'

" 'We don't have much to work with,' I told him, but I said I'd do my best with the little material available to me.

"I collected scraps of wood and boards that I found scattered in the yard of the coal mine. At the end of my work day I went about making the cradle for the *Kommandant*. Upon completion of the cradle I received three large loaves of bread from the happy future parent.

"Des war was wie ich des Brot grigt hab. Alli sein kumm. – That was something when I got the bread. Everyone came. I cut the loaves and gave my friends each a piece. With sixty people in the room, there was not enough to go around. Every crumb disappeared instantly.

"During the time I worked on the cradle, my other boss, *Dovarisch Natschalnick* – everyone was called *Dovarisch* – which means comrade – happened to be at the camp one day and saw the work I was doing. He liked what he saw and asked me if I could make windows and doors. 'I'm no carpenter and I don't know how to begin,' I told him.

" 'Would you be willing to try?' he asked. I told him I'd think about it.

"In the evening I told the *Kommandant* about my conversation with *Dovarisch Natschalnick*.

" 'Ivan, don't agree to anything unless he gives you *Tallons*,' the *Kommandant* told me.

"Tallons were coupons. In each Brigade or camp, the *Natschalnick* was allotted coupons from the government to give to workers for additional work done outside their daily job. The coupons could be used like

money for certain foods from the village market.

"The next morning, I told the *Natschalnick* that if he gave me food coupons I'd do my best to make the doors and windows that he requested.

"Soon I began to produce windows and doors for houses in the small shop next to the mine instead of frames for the mine shaft. My men and I had very little to work with. Sometimes we didn't even have nails; to compensate we snipped wire into different lengths and used it instead. And because there was no ruler to measure with, I made my own by approximating the centimeters on a long straight piece of wood. These were the working conditions for everyone, slave laborers and Russian citizens alike.

"The only piece of machinery in the shop was a broken circular table saw. Before we could do anything, this saw had to be fixed. I and my fellow prisoners took the whole saw apart, made a new frame, worked on the motor and somehow managed to get the blade spinning. This was essential to our operation, for all of the wood came still in its natural shape — tree trunks.

"The wood was brought in from a different part of the country. The logs had to be brought from the train station down below to the mine up above. Two crews were responsible for keeping us supplied with the wood. Each consisted of one man and five or six women to pull the logs up from the train station to the shop. These human pack horses, many of them only sixteen or seventeen year old girls, did nothing all day but trudge up the hill with their burden behind them.

"Once the tree trunks were at the workshop, they had to be turned into wood boards. The machine was kept running all the time. Logs were cut and the boards stacked in piles. Although crude and rough, they were boards nonetheless.

"Soon everything was ready and all systems were in full production. We turned out windows and doors for the houses that were being built for the Russian workers, but the slave laborers' living quarters remained just as they had been when we came here. And the daily ration of Borscht and black bread was doled out the same as before. Only once did we receive a special treat: fresh meat in the soup; the feet of a poor horse, hoofs and all.

"But we always managed to get a little extra food somehow; and we learned to deal with our situation. Everyday life became a little easier. Sometime there was even time for a laugh or two. In the unsanitary conditions, bedbugs and lice lived and dined on us. So in the evenings, to help pass the time, we held races between two lice. We picked sides to cheer for. Usually a louse needed a little prodding from behind with the tip of the referee's index finger so it would jump ahead of its competitor.

"I will always remember this one particular race. After my side had won, I was relaxing on my bunk, when suddenly the doors flung open and my friend, the *Kommandant*, stormed over and started kicking me and calling me names. He grabbed me and pushed me out the door, punching and kicking me in the rear end with his foot until we came to the small guard house at the gate. At that, he shoved me inside and locked me up.

"Still loudly cursing, the *Kommandant* went back into the stone prison building. I had no idea what I had done to get this kind of treatment. After all was quiet, I called to the guard who was stationed at the gate. His name was Woloja, and he was the only male guard among the Russian women camp guards. When he came over, I asked him if he knew why I was locked up. But he had no answer.

"Evening turned into night and soon the moon was high. Sitting on the ground, I waited. A long time passed until I heard the key in the door. When the door opened the *Kommandant* softly called, 'Ivan come out.' Not sure what to think, I stepped out of the small house.

" 'What have I done?' I asked.

" 'You were going to be taken away,' he told me. 'The only way I could think to keep them from taking you was to show everyone that I was angry with you and lock you up.'

"*Politicians* came on a regular basis and took people in for questioning. No one knew what happened during this interrogation, but most never came back. If the overseer had not used his head, who knows where I would have ended up — maybe I would even have been put to death."

"In spring of 1946 I stood outside the small woodwork shop and watched three trucks come rolling into the mine yard.

"*Was is jetz los?* – What is going on now?" I thought to myself. A crew of Russian men unloaded an enormous 4' x 4' brand new motor off the first truck and put it down in the middle of the yard. No effort was made to see to it that this fine piece of machinery was kept free of the dust and dirt from the stone-strewn ground. It was treated as if it was just a piece of wood.

"When the next two trucks were unloaded I saw what was going on. They were unloading parts to a gigantic gutter saw. Now we were going to mass-produce wooden boards as well as coals at Brigade Bene, I thought.

"I kept on watching as the *Markscheders* – engineers – came to install the machine. They looked and measured and prepared to put this apparatus together. When the machine parts were assembled, four large posts were pounded into the ground. The machine was going to stand on these posts.

"This is never going to work, I thought. Accuracy was needed for such an intricate machine.

"Russian engineers and workers swarmed over the saw for more than a week, trying to get it to start. They took it off and put it up again. Then they took it apart. Everyone tried and tried, but the equipment simply did not co-operate. The young *Kommandant* and I were leaning on the doorway and watching the engineers. 'This will never work,' I told my friend. The Russian agreed that they were not going about it the right way. Anyone who had any knowledge of the workings of electric motors could see in an instant that this crude makeshift setup would never bring the motor to life.

"As the two of us stood, still talking, the *Natschalnick* from the coal mine came up to me and asked, 'Do you know anything about setting up a saw like this, Ivan?'

" 'I have no idea. I've never worked on a machine as big as this one before,' I said.

" 'Are you sure?' he asked again.

" 'Da' was my answer.

"The *Natschalnick* turned and left me and the *Kommandant* and returned to his post.

" 'Don't you show the *Natschalnick* anything unless he makes it worth your while,' the *Kommandant* told me as he walked off.

"A few hours later *Dovarisch Natschalnick* came back.

" 'Ivan, you've worked with electric motors before. You understand something about them,' he said. 'I can't give you any money, but I will give you Tallon so you can go to the warehouse and get things like fabric and dry goods, not just food. Do what you can to make this thing work.'

" 'I considered his proposal and thought, why shouldn't I make life a little easier for myself? 'I'll help you out,' I told him. 'I'll try my best to get this thing going. But I want all Russians off the job. I want to make sure to communicate exactly what should be done. Give me five or six young boys from my town as helpers. I know what they can do.'

" 'Good, do whatever you can,' he replied.

"So the boys and I went to work. I had no idea where to begin, I had indeed never seen a gutter saw before. One thing I did know: the motor would not work unless it stood level. Having no tools such as rulers or a *Wasserwoch* – level – I took a stone and tied it to a string to make a plumb line. I measured to see how far off the ends of the saw stood. One side sat much higher than the other. With the use of the plumb line we set the machine level. Now we tried our luck.

"The machine started to hum. We picked up a log and started to push it through. Slowly the eight blades of the saw split the log into eight boards. But about two feet into the tree trunk the machine stopped. So we took the blades out, re-adjusted and sharpened each blade, and started all over again. This time the log was cut into eight long boards.

"Russians, Germans, all stood and watched. The one person who was especially dumbfounded at how beautifully the saw worked was me.

"One after the other, logs slid through the blades and were cut up as easy as if they were loaves of bread. Soon twelve logs had been cut and stacked neatly. Now the president walked over to the young boys and told them to stop. He then assigned a work crew to cut the wood.

"Shifts were set up to cut wood day and night. Wood was brought in and stacks and stacks of boards piled up fast. There was enough lumber for use in the mine as well as for building workshops and storage sheds.

"Life became livable. My boss looked at me in a new light. No longer was I considered just one of the slave laborers. I had become a valuable worker, someone who made the *Brigade Bene* earn more points and helped the *Natschalnick* and vice president look good.

"One day the *Natschalnick* came to me and asked, 'Ivan, what would you say if I made arrangements to have your family brought to Russia?'

" 'What do you mean?' I said.

" 'If you accept, you would no longer be a slave laborer. I'd make sure that you'd have a house in the village and be one of the top workers in *Brigade Bene*. Think it over before you give me an answer.'

"I didn't have to do much thinking. My answer to this proposition was *'Njet.'* I wanted more for my family than what I had seen here. Conditions here were so bad that I felt the only difference between myself and the regular population was that they lived on the outside of the fence and I and my fellow prisoners lived on the inside of the barb wire. True, some of the villagers might have had more food to eat and a bed to sleep in, but this was not enough. Of course I didn't know at the time what the conditions were back home. I thought all was as I had left it."

If my father's answer would have been yes, I would now be fluent in Russian instead of English. And we would never have set foot in America. Thank God his answer was *"Njet."*

He and his crew not only made doors and windows, they also built the elevator tower for the coal mine. Upon the tower's completion their new job was to help build housing for the Russian workers, since more workers were needed as the mine became more productive.

Although most of the prisoners had never worked in the building trade, the men did have knowledge of tools for most had been tradesmen of some kind or other back home. In a few months they became accomplished carpenters. Since the work was equally divided among men and women, women as well as men became experts in masonry, carpentry and the general use of tools.

Other machinery was given to the Russian government from America. Little did the Americans know what happened to much of that intricate motorized machinery. Communism, being what it is, made it very hard for its people to remain honest. The word most often used in everyday life was *Zabzerab*, which means to take, or appropriate. Everyone stole. Maybe the word "stole" is too harsh, and should be changed to "acquired." For this was the only way one could survive. From the biggest officer to the smallest peasant, if you didn't acquire, you didn't have. Almost as soon as a machine was delivered, it was as quickly dismantled. Nothing was safe. Tires from brand new trucks were cut up to use as soles for shoes. Belts that turned the engines were taken. This left a lot of machinery useless. That's why there were never enough nails or tools.

But woe to any who were caught. The penalty was very grave. More than likely the person was shipped off to Siberia. It didn't matter if you were an officer, engineer or peasant. Of course, all were expert thieves, so very few got nabbed. Having "friends" in every part of the system helped the most.

Windows and doors that were installed on houses by my father and his workers during the day were often not there the next morning when they returned. Because of shortages on everything from food to clothing to housing, this was the way of life. It was the only way one could survive.

CHAPTER
15_____

Life in München and Out of Russia

When we arrived in Munich, bombs had destroyed most of the buildings, and the city lay in ruins. Refugees were streaming into Germany from Eastern Europe. People were lucky if they had a room, let alone an apartment. Times were hard.

My father had been trying to find a place without much luck. One day he heard through the grapevine that a Herr Ruprecht was looking for people to rebuild his three story apartment building located at the back of Heberl Strasse # 8, a few blocks from the park known as the Theresien Wiese, where the famous *Oktoberfest* takes place yearly.

The front building had survived the war without much damage, but the smaller rear building had been almost totally destroyed. The builders were given no materials or money, but as payment for this job they would be allowed to live in the apartments and pay rent once they completed it.

"Not a bad deal for the landlord," Tati said.

Without money but with plenty of willpower, my father and three other men – Hechele's Ignatz and Sepp, two brothers from our home town, and Herr Ziessler, also a Danube Swabian from Kernei, Yugoslavia, agreed to do the job.

It was hard work. They spent every minute of their free time restoring the leveled structure to its former condition, re-using materials that remained from the demolished structure and bartering for nails, doors, windows and plumbing. They traded cigarettes, soap, and other scarce items. Even the black market came into the picture. Some things were impossible to acquire legally; in fact, right after the war, many everyday commodities fell into this category.

Out of the rubble the four men re-created a place fit for their families to call home. The very day that we arrived in Munich, my father was putting the finishing touches on our new apartment, right in time for us to move in. He had gotten word only the week before that we were coming. Considering that when he began to build, he had no idea if or when we would ever come to Germany, our timing was perfect. Although our new home was a mansion compared to the wretched existence we had led the past few years, there still were only two small rooms too small for seven people to live normally. Basl decided it would be best for Marie, Andres and herself to reside somewhere else.

Easier said than done. It was no use searching for a *Wohnung* in bombed out Munich. Basl had no way to pay for an apartment even if one were available. And the refugee camps located outside the city were overcrowded. So my aunt and cousins had to leave Munich and move to a *Flüchtlingslager* outside the city of Hof, a few miles from the East German border. While the refugee camp was only three hours away by train, it might as well have been in another country. Train tickets cost money, one thing we had very little of.

When the hour came for parting, it was hard to say good-bye. The two sisters embraced.

"Irgend wie were mer uns wieder sehe," Mami cried.

"Somehow, we'll see each other again."

"Ja, *Schwester*, maybe it'll be in just a few months," Basl answered tearfully.

"Marie, I'm going to miss you," I said.

"I'll miss you too," she told me as she pressed me close to her. "But we'll visit – you'll see."

"Are you sure?" I asked.

"I'm certain!" she exclaimed. With a hug and a kiss we all said, *"Auf Wiedersehen."*

The six of us had clung to each other when life offered nothing but despair: our love bound us together to survive pain, fear, hunger and even death. Now we had to part. It was hard for us children, but much harder on our mothers. To lose one's sister was not easy, but losing your best friend was even harder. Many miles would separate them, and their only connection would be paper and pen.

"Bettzimmer, Kuchel, Speiss, Halle und Klo mit Wasserablauf." Bedroom, kitchen, pantry, hallway and a water closet: for the first time in almost three years we lived in more than one room with less than fifteen people sleeping on the floor together. The rooms were for our use alone. We slept in beds!

In the center of our apartment was the hallway with five doors, the only doors in our home. Like the main cavern in a cave, it was the darkest part of our dwelling.

Our bathroom was a narrow, windowless room, at the far end of which was a white porcelain toilet. I was in charge of cutting newspapers into squares and hanging them on the large hook on the wall next to the toilet whenever we ran out of toilet paper.

On the other side of the toilet was a hose connected to some pipes. To flush, you had to turn the hose on and spray the water into the bowl. Presto, everything was gone. This was magic to my eyes. Tati said that this was not the way it operated originally, but it was the only way he could think of to make it work, for the tank was missing and there was no new one to be had. That was fine with me. What a luxury. It belonged only to us.

The room we lived in the most was our kitchen. The small green table that stood in the middle of the room taking up most of the space was our family headquarters. We used it for everything – eating, homework, cooking, a repair bench, playing games, visiting with friends, and of course, sitting around and listing to our radio. I'd sit at the table captivated by the sound coming out of the square box just three feet away. Our radio stood on the counter top of our *Kredenz* or china cabinet, between the glass doors and the two large drawers. I would listen every chance I had. At first I thought small people lived in it that did all the singing, talking and story telling. But I was soon informed I was wrong. It didn't matter: I still pretended it was so.

Mami was always in the kitchen where she spent most of her day. Every morning she'd light the fire in the large wood burning stove which was used for both heating the kitchen and cooking our meals. Before she set the pot on the stove top, she'd lift one of the four round covers with a bent-tipped rod and look inside to check on the fire.

The best part of the stove was the hot water reservoir that fit snugly into its cut out place on the top of the stove. I loved its warm copper cover. Mami rubbed it with ash every day to make it sparkle.

The water faucet and sink was the other *Zauberei* or magic in our new home. All one had to do was turn the handle, and *Simsalabim!* – abracadabra! – water came rushing out of the pipes.

Outside, on the window sill, was our garden. Tati had made a window box, and in summertime, Mami planted herbs and parsley between a few red geraniums.

Below this same window was a tiny, enclosed cobblestone yard. I can also tell you that the yard was quite far down from our window. I was warned not to stand on the chair when I leaned out the window.

Mami always said: *"Der nicht hört muss fühlen.* – He who doesn't heed must feel." I didn't heed. So I felt. I fell over, out and down onto the hard cobblestones.

Our bedroom, the largest room in the apartment; was heated by a beautiful *Kachelofe* – a shiny tiled stove. The tiles were just as beautiful as the ones I had found that day in Novoselo. The large bed took up half the room's space. Tati had made the bed, which was really two large single beds side by side. Mami and Tati slept on the left side and I slept on the right side. On either side was a *Nachtkastl* or nightstand.

My mother in the kitchen with a view of the bedroom.

My father in our kitchen on Heberl Strasse.

My brother slept on the other side of the room in a bed that served as a couch during the day. On the wall over the bed hung a small picture of the Last Supper; my brother got it when he made his first Holy Communion, in the Spring of 1948.

Every time I gazed up at it I always thought to myself, one day I'll make my *Erste Heilige Kommunion*, just like Seppi, then there will be two beautiful color pictures of *Jesus* hanging in our bedroom.

At the end of his bed was a small desk. On the wall between the end of the bed and the desk hung a large crucifix that Tati had carved himself.

My mother had vowed to God that if he led us safely to my father, she would offer up in thanks the largest candle she could find. When He answered her prayer, she searched all over Munich, but not even a small candle was to be found. So she and my father compromised with God. In place of the candle, my father carved a wooden cross from a choice piece of mahogany, attached a fine bronze figure of Jesus to the crucifix, had it blessed, and hung it on our bedroom wall.

The small two room apartment was where my family lived for two and a half years. We were very poor, and had very little, but I didn't know it at the time. I was happy.

Evenings we usually sat together after our meal and talked about the day's event. I'd listen as my mother and father talked about *Derham*. If the conversation about back home was about our family and our house, I'd usually know who or where they were talking about, but most of the time I didn't know the people or places the conversation was about. Back home to me was mostly memories from concentration camp. I can't recall my mother talking much about our experiences, maybe because I had lived through it with her, but when Tati told us about Russia I'd usually pay attention. Although I took it in as a matter of fact – not disturbed or shocked about his ordeals in Russia, but only as Tati's story.

"By the summer of 1946 I was once more hoping to become a free man," my father told us. "I not only worked outside for the coal mine boss, I also worked in the small shop that had been set up in the confines of the camp yard. Once a week, an older gentlemen dressed in a red army uniform with stars on his shoulder pads, came and inspected the going's on in the prison camp. I was usually inside the shop when he came in. The man just looked and observed the prisoners at work. As time went on I began to greet him and address him as *Otaz* or Father and soon we started to chat about our daily life, and the inspector began to call me 'Son'.

"One morning, on my day off, I stood looking down the hill. There were no Sundays. To determine when a worker had a day off, names were written on the calendar and then a line was drawn across the middle. Whoever's name the line crossed had that day off. On this particular day off, I spotted two trucks coming up the slope.

" '*Wann die nur endlich for die Kranki were.* I thought in jest to myself – if only they were finally coming for the sick.'

"The trucks stopped inside the gate. The drivers stepped down and went to the office of the new *Kommandant* of our camp Bregade Bene. (The *Kommandant* that I had befriended had been transferred.) A few minutes later all prisoners were ordered to go outside and stand at attention. The *Kommandant* then read names off a list and all on that list were told to step forward and get their things. Among the names called was 'Ivan Hugery'.

"As soon as I heard my name I ran and got my bag and joined the group outside in the yard. Not once did I stop to question why I was called. Deep down I 'knew' what was happening. A year had gone by since the medics inspected the sick in our camp and made a list of those who were to be shipped home. Now they finally got the approval to send us back home. It didn't matter that by this time the ones that had been sick had gotten well or died and the ones that were now sick were considered well and had to stay.

"All those on that sick list were loaded onto the trucks. But before the tailgates were shut, I saw the *Natschalnick* and Vice President from the coal mine come out of the office. I turned to the woman next to me, who happened to be one of the best bricklayers in the prison camp, and said to her: 'Emmi, watch, they won't let us go. We're too valuable to *Bregade Benne.* See, here they come.'

"Both men walked over towards our vehicles. I was sure they were coming to get the two of us. But I was mistaken, I breathed a sigh of relief, as I watched them board the other truck to serve as escort. Soon the engines were started and we rolled down the hill and rambled on for about four miles until we came to a large factory building in the city of Kadjewka, which was used as a regional Government headquarters for all the prisoners. We drove through the factory entrance and into the courtyard. We were unloaded with bag and baggage in the yard and ordered to sit down on the ground and wait.

"I still felt in the pit of my stomach that I'd be stopped from going. You can't imagine what that was like ... how alarmed I felt. I looked across the yard and saw the *Natschalnick* and a young *Leutnant* coming towards me. The Lieutenant was in charge of all the prisoners at this military headquarter complex in Kadjewa. I knew him well, I had made furniture for the young man's wife and two children.

"Now you're done for," I said to myself, as both men stopped in front of me.

" 'Ivan, you're staying here,' the young Lieutenant declared sharply.

" 'Oh no,' I replied daringly. 'I'm not staying here.'

" 'YOU'RE STAYING HERE. Take your things and come along,' the Lieutenant shouted.

"I refused to comply. Once more he ordered, 'Ivan, get up and take your things.'

"Now I got up and looked directly into the young man's face, and told him point blank: 'Look, I know you, and you know me. You have a wife and two children and I have a wife and two children. If you would be standing on my side and I on yours, what would you say?'

"*Job dwoje musch,*" he swore at my father. "Sit down."

"I sat down. Now the Lieutenant was convinced but the *Natschalnick* still kept on trying. He talked and argued with the Lieutenant, who just kept on shaking his head, until finally both men walked away.

"A little while later came *Otaz* – my friend, the old inspector. The old man asked, 'What did they want with you?'

" 'They don't want to let me go home,' I replied.

" 'Son, as long as I'm here, I'll see to it that you're going home.' The old gentleman sat down next to me and did not leave my side until it was time to go to the train that was to transport the "sick" home."

My father was one of the laborers picked to load the train with food supplies that were to be distributed among the passengers. "Do you know what good food we loaded into the cars that day?" my father marveled as he told his story. "All kinds of canned goods. Meat, fruits, vegetables of all kinds and loaves of bread."

When they were finished loading the food, which was from the American government, my father boarded the train with his old friend. The two men sat at the open cattle car door with their feet hanging out freely. The old gentleman meant to keep his promise to my father.

"The train rolled out of the Kadjewa station and headed back to Almanza, the town where we had just come from," Father said. "There it slowed down and stopped."

"Wer denkscht hat dort g'wart af mich, niemand annerscht als dr Dovarisch Natschalnick. – Who do you think was waiting there for me? None other than *Dovarisch Natschalnick!*

"Once more he commanded me to get off the train. But my friend, *Otaz* the old gentleman, countered. 'No, he is going home,' he said, knocking on the floor with his knuckles to emphasize his point. 'I'm staying at his side to make sure no one takes him off this train.'

"But the Natschalnick did not give up. He was there waiting at every stop the train made, trying to get me. He had a lot to lose. I had helped him make not only points but money on the side. The president had received money and returned favors for some of the furniture I had made for the Natschalnick's friends during my free time. Now this was all to stop.

"At the train's fourth stop since Kadjewa, I saw Woloja, the guard from our camp who was assigned to escort the sick back home. 'Dovarisch Natschalnick is here again,' he told me. Sure enough, I saw the president heading in my direction.

"This time he put his hand on my shoulder and said, 'Ivan, here, take these two-hundred and seventy Rubles.'

"The Natschalnick had finally given up. He shook my hand and wished me luck. 'Buy food wherever you can, even if you have to sell your shirt. For none of you will get any of this food supply that is on the train,' he told me. 'All of it is going to be stolen.'

"I thanked him, and the Natschalnick turned and walked away. And sure enough, the only food we received was a small piece of hard bread once a day.

"When the train stopped in the city of Debalzer, Otaz shook my hand and wished me luck. I thanked the kindly old gentleman and watched him get off the train. I owed the good hearted man a lot. He had given me my freedom.

"When the train halted in Kiev, the passengers were allowed to get off, since it was stopping for a few hours. I went with three other Karlsdorf men, Stembers Nikolaus, Deckerts Josef, and Balsvetter my uncle. The four of us headed for the market to purchase food.

"The strange thing about Russia was that I never saw any stores. You could buy food and other items only in the government-run warehouses or at the market. In the warehouse you used *Tallons* instead of Rubles. Everything was much cheaper than in the market place. What was just a few Rubles in the warehouse cost hundreds of Rubles more in the market place. Since one pound of bread cost about fifty Rubles at the market, the two hundred and seventy Rubles that I received from the Natschalnick disappeared in no time. So the shopping spree was over very quickly. Carrying our bundles under our arms, we returned to the train, which then continued on to the next stop, the city of Minsk.

"Along with the common passengers in our freight car was a Countess, an older woman who had become enslaved with the rest of the Germans in her community. She looked like everyone else on the train, but her highborn bearing showed through her speech and carriage. Because of her age and dignity, we treated her with a special respect. When the train came to Minsk, she asked me, 'Would you be so kind and get me some water to drink from the station.'

" 'I'll be happy to,' I told her, 'it's been a long time since our last stop. I need to stretch my legs anyway.'

When I stepped down from the cattle car, what I saw made my stomach turn. Never before in my life had I seen so much filth. The platform as well as the railroad tracks were covered with human excrement. There wasn't any way you could avoid stepping in it. The smell was enough to gag you, and I quickly stepped back up.

" 'Madam, I'm sorry," I told her. 'Due to the filth all around us, you'll have to remain thirsty until the next stop.'

"At every stop, more people were put on the train. German slave laborers from different camps as well as hundreds of German soldiers who had been prisoners of war now were being sent back home, most of them weak, ragged and sickly. Soon all the cars were filled, people packed so closely together that it was almost impossible to move. The journey back to the west was long, and because of the inadequate amount of food, many people died. Most of the dead were German solders. Who knows what hardships they had suffered since they had been captured. Maltreatment was high on the list for war prisoners.

"Every day the train stopped in the middle of nowhere to unload dead passengers. The doors opened and the bodies were cast outside, left to rot on the side of the tracks as if they were nothing more than bags of garbage. Hundreds of bodies were left behind in this manner as the train sped on towards Poland in the summer of 1946. We survivors became so familiar with death that we became frozen emotionally. Once I awoke in the middle of the night and noticed that the man next to me was dead and had grown cold. I removed the dead man's jacket, put it on, turned around and went back to sleep."

Weihnachten was getting closer and closer. Our first Christmas together. It was the middle of December, 1947. I had no idea what it was to get ready for this special *Feiertag*. Holidays were strange to me. I could barely remember celebrating one of them. Tati was standing on a chair next to the desk, hanging or fixing something over it. I stood at the desk and started to fool around with the drawer, opening and closing it as we talked.

Tati got off the chair. As he turned to walk away, I pulled the drawer open. When I started to close it, something round rolled forward from the back. My eyes couldn't believe what they were seeing: a ball, made from red rubber and no bigger than my fist. I picked it up and turned to my father.

"*Schau, schau was ich hab,*" I cried out, all excited. "Look, look, what I have, oh Tati it's a real ball!" My father didn't say anything for a moment.

"*Christkindl* must have put it there," Tati answered.

I got to keep the ball, even though it wasn't Christmas yet. It bounced as if it were alive, popping up and down on the floor over and over. The old rag ball I had received a few months before in Novoselo only sprang off the wall. This one hopped like a rabbit. For the next few weeks the round little sphere accompanied me everywhere, safely riding in my apron pocket.

Heiliger Abend, our first Christmas Eve together since 1943, Mami and I were in the kitchen, baking *Weihnachtskuche.*

"*Wann kummt des Christkind, Mami?*" I asked my mother.

"When is the Christ child coming?"

"Oh, when the first stars come out."

"Why has the bedroom door been closed all afternoon?"

"Tati and Seppi have to fix something in the room."

I was satisfied with that answer. I believed with all my heart that today *Christkindl* was coming, tree and all. I had a picture in my head from long ago, but the vision was not very clear.

Then Seppi opened the door to the kitchen.

"Kummt ins Zimmer, es Christkindl war do," he cried out all excited. "Come on, come on, the Christ child was here, hurry." He grabbed me by the hand and ran with me to the open bedroom door. I stopped in the doorway. A tree, almost reaching to the ceiling, stood in the corner by my side of the bed. It glowed with candlelight that shimmered like stars in the dark room. Never had I seen anything like this before. I stood in front of the soft glowing candlelight dancing in front of me: such splendor. I never dreamed it would look like this. The shiny glass point on the very tip of the tree was like a jewel.

Silver strands of tinsel shimmered as they hung from the branches. We stood in front of the *Weihnachtsbaum* and prayed *"Vater Unser"* and a *"Heilige Maria."* When we finished the Our Father and Hail Mary, we sang "Silent Night" and the other Christmas carols that I had been practicing all Advent. I kept my eyes riveted to the tree when Tati lit the *Spritzkirzen.* The crackling sparklers turned the room into an unbelievable fairy tale. Never before had I seen such magic. Round balls of tiny white shooting stars bounced of the lit center and disappeared. When they were finished I just stood there.

"Aren't you going to look under the tree?" someone asked me. Oh, I had almost forgotten the presents. There at the base of the tree sat a rag doll. It was a *Kasperl,* dressed in a colorful outfit, like Punch should be. I decided then and there to call him Sepp despite the fact that he was already called Kasperl.

Punch and Judy are known all over Europe by different names. In Germany they are know as "Kasperl and Gretel." Gretel never came to live with me, just her mate, Kasperl.

That Christmas in 1947 was the most memorable in my life. Never has a tree cast its magical spell on me like the first one in Germany, forty-nine years ago. I woke up during the night to look at it. The shiny ornaments caught the moonbeams streaming through the window. What a wonderful sight!

Saturday night, bath night. Tati set up the large wooden *Mulder* – the tub – that he had made just for us and filled it with hot water. The kitchen was turned into the bathroom, all steamed up and ready for its first customer. Me.

This was luxury at its finest. Along with the warm water and suds, there was entertainment from the radio. I could hardly wait all week for this special treat. The bath was not as important as the staying up late and listening to the weekly comedy sketches that came floating over the radio waves from *Kabaret am Wochenend* – Cabaret on the weekend.

Tati and Seppi sat around the table, taking in every word. Mami and I listened as she washed my hair. She paused whenever a good joke came across the radio.

Seldom did I get to hear all of the program. It was not over before my bedtime, so from the dark bedroom I tried to hear the rest of the program through the closed kitchen door. I fell asleep to the sound of laughter.

Aside from the radio, another entertainment we could afford was Tati's wonderful stories.

My Tati told the best stories in the world, especially stories of Indians, settlers and the American Frontier. He was a gold mine of tales, our living library. We could not afford books. But Tati had read hundreds of books back home.

Every chance he had gotten back home in Karlsdorf he'd used to steal away to the john and read. My mother has often told how in the middle of the day Tati would disappear and was nowhere to be found. That usually meant he was in conference with one of his favorite authors.

James Fennimore Cooper's *Lederstrumpf* – Leather Stockings – and *Der letzte Mohikaner* – The Last of the Mohicans – were my father's favorite books. He also read many, many books by Karl May, a German author who wrote about the wild west at the turn of the century. Although he was never in America, his stories are very popular in Germany to this day.

We spent many weekends in our little bedroom listening to Tati's *G'schichte.* I usually was on his left, with Seppi next to me and Mami on his right. We'd cross the American continent with Tati. His old friends became our heros. Old Joe, Old Shatterhand and Old Waverly (all names said with German accents, of course) were in almost all his stories.

As he told the tale of *Old Waverly und die Sioux Indianer im Wilden Westen,* I saw the Indians come closer and closer, surrounding the wagon train's protective circle. I felt the fear of the pioneers as they fought to stay alive and keep their scalps. Once more the four of us, crowded together in one bed, traveled with Tati to another world. Light faded, day gave way to evening, and I hung on to every word of Tati's story, which came alive with the approach of darkness. My heart pounded as the visions in my head became real. Not only did we get to know his books, we heard the stories of the many movies he saw "*im Karlsdorfer Kino*," and of the few plays he attended in Belgrade as a young man. *Der Bettelstudent* – The Begger Student – was his favorite play, and also mine, just because it was his. I had never seen a play in my life.

But the best adventures were the ones he made up. *Daumelanger Hans* was his star. Tom Thumb had hundreds of adventures, although the Brothers Grimm had written only one. Tati made up the small hero's sagas as he went along, "*aus'm Bauch*" as we referred to made up stories in our dialect. The tales were never the same, even if we asked him to repeat them, for he usually forgot what he had told before.

Then there were his stories from *Schlaraffenland*, where sausages grew on trees, where roast chickens, pigs and ducks ran around crisp and hot, ready to eat. Candy flowers and candy paths lined the fields and mountains, while rivers flowed with chocolate sauce and honey.

This was the place I wanted to go. I wanted the food that I only heard about in stories and never got to taste in real life. Most of the stories that my father told us were tales of fantasy and things he did and saw as a young man. Sometimes he'd continue telling us about Russia.

Being a child at the time, I never really knew exactly what had happened to my father. I had misunderstood or had not cared to hear many things about his ordeal. So when I interviewed Tati for my book I finally found out exactly what had happened during thoes years as a slave laborer, and how he got out of Russia to Munich.

The train's iron wheels rolled over the Russian border and into Poland, and at every station, peasants came to sell their wares.

"*Wurscht, Fleisch, Milich, Obst aller Art, alles was m'r nur sich g'wunsch hat, hat m'r kaufe kenne.* – Sausage, meat, milk, fruit of all kinds, everything one could wish for one could buy," my father told me. "That is, if you had money. Since money was in short supply among us, not many deals were made.

"Poland was much cleaner than Russia, maybe it was because the Polish people had not been under Communism's iron fist for almost thirty years.

"The train rambled over the Polish border and into East Germany, its final destination the village of Halle-an-der-Saale, where the sick prisoners were handed over to the East German Government.

"Ah...free at last...no, not yet. The East Germans shipped all the ex-slave laborers off to Frankfurt-an-der-Oder, to a large building complex that once had been a hotel. More than eight thousand men and women were stuffed in the building like sardines, sometimes thirty or forty people to a room.

"Our daily food ration was only 272 calories, just like the citizens of Frankfurt-an-der-Oder. However, the people in town could add to this ration by buying or trading. And some people had land of their own on which they were able to grow fruits and vegetables.

"At first we were permitted to go outside, and we did what all hungry human beings would do. We went from house to house, begging for food to still the pains in our bellies. You can imagine what happens when eight thousand people fill the streets in any community. The East German inhabitants hardly had enough food for themselves and certainly were unable to share the little they had with thousands of extra hungry people. The only solution to this problem was to lock up the beggars inside the hotel yard.

"There were mostly seventeen, eighteen year old girls, older women and young men, all suffering from malnutrition. People were still starving.

"We did everything to stop the gnawing hunger. People stripped the bark off the trees in the courtyard, boiled and ate it. Once more, or I should say still, we did not have enough food. Here it was the summer of 1946, almost two years since we were forced to leave our homes and families. Now we were out of the clutches of the Red Army, but still we were imprisoned and in danger of starving to death.

"One night, sitting in the darkness with my stomach knotted with hunger, I resolved that since I made it this far, no way would I give in and die of hunger here. I woke my uncle, Balsvetter, and the other two men from Karlsdorf, Deckerts Josef and Stembers Nikolaus, who slept in the same crowded room. *'Do sterb ich net.'* I said, 'I'm not going to die here."

" 'What do you want to do about it?' Balsvetter asked.

" 'I'm going to escape. Are you coming with me?'

"So it was that all four of us agreed to break out that same night. We crept out of the building and slipped into the dark yard to the large iron gate. The gate was open. Four policemen were stationed outside. Two and two, the guards walked back and forth in front of the entrance, it was a cold night and the men were moving to keep warm. Across the road was a forest.

"We waited until the guards had their backs turned. Quickly I gave Balsvetter a helping shove and the older man ran unnoticed across the road and into the dark forest. One by one the rest of us did the same. Free at last, we walked through the woods with nothing except the clothing on our backs. That night we walked for quite some time. With no map to go by, we just kept going due west.

"We came to a small town and stopped at a *Gasthaus*. We entered and asked the innkeeper if it were possible to sleep in his barn. '*Raus mit Euch verdammtes Bettelgesindl!*' He screamed. 'Get out you damn beggars and stay out!' Red faced with anger, he raised his fist, chased us out and slammed the door.

" 'Now what shall we do?' we asked each other as we stood together outside the door of the Gasthaus. Before an answer came, a woman called to us from across the street.

" '*Kommt rueber.* – Come on over.' She opened the door. '*Kommt herein. Ihr seid willkommen diese Nacht hier zu verbringen,*' she said 'Come on in, I welcome you to spend the night.' She showed us to a small room with two very clean beds. Not since we had left Karlsdorf had we slept in clean, white, soft beds. Before we went to sleep that night, the *Hausfrau* provided dinner so that we need not go to bed hungry. And the next morning before she bid us '*Auf Wiedersehn*' she also gave us a hearty breakfast. This might not seem a lot today, but back in 1946 what the woman gave us is almost impossible to measure. I'm sure she did not have much food for herself, and yet she gave of the little that she did have.

"We weren't very clean. We hadn't taken a bath for months and months. If we had a chance to take a sponge bath, they usually had to be taken without soap. We were lucky to have water to drink, let alone to cleanse our bodies with.

"We were full of head and body lice. When we left the kind woman's house, I'm sure many of them stayed behind in the crisp clean beds.

"Again we were on our way, pressing forward to home and family, hoping all would be well at the end of the journey. Traveling over fields and through forests, we had to live off the land. Once we came upon a field of sugar beets and tried to eat them raw, but we couldn't. Cooking them over an open fire didn't make them any more palatable. When I brought the sweet sticky substance up to my mouth, I couldn't swallow it.

"Balsvetter was not well. He was getting weaker and had a hard time walking, as we traveled over the East German countryside. Something had to be done. At the next village, we went to the railroad station. I walked up to the ticket counter and told the young man behind the window. *'Wir kommen vom Ivan* – We're coming from Ivan - (which meant we're coming from the USSR), and we want to go to the west zone but we don't have any money or papers.'

"Without saying a word, the man turned and took four tickets and four individual papers out of a drawer. Smiling, he slipped them under the ticket window. 'Take the next train that stops here. Then get off just before it crosses the border. You must cross the border on foot.'

"We did as we were told, and crossed over to the western zone without difficulty. Still walking over fields and open land, we came to the city of Goettingen which was in the English zone. It was a warm Sunday morning. People were going to church and all was peaceful. We decided to split up and beg two and two instead of all four together. Balsvetter and I walked through the town and out past the city limits, begging but with no luck. After a few miles we came to a big *Bauernhof* or farm.

"We walked up to the door and knocked. A voice asked to come in. In the middle of the dining room stood a long table and sitting around it was the *Bauer* and his family and all of the farmhands eating Sunday dinner. Everyone stopped eating as we walked in and all eyes turned toward us.

"'*Habt ihr Hunger?*' the farmer asked. And before we could answer, in walked Deckerts Josef and Stembers Nikolaus. The farmer greeted them just as cordially as he had us and invited them to dinner. A woman brought out an enormous tureen of soup and all the courses of meat and vegetables that had been served before.

"'Eat until you're full,' the farmer told us. When all was eaten and cake had been provided for dessert the farmer asked us, 'Are you full?'

"'No' was our reply. I could not tell if I was filled up or not.

"'Bring in more food,' the farmer told the women, and we began another meal. My stomach had been empty for so long that I could not remember what it felt like not to be hungry. Food was scarce all over

Europe. But the luckiest people were the farmers for the good earth provided, war or no war.

" 'Now you must be full,' the kind man said when we had once more finished everything on the table. 'Where are you headed?'

"We want to go to the American zone." I said. The generous *Bauer* handed each of us 36 marks and told us to take the train to the American zone. He shook our hands and bade us good-bye and good luck.

"We rode the train through the English zone to the American zone, where the train halted and all passengers had to disembark to be inspected. Each carload was to remain together as a group while the authorities made sure everyone was crossing legally. "As we waited a conductor came around and asked where were going.

" 'We came from Ivan and wish to cross over to the American zone,' I said.

" 'Wait in the station,' he said, 'When you hear the departing train whistle, then board the train once more.' "We did as we were told. But during the time we waited in the station, another train had pulled up next to the one we were to get on. So when the shrill whistle sounded, we had to run like mad around the other train to reach ours. When the conductor saw us, he yelled and pulled us up the ramp and into the train. Still screaming and swearing, he pushed us into a washroom and closed the door. This was a ploy to get us into the American zone without inspection and without a ticket. We stayed in the washroom, even when people were pounding to get in. But we did not budge from our safe place until the train pulled into the *Münchner Hauptbahnhof*, the same Munich train station where Mami, Seppi and you arrived a year and a half later.

"We got off and headed into the main bombed-out depot. Again we had to look for food. By this time begging for food was an everyday event.

"It was decided that my uncle and I would go panhandling and the other two would stay in the train station. We traveled down the street, going from house to house without much success. By this time our path had taken us quite far from the Innenstadt or inner city. We came to a high, fenced-in yard with a large open entrance gate and walked in. In the middle of the yard was a small house; a *Hausfrau* was busy hanging out her wash.

"The woman's back was turned. Politely, I asked, 'Can you spare a few morsels of food.' When she turned from her work to look at me, I stared into her face in disbelief. Two familiar eyes looked back into mine. She was Tersep's Kathi, a neighbor from back home.

" *'Kathi, kennscht mich net?'* I cried. 'Don't you know me?'

She looked at me without recognition, then her face lit up.

" *'Jani, bist's du?'* Then she turned to my uncle and smiled, recognizing him at once. We were a sight to behold. I wore a Russian army hat and a torn quilted jacket to match. My feet sported a pair of torn rubber galoshes with no shoes inside. Unwashed and unshaven for weeks, my own mother would not have recognized me.

" 'What are you doing here in Munich?' she asked. I told her that Balsvetter, Deckerts Josef, Stembers Nikolaus and I were coming from Russia and now were heading back home.

"Kathi looked at me for a few seconds before she asked; *'Du waascht net was los is drhahm?'* I shook my head, no. 'What's going on back home? I haven't heard anything from my family or Karlsdorf since they took us to Russia in '44.'

"She told me that there was no more 'home.' They had taken everything and put everyone in concentration camps. 'You would be best off if you stayed here in Munich, made a new life for yourself and kept up your hope that your family would one day be able to escape to the west,' she said.

"I was in total shock by what I had just heard. Thoughts raced through my mind like a whirlwind. Where is my family? Are they alive? Dear God let me see them again. I begged in silence. But to my old neighbor Kathi I spoke calmly. 'Make a new life with what? I own nothing except these rags on my back.'

" 'You'll find a way, I'll help you.' she said.

"I went back to the train station to get the other two men, and all four of us spent the night in the one-room house along with Kathi's family. Although the mattress was only the hard floor, it was comforting to sleep under a friendly roof.

"So it was that I came to live in Munich, knowing there was nothing for me to do but hope my family would be alive and well. I also believed that one day we'd be together again."

I'm still amazed at how my family, as well as the rest of the *Schwabos* survived. My father and I have talked about how enduring our people were. Many of the *Donauschwaben* managed to pull through somehow. For example on the train on the way back from Russia, my father says that most of the dead who were thrown from the train were German soldiers and Germans from other regions of Eastern Europe. The *Donauschwaben* seemed more often to survive. Maybe it was because of the way we had to struggle back home to come as far as we did.

A determined man, my father set out to have everything ready for that hoped-for day when his family would come. He got a job as a cabinet maker and soon earned enough money to rent a room. Luck was on his side when he found Tante Mitzi. She was a kind hearted older lady: she not only took my father in as a boarder, she cared for him like a son.

Now he had to face the biggest task of all. If his family made it to freedom, he knew he had to find a place for them to live. This was nearly an impossibility in a city that was almost flattened during the war, and in addition had thousands upon thousands of refugees.

Most of the people who managed to escape from the clutches of the communists ended up living in refugee camps. These were wooden barracks with one-room dwellings and no running water or toilets. Some had only walls of blankets to separate each family. Tati wanted more than this for his family. Somehow he was going to find a way. And find a way he did.

My father was and still is a very clever man, and when he puts his mind to something, he accomplishes what he sets out to do.

"Elsa, schau. Die nummer 4 is doch so leicht. Sie is sowie a verkehrter Stuhl. – Look, Elsa. The number 4 is so easy. It's nothing but an upside down chair." I watched Tati's pencil as it drew the upside down chair on the paper. It seemed like hours since he had taken me on his lap to help me learn to write numbers and letters. I knew I was not going to be able to do it. I hated school. Maybe this number was easy, but not the rest.

Everyone in my class could write and read, but not me. Tati and I spent almost every evening at the kitchen table as he tried to teach me the scribbles I was to learn. I liked it much better when he drew his silly ladies with big hats and fancy scroll-like designs just for fun.

I had a bad start in school. When we arrived in Munich, school had been in session for almost half a school year. I was put in first grade and Seppi in third. Everyone in my class could already read a little: I didn't even know the alphabet. No help was given to me in class. My father and mother had to help me catch up. I'm sure that this would not have been the case a few years later, but at that time school was not yet normal. The school had been bombed during the war and only half of it was standing. Some rooms were not fit to teach in.

Boys and girls were separated and classes were held in two shifts, one in the morning and the other in the afternoon, six days a week. And when it rained, school was out for the day, because the building had no roof.

School days were a new way of life. I now had to be present in a certain place every day. This was all strange to me. For the first time since kindergarten, almost four years before, I became part of a group of children my own age. The going and coming at the same time of day made life different. Routine set in. Things became part of a whole.

One part of the school week was having to line up for *Impfungen.* Shots were handed out like candy. I never knew what they were for, only that they were necessary to stay well. Sometimes one and sometimes more needles were stuck into my upper arm. It happened almost every Friday.

Once a week we had *Handarbeit.* I usually enjoyed the crafts that we learned, from folding paper into stars to learning how to knit a pot holder or stitching a decorative doily. I was working with my hands, and didn't have to learn abstract patterns. Little did I know than that one day I would love to put those scratches of symbols, representing words, on paper.

During school I would struggle to learn to read and write. Writing the letters over and over on one line wasn't so bad, in fact, I sort of enjoyed penmanship. But spelling was another matter. I could hardly wait for the time to end.

I liked singing and *Turnen*. Gym consisted only of playing games out in the school yard. We had no equipment, not even swings or slides, only a gravel area in back of the building.

My favorite subject was religion. I liked the Bible stories and I also liked Pater Pazifikus, one of the Capuchin Monks who came to our school each week to teach religion. His smiling eyes twinkled. He had a long beard, which he stroked constantly. When he was deep in discussion, he sometimes rubbed it between his fingers and flipped it across the tip of his nose. His dark brown hair had the customary shaven spot at the back of the head, like all the monks from his order.

After each story, he took large felt cut-outs that illustrated the story and placed them on a felt board. Then he handed out sheets of paper and instructed us to copy the picture as best we could. This was the moment I had waited for since the good monk walked into the class room. I could duplicate the illustration without any difficulty. I was good at it. I could draw the picture on the paper almost as well as he had done on his "felt drawing." Soon the girls around me asked me to do "theirs." I obliged, and my ego soared.

That was my introduction to my artistic abilities.

Ruins were a part of the Stadt. In fact, I thought that was the way cities had to be. On our side of the block, more than half the buildings were nothing but hills of broken bricks and mortar piled up among the still standing walls. The other half were bomb-damaged two-and-three story apartment buildings pock-marked with shrapnel. Across the street, two hastily-built one story wooden *Buden* – huts – stood at the corner. One housed an ice cream stand and the other a small confectionery store.

The large, cleared space between the new stores and the remaining three-story buildings stood out like a gap between teeth. This was our short cut to the *Tummlinger Schule*, the neighborhood school we attended. We passed through the empty lots and entered the school yard at the back.

A nasty, pea soup colored puddle was located in the middle of the empty lot. Its greenness looked strange, for the rest of the ground was covered with grey dirt and gravel.

Seppi, who also went past that spot daily, said that if I breathe the air near the water, I'd probably get sick and die. So I always held my nose and ran past this place as quickly as I could.

Up the block, on the third floor in a small room, lived Herr Bursch, a friend of my family from Karlsdorf. Every time we visited, he gave me *Lebertran*. He said I was sickly looking and it was good for me. The cod liver oil tasted ghastly. But not wanting to make a fuss, I took it, nearly choking every time.

A few doors from our building was the *Milch Laden*, tiny milk shop no bigger than a wide hallway, in the middle of which was a large tin vat that contained the milk. Oh, how I hated the watery blue *Magermilch*. The smell of skimmed milk made my stomach turn. But every day I had to take the *Milchkann* from the kitchen shelf and bring it to *"Milch Anna"*, the lady of the store. Skim milk was all we had after the war, and my mother made me drink it daily. On certain days, Mami sent me to get *Rahm*. Now, *that* I could hardly wait to bring home from the milk shop. I loved to dip my bread into the thick, sour cream and savor it on my tongue. If only the milk had been half as good.

The Saturday before Easter, my first in Munich, I went to the *Theresien Wiese* and found the first green grass of the season. I had to make a nice soft nest so that the *Osterhas* could lay his eggs without breaking them. Grass was not that easy to find, as it was just starting to grow.

After my Saturday night bath, I carefully lined a soup plate with the sweet-smelling grass and put it on the nightstand next to my bed. I wanted to stay awake all night so I could get a good look at this bunny that was going to bring me my Easter eggs. I envisioned the *Osterhas* coming into our bedroom through the window and putting the eggs right next to my bed. But as all children do, I fell asleep.

When I opened my eyes the next day, bright colors glowed in the grass-lined dish. I got only eggs but what Easter eggs! I didn't know that colors on eggs could change the whole personality of the object. Bright red, yellow, blue and all the other magic colors that the Easter Bunny used were right here in my lap.

CHAPTER
16

Our Neighborhood

We lived at Heberlstrasse #8, *Rückgebäude* – rear build ing – for two and one-half years. Our family was one of four that occupied the two-story apartment building. A court-yard separated our building from the three story apartment building that faced the street.

A foot-high cement wall partitioned the courtyard. Half was paved with cobblestones and the other half was packed-down dirt, embedded with rubble. At one time this area must have been a garden , but now all that it produced was a fuzzy moss cover .

A set of doors, located in the front building, opened up into a high, wide archway, forming a tunnel right through the center of the building. At the end of the archway was another set of doors that led to the street. Stepping out of the large two-door gangway was sometimes a hard thing to do.

During those years, I got a little street-smart about life in the big city. Outside our building a whole world of magic and good food was to be seen and smelled, although I usually didn't have the money to buy any-thing. On the corner across the street was an ice cream stand. A few doors down stood a make-shift candy counter no bigger than a table. I never had enough money for anything but a piece of caramel, hard and chewy. I liked it because it took so long to melt in my mouth and it only cost 15 Pfennig – 4 cents.

On Lindwurm Strasse, around the corner, was a *Tabak* stand. Once in a while Tati sent me there to get him a small pack of "Old Joe" cigarettes. We pronounced every letter in the name, calling them Old Yo-e. Tati usually rolled his own, but when he had a few extra Pfennig he bought the cheapest cigarettes on the market.

At the end of our block, the three streets crossed each other: Lindwurm Strasse, Göthe Strasse and Heberl Strasse. This intersection was known as Göthe Platz.

Every morning a vendor would come and place a large two-wheeled cart on the corner of Heberl Strasse. To get to any other street you had to pass by this cart of apples, pears, cherries, peaches or whatever fruit was in season.

The wagon was filled from end to end. I'd stand a few feet away and let my eyes feast on the fruit. Every kind looked good. I can't remember ever eating fruit from the cart except for one time on a special day in early summer.

The wagon was full of cherries, round and dark red with little green stems. I wanted just one cherry: I could almost taste it with my eyes. Hypnotized by the red fruit in front of me, I couldn't move. Just to look at the perfect fruit was almost as good as being able to put it in my mouth.

"Kleine, magst Kirschen?" a voice said from far away. "Little one, do you like cherries?" Startled, I saw the lady standing by the cart smile at me. "Ja," I replied. Still smiling, she stretched out a hand-full of the ruby red cherries. *"Hier, nimm diese,"* I hesitated, and she repeated "Here take these. Hold out your hand." I cupped my hands and received the treasure. Thanking her, I hastened back home, unable to believe my good fortune. In the courtyard I sat down on the small cement wall and stared at the six cherries I had placed on my lap. I picked up a pair and dangled them in front of my eyes, admiring them as if they were fine jewelry. I hung the scarlet cherries on my ears like earrings, one pair on each side.

That left me two more. I put one in my mouth and felt its smooth roundness. Still holding onto the stem, I pulled the cherry out of my mouth, so that it would last longer. I repeated this over and over until the fruit burst and its juice ran down my throat.

Savoring every juicy drop and taste of the six delicious, red sweet cherries, I made them last for almost an hour.

Not only was there food all around outside our house, but also small toys and balloon stands. On almost all the corners of the square, vendors sold everything one's heart desired.

I knew we couldn't afford any of the things outside our house, and most of the time I accepted that fact. Not that I didn't crave the things offered. Sometimes the want was so great that I was mesmerized by the object. Had it been possible to make the wanted item mine through sheer longing, I would have possessed many things. But I knew I had to be satisfied with just looking. And I usually was.

My desire was to have a whole round balloon, although I usually had to make do with the pieces I found on the street from balloons that had blown apart.

Down on the ground is where my eyes traveled any time I went outside. Sometimes I found a piece of balloon as big as my hand. That was the best piece, for it was big enough to stretch over your mouth and form a small bubble between your teeth and tongue. By clamping your lips shut and twisting the latex tight you could make a balloon the size of a very large button. It didn't matter that it was dirty or small. I rubbed it on my sleeve, to make it squeak.

The *Theresien Wiese* was a few blocks from our house. The large grassy meadow surrounded by a tree-lined walkway was one of my favorite places in Munich. At the back of the field stood a colossal

Tati, Mami and I in front of the Bavaria in 1949.

statue of a stately lady holding on to a large lion with one arm, the other extended to the sky. This was the *Bavaria.*

A two tier stairway led up to the Bavaria with a wide slanting slab of white marble on each side. Since the park had no playground equipment, we children used this spacious, slick banister as a slide.

Inside the statue was a circular staircase that led up to her crown, where for a fee, one could look out and see all of Munich. The yearly *Oktoberfest* was held down below, at her feet, as well as the lesser known *Frühlingsfest*, or Springfest.

Everyone all over the world thinks of beer when *Oktoberfest* is mentioned. But beer was a small part of it. It was a big fun fest of rides – roller coasters, carousels, ghost train – to name a few. Side shows with dare devil motorbike riders, midget shows, calliope wagons, and dog acts.

Music and food were everywhere. We went from one sweets-stand to the next, looking longingly at the *Lebkuchenherzl.* Gingerbread hearts came in all sizes: big ones, almost a foot high, small ones only as big as my hand and in-between ones. All were decorated in bright colored sugar icing, with ribbons strung through the middle to hang around ones neck. The messages, *"Ich hab Di Gern," "Sei Lieb zu Mir," "Du bist Mein Schatz. "*, proclaimed for the world to see "I Like You," "Be Sweet to Me," "You're My Sweetheart." Some had no sayings at all, only colorful decorations of hearts and flowers.

I dreamed of the day I was going to get to wear one of the biggest *Lebkuchenherzl* around my neck.

Everything cost money, so we just gazed and wished. We would go from one ride to the next. After we had covered the whole Fest we went to the one place where we knew we could buy a ticket. At the end of the midway was a small tent where the *Spiegl Saal* was housed. The "Hall of Mirrors" was the cheapest attraction at the Fest. We handed over our 15 Pfennig and happily joined the rest of Munich in celebrating *Oktoberfest.*

The first time we went back to Munich I wanted to see if my beloved *Theresien Wiese* was still as I left it. The *Wies* – meadow – was always full of people playing or sunning themselves back when I was a child.

Although it was late June and no fest was being held, I wanted to show my family the place I had so often told them about. When we got there, the park was empty. We were greeted by the stately lady, *Bavaria,* just as I had left her. But what had they done to the meadow?

On the spot where *Oktoberfest* reigned, slabs of cement had replaced the green grass. Between the cement, gravel pathways criss crossed each other like streets. Sadly I walked on the paths as my children ran ahead of me. Why must progress always ruin the beauty of a place?

We came to the spot at the far edge of the park where the old gothic church loomed against the sky. The last time I had seen the church, only one side of its steeple pointed towards the heavens. The other side, which had been damaged by a bomb, looked as if a big animal had bitten a chunk out of its side. Restored to its pre-war elegance, it was whole again, reaching up through the tree tops.

I was transported back in time when I was a barefoot child walking across the field. The grass and surrounding trees were bedecked in their fragrant, new spring growth. In the distance I saw a man sitting on a stool and as I came closer I saw that he was painting. He was so engrossed in what he was doing that he didn't even notice me.

I watched as he recreated the scene in front of him, adding color from the small table next to him. I had never seen an artist before or, for that matter, oil paints. My father and mother had used paint out of a can to paint our room but this was different. I liked what I saw.

As his paintbrush moved, the objects began to look real. Especially the church. With just a few strokes, he duplicated in miniature what stood before him life size. The colors made the picture come alive. I watched until he completed the picture. Maybe one day I could try painting with bright colors and create a picture just like him.

At the time I had no idea that art would play such a big part in my life. I became not only an artist but an art teacher.

Not everyone in Munich was as poor as we were. Opportunities to spend one's money were endless, especially during Advent, at the *Christkindlmarkt*, a fairy tale come to life. Here at the Christmas market my eyes took in more treasures than was possible for the mind to comprehend. I had not been aware that there were so many toys and Christmas glitter in all the world.

Stars, angels, glass trumpets, birds, bells and ordinary round ornaments hung from the top of the stall or were displayed in their boxes. Silvery tin foil icicles, garland and white angels' hair. Everything for the *Weihnachtsbaum*. I was certain that the *Christkindl* came here first before it brought the Christmas trees and toys to all the good children in Munich.

But the most important stands were the ones which displayed the toys, stuffed teddy bears and *Puppen*. Dolls of all sizes and dress occupied the little store like booths. Some were almost one and one half feet tall, with long golden locks or braids, dressed in satin and lace. Pretty glass eyes of blue, brown or green looked back into mine from the crowded shelves. It was as if they were capable of winking at me with their thick lashes. Some even opened and closed their eyes.

Others called out "Mama" when they were picked up and put down. I had never seen so many beautiful babies. With all my heart and soul I wanted one of those lovely pretend children. Even if it was the smallest doll from all the doll population in this Christmas fairy land, I would have been the happiest girl in all of Munich.

I hoped that maybe on Christmas Eve my wish would come true. But it was not to be, I had to be content with my rag doll, it seemed that *Christkindl* just couldn't get enough money together to make my dream come true in 1948.

Miles and miles of rubble made the middle of the city look open and airy. Block after block, the remains of the war were written all over the Stadt. In some streets all the buildings had vanished; in others only one or two structures remained. Some had more than half standing, depending on how "lucky" the bomber had been.

I thought that this is the way it was supposed to be. At the corner of our street, facing Göthe Platz, was a brick mountain higher than any other in the neighborhood that my best friend Käthe and I used to climb. It was almost two stories high in the middle and had nothing but fallen bricks on all sides, with no walls standing. At the base of the ruin, all around the ground, every last brick had been removed and swept clean to make room for all the little stands located there.

It was hard to get to the top of the ruin because of its height. That didn't stop us, and when we got up there, it felt as if we were on top of a mountain, looking down on the small people and streetcars going by. At the top, facing Göthe Platz, was an opening that looked like a cave. We dared each other to go in, but both of us were too afraid of the *Rauwer* that might be living in there. Sometimes we'd make up stories about the robbers down there and how they came out at night. They were so real to us that I still can see their imaginary room in my head.

One slip and we could have rolled down the brick and mortar hill in no time. If our poor mothers had known what we were up to, they would never have let us out of the house.

When I got older I started to understand that the piles of bricks had made up walls and rooms where mothers, fathers, children, even babies had once lived. Maybe some or even all had died there when the fiery bombs hit.

I recall walking home with my brother, deep in discussion about the future. Seppi was saying how in the next ten years Munich would be rebuilt and no more trace of *Ruine* would remain. This was hard for me to believe. In my young mind the ruins were a part of life and I just didn't want things to change. I had seen too much change in my lifetime. And now he was telling me that change was coming again.

"Do you really think we will see no more ruins in ten years?" I asked him.

"Maybe even less than ten years," he replied.

"I don't believe you," I said. Besides, ten years was a long time off. By that time I'd be old.

This, then, was city life after the war. Little did I know at the time that we wouldn't be here to see the city being restored. My family would be across the ocean far away in a much bigger city: Chicago.

If it were possible to go back to visit the Munich of 1947 to 1950 and view the city as it was then, you as well as I would see how poor conditions were, compared to today's standards. But at the time, I could only relate to the conditions I had seen and experienced before November 1947. Compared to the life that I remembered from Yugoslavia, I now lived in paradise. Although debris was on every street, I didn't see the ruins as anything out of the ordinary. I saw them only as places to climb over, and play in. I had never seen the city when it was "whole".

I had my family and food to eat. Even if occasionally oatmeal cake and rhubarb were the only things on the menu for days, I never went to bed hungry.

I had the most important ingredient, one that sometimes is missing in today's modern world with its profusion of monetary wealth: people who cared for and loved me, and I them.

In my childish eyes, this city life was wonderful. They were happy, innocent years and I loved living in Munich.

CHAPTER
17
Routine Sets In

Mami worked at home in her trade as a seamstress. She sewed for friends and neighbors right here in our kitchen and that helped put a little more food on our table. People came and went through our small entrance door for estimates, fittings, and pickups.

New fabric was sometimes a luxury that one could not afford. For some of my mother's customers, the trick was to make a new garment out of the old: from bits and pieces of unraveled dresses, coats and skirts. Mami was an expert at renovating old clothing as well as making new clothing from scratch. I was glad that she did not need to leave our house, instead of empty rooms I liked to come home from school to find Mami there, alone or with customers. I had enough of being alone in Yugoslavia.

Next to sewing, the work my mother liked most was to chase the dirt and grime resulting from daily family living. Armed with tools of her trade she would turn from *Schneiderin* to *Hausfrau* as often during the day, or night, as needed. Our surroundings were always neat and polished. Mami was as precise in washing her floors as she was in tailoring a frock. Tati always joked that if she continued to scrub our wooden floor so often it would rot from always being wet. He was right; it eventually did, since it was raw wood.

Not only did she clean our apartment, she and the other *Hausfrauen* in our apartment complex took turns washing down the stairway in the building. It was my mother's chore every fourth week, since there were four families occupying the building.

Because of the many bombed-out buildings surrounding us, Munich was a great place for the large population of rats to live: under and over the rubble still covering half of the city. Most preferred the dusty blackness of the brick hovels outside our building, but some liked the cleaner surroundings of our hallways instead and took up residency there.

When the ladies cleaned the hallway steps, the rodents usually scurried out of their way. There were at least a half a dozen *Ratze* living under our roof. The rats came in different sizes, some as big as a small dog or a cat. Battle scars and loss of fur marked their bodies. They were recognizable by these emblems and given names with their trademark in mind. Mami sometimes called them our *Haustiere* or house pets and mentioned which one she saw this time around when scouring the stairs.

Under our apartment was a dank, old-fashioned cellar. The floor was packed-down dirt and the walls were made of large cut stones. Tati had made a large wooden box, filled with sand, where we stored our small supply of potatoes and sometimes a few carrots, if we were lucky enough to have any.

It was my job to go down and get the vegetables when Mami needed them. I was scared every time. I would walk hesitantly down the small set of dark stairs and into the black hallway. The only light was in the small room at the back of the cellar. I didn't always manage to find the light switch right away, it was located just on the right hand side of the entrance door. And even so, the naked light bulb shed very little light, not more than a small candle.

I got the object I came for as quickly as possible, I was always afraid that one of our "house pets" would run over my feet. Luckily I never encountered one of the large rats.

My mother, who is afraid of rodents, toads, or small unsavory critters of any kind, took the rat problem in stride. She could do nothing but live with it.

Since I was always at my mothers side when she was sewing or doing her housework I never regarded her in any other way except as my mother. She seldom talked about her childhood. That was my fathers department. But one day Mami and I were in the kitchen. She was busy with her work and I sat at the table keeping her company, chatting about this and that. We got on the subject of playing ball. Mami told me when she was a my age, girls played the game of *Abfange* with their *Schürtzel*.

"How can you play catch with an apron?" I asked.

"Kumm, ich zeig dir. – Come I'll show you," Mami said and told me to go get my red ball.

I did as she asked. I didn't want to miss this. I was not used to Mami stopping her work just to play.

She held up the two corners of her apron and told me to toss the ball.

"Oh, that's so easy," I told her a little arrogantly. Anyone can catch a ball like that.

"I'm not going to catch it the way you think. Just watch."

I tossed the ball overhand. Mami lifted the hem of her apron and snared it in mid-air, wrapping the apron over it like a hook.

"Now you do it." She got ready to throw the ball back to me. Since I had only a dress on, I used that as my "hook."

Mami tossed it and I tried and missed. "This is not as easy as I thought," I said.

"Übung macht den Meister," she said laughingly. "Try again." So the two of us played ball in the tiny hallway, laughing and giggling, tossing the small red sphere until I got the hang of it. *"Übung hat mich Meister gemacht,"* like my mother said. Or in English, "practice did make me a master."

This is one of my fondest memories of Mami in Munich. She was a young girl once more, and for just a few minutes the two of us were the same age.

The entrance hallway was the only unused space of our small apartment. By "unused" I mean it had nothing except doorways through which we walked to get from one room to the other.

Usually what fathers do is interesting. A lot more so than whatever mothers do. Is this because children are most often around their mothers and have seen them do their chores a hundred times?

I can recall Tati having to fix something on the bedroom door. I watched, keeping my distance, as he got ready to work on the hinges near the bottom of the door. He had the strangest contraption called a *Schweisser*, and I was curious to see how it worked. It looked like an oblong metal balloon with a bent pipe extending from the top.

Tati got out some matches and lit one and held it to the end of the pipe. As soon as the flame touched the opening, a small bluish flame shot out of the thin tube.

"*Bleib dort stehn – net kum naecheder.* – Stay over there – don't come closer," Tati said. "I don't want to burn you."

I craned my neck to look over his shoulder from three feet away, not knowing what to expect. My father turned a small knob in back of the pipe.

The tiny flame "whooshed" into a fiery bluish tongue as it shot out of the small pipe. Startled, I jumped. The whole hallway was lit in an eerie light. Like the burning blue breath of a dragon, it continued to spit out the flames.

"Are you going to burn the door?" I asked. He laughed and reassured me that he would only *schweiss* together the broken parts. I watched the whole time as Tati worked with the torch until he was finished welding together whatever had needed to be fixed.

The smell of hot metal mixed with flaming butane nipped at my nostrils. Even now I still can remember the odor.

Besides telling stories, Tati loved to sing and whistle. One of the nicest times we had together was Sunday afternoon or evenings when we sang together. The first song he taught me was:

Regentropfen, die an dein Fenster klopfen,
Das merke Dir, es ist ein Gruss von Mir.
Sonnenstrahlen, die an dein Fenster fallen,
Das merke Dir es ist ein Kuss von mir.

Translated:
Raindrops knocking on your windowpane —
     take note of them —They are greetings from me.
Sunbeams streaming through your windowpane —
     take note of this — It is a kiss from me.

I considered this to be my song from Tati. I took its words literally.

Sitting around the table in the kitchen we all joined in and sang along. Included on our song list were all the old German folk songs as well as the popular songs of the day: "*Mariandl, -andl, -andl*" "*Du Bist die Schönste Vom Wörther See*", "*Am Strande Von Rio,*" and the one I liked best of all "*Halt dich Fest, Marie.*" Little did I know then that the melody from that song was also a big hit in America. "Jingle Bells" will stay on the children's pop chart for many more years to come.

Tati told us his favorite song was *"Möwe Du ziehst in die Heimat."* He sang that song in concentration camp when things got too hard to bear. It tells the story of a lonely sailor out at sea. And when he sees the seagulls flying up in the sky, he sends the following message back home with them:

Möwe, du ziehst in die Heimat.
Grüss sie recht herzlich von mir.
All meine guten Gedanken
Reisen stets Heimwärts mit dir.

Translated:
Seagull, you're returning back to my home.
I send my greeting along with you.
All my good memories and wishes
Travel back home with you.

Although I was not even ten years old, I fully understood how my father must have felt during those times of despair when he sang *"Möwe du Ziehst in die Heimat."* We had all been there.

I had slept most of the day and my body hurt all over. I had *Die Grippe* – the flu. Mami tried to get me to eat something but I just didn't feel like eating. Every part of my body ached, but my throat hurt the most.

Even if I had been served one of my favorite meals *Dampfnudl mit Vaniliesosse,* I think I would have refused it. *Dampfnudl,* a Bavarian dish that Mami had learned to make in Munich, was a big dumpling, bigger than my fist, covered with a sweet vanilla sauce. The vanilla sauce was what made the dish my *Leibspeiss* – my favorite.

The next morning Mami placed the thermometer under my arm to take my temperature again. A few minutes later she checked it and said I still had a fever and couldn't go to school.

Being sick didn't make me happy, but not being able to go to school didn't make me sad either. Seppi came into the bedroom and said Mami had written the teacher a note to explain why I would not be in school. He held the piece of paper in his hand and asked if he should read what it said.

"O.K. if you want to," I said.

"I don't know if she will be able to read this," my brother said in an alarming tone.

"What do you mean?" I said, swallowing the bait.

"Listen to what it says." My ever-teasing brother started to read: ".......UARF EBEIL

..ELUHCS RUZ THCHIN NNAK DNU EPPIRG EID TAH ESILE EID.

"That's not what it says," I interrupted. "It doesn't make any sense."

"That's what Mami wrote," he insisted and continued to read the strange sounding note.

I yelled at him to stop. Mami heard the commotion and came into the room. *"Was is do los? Warum schreit ihr so rum?"* "What's going on here? Why are you screaming around?" she scolded.

"The excuse you wrote is written all wrong," I fretted. "The teacher won't understand it."

"What do you mean she won't understand it?" She took the note from my brother, looked at it, fixed her gaze on Seppi and asked, "What did you tell your sister?"

"Nothing. I just read the note out loud to her – backwards."

Mami told my brother to hurry up and see to it that he got himself off to school.

"You want to know how to learn to read backwards quickly?" Seppi asked just before he left the room. "Hold the writing next to a mirror and read what you see there."

My brother went off to school with the note, and I, snuggled between the covers, drifted off to sleep.

I deduced that Seppi was quite smart to be able to turn the word around in his head as he had done. And when I felt better, I was going to practice that mirror trick and be just as good as he was at backwards reading.

Like most siblings, my brother and I loved and disliked each other at the same time, fought one minute and the next minute behaved kindly towards each other. If any one ever said anything against Seppi, I was right there to defend him. And he did the same for me.

Where was Seppi? It was getting dark and he had been gone all day. I knew Tati and Mami were worried and so was I.

No one had seen him since morning when Mami had given him the chore of polishing the boots he had borrowed from a neighbor to wear for *Fasching* – Mardi Gras. He complained and said he didn't see why he had to polish them.

He was told by my mother in no uncertain terms that the job had better be finished when she came back. Then she left the house to do some errands. When she returned, the boots were still on the floor, untouched, and Seppi was gone.

The day turned into evening and still no sign of my brother. The three of us sat at the dinner table eating but not tasting the food. I listened silently as my parents worried out loud.

"Wu is' er nur dran? – Where is he?" Mami asked no one in particular. They wondered if he was lost. Worse yet, maybe he had met up with the unspeakable misfortune that parents fear the most, especially when their child is not where he is supposed to be and the moon is already high in the sky.

I was just as worried as they were. What if he never comes back? What if he is dead? These thoughts kept going through my head as I lay in my bed, unable to fall asleep. It was close to ten o'clock and still no Seppi. I strained to hear the smallest noise that entered the room as I lay motionless in the darkness, waiting to hear the front door open. At last I definitely heard what I had been waiting for; the rattle of the door knob.

Finally I fell asleep with a lighter heart when I heard my brother's voice and my parents' raised voices, which were then muffled as they went into the kitchen and closed the door. Seppi was not hurt; otherwise he would have been brought into the bedroom right away and not yelled at in the kitchen.

Almost a teenager, my brother was going through one of his rebellious stages. He had determined he was being bossed around one too many times and decided to run away from home.

He left boots and polish behind and set out see the world. When he reached the *Bahnhof* he waited for the next train in. From the platform, he watched as the passengers got off the train and started to leave the station. One of the last people to get off was a kindly looking old gentlemen. Getting his courage up, my brother walked over to him and told him he had lost his money to go home. The man took pity on my brother gave him money to buy a ticket "to get back home." He went to the ticket window and bought a ticket for the amount of money he had. It only bought him a seat on the train to the next town.

He got off the train and walked around the town the entire day. When evening approached, Seppi had a change of heart and wanted to be back home.

He sat at the train station trying to figure out how to get back to Munich. Since it was winter, it got dark early. Night was upon him and he was still at the train station. A man had noticed that my brother was in trouble, he had been at the station a long time. The stranger asked if he could be of some help.

By this time my brother had lost all his courage and desire for freedom and told the man the truth. The two went to the window and the man bought Seppi a ticket back to Munich. When the train came into the station, my brother got off, but was afraid to go straight home. Finally getting his nerve together he decided to take his punishment like a man.

When he walked in the door, he was sure he was going to get the licking of his life. He was wrong. My parents were so happy to see him that after a few sharp words and a lecture, he was sent to bed.

Later my father told my mother that he thought Seppi had been punished enough. Going without food all day was a penalty to fit the crime. When I heard this, I was flabbergasted by their leniency, I was ready to kill him for all the worry he caused.

Weihnachten was here again. All day I anticipated the first evening star in the winter sky. I was ready to walk through our bedroom door to see what enchantment was waiting there for me this year.

When finally the moment had come I slowly walked through the bedroom door with the rest of the family behind. The tree was just as lovely as it had been the year before, but this time my eyes darted to the place underneath it to see what *Christkindl* had left there. There under the flickering lights was a gleaming, white doll stroller with four solid wooden wheels. The stroller handle was made just the right height for me to push my doll Sepp around like a real mother did her real baby. For my brother there was a solid wood *Schliede* to go schussing down on snow covered slopes. The sled seemed so big in our small room.

Christkindl was extra good to us that year, we had not expected anything this big. My rag doll with his big grin and red cheeks looked as happy in his new buggy seat as I felt.

The next day Mother Nature co-operated and covered our streets with the a thin layer of snow. Although the cover of snowflakes was not deep, enough came down from the sky to try out a new sled.

As children, we often don't realize what parents do to make us happy till we grow up and fulfill our own children's dreams. *Christkindl* had a lot of assistance from a certain "helper" to make and deliver the doll buggy and sled under our tree. The assistant's wife also did a lot of the work in fulfilling wishes and dreams in the name of *Christkindl*, just like parents all over the world do.

Mutter, my father's mother, had been married at the age of sixteen to Franz Haag. They had two sons by the name of Franz and Peter. Shortly after Peter was born, her husband was killed in a train accident. Mutter was remarried in her late thirties to Johann Hugery and had another son Johann, my father. My father's half brother Peter, had left home at the age of seventeen to seek his fortune in *Amerika*. Tati was only eight years old when his brother left, so he hardly knew him. But the brothers kept in touch through letters.

As a teenager my father bought a camera and became a photography buff. Since he also developed the pictures himself he sent many family photographs to his brother. Lucky for us, when we came to America Peter Onkel gave them back. Since all of the pictures were taken before 1940 there were none of me. I was told during the war Tati's hobby came to a halt for film was almost impossible to get.

One day we received a package. We stood around the big fabric covered box that had our name and address written on it in big block letters. In the upper corner on the right side was another address. Underneath the address were written three big letters ... U. S. A. They stood out large and clear, proclaiming to the whole world that the package came from the land of plenty.

"*A Packet vom Peter Onkel,*" Tati announced when he carried it into the bedroom and placed it on Seppi's bed. A package from Uncle Peter in America.

"Why is the package sewn-up in cloth?" I asked. "So it won't rip open easily," I was told.

Quickly Mami got her scissors and cut apart the large thread stitches – careful not to cut into the covering, for the fabric could be made into dish towels, aprons or other simple household items.

Mami took out each item, ceremoniously held it up and passed it to

Tati. Although the box was not big, it was packed tightly. It was hard to believe that so much could be contained in that small carton.

There was clothing and boxes of food as well as one box of American Family Soap Flakes. This made Mami especially happy, the only soap available was a hard, gritty, grey bar soap. It was like the Lava soap we use here in America for grimy hands. We used this for bathing as well as washing our clothes. I remember Mami, who washed all our clothes by hand, always complaining about having to wash with this poor excuse for soap.

Inside my mother's treasured box of soap was concealed a small fortune in American cigarettes. My clever relatives had opened the box and re-sealed it so that it was almost impossible to detect it had been opened. Back in the late forties, a pack of *Ami Zigaretten* was almost worth its weight in gold. Tati was able to trade them in for a lot of food.

"Schau mol, a Kann Kakau." Tati held up the can in elation. A can of cocoa. I had never had cocoa before and didn't know what it was. But I soon found out. It was the best part of the whole *Packet von Amerika.*

The packages from Onkel Peter were not the only ones we got from America, once my brother received one from a teenage girl.

One day Seppi came home all excited from school carrying a *Paket.* It was only a small 12" x 12" square box that came all the way across the ocean from *Amerika.* He had received a package from *Karitas.* Everyone in his class had received such a gift from Catholic Relief of America.

We gathered around my brother and watched him take out each item one by one. The first item in the parcel was a letter written by a young girl. The letter was meant just for him. She had written that she was sixteen and attended high school. Since my brother could only read German I believe it was in German or a translation.

The rest of the contents were soap, a toothbrush, toothpaste and other toiletries a boy could use. Seppi beamed as he held each one up for us to see. The girl across the ocean had made my brother very happy.

It's too bad that people in America could not have been present when the packages sent to families like us were opened. The young sender of my brother's parcel would have been just as delighted at our joy as we were.

Many people received these kinds of packages from religious groups such as Catholic Relief as well as protestant organizations.

Not only did the "gift" provide us with ordinary everyday needs that were not readily available, it also showed that someone cared.

My father's brother Franz and nephew Hansi were drafted into the German army in 1943. A few months later my father heard that his nephew was declared missing in action and his brother a prisoner of war.

One evening when I was already tucked in for the night, there came a knock on our front door. A few seconds later I heard Tati call out joyously, *"Mein Gott, Franz..."* Loud, happy voices echoed throughout our apartment. Mami came and got me up from my bed.

"Dr Franz Onkel is do." she informed me. "Get up! *Onkel* is here."

Who is this *"Onkel"?* I wondered as I entered the kitchen.

An older man sat at the table talking. As soon as he saw me, he picked me up, hugged and kissed me.

"Elsa, Du bischt jo schun so gross!" He laughed. "You're such a big girl now. The last time I saw you, you were only three years old."

I didn't remember ever seeing this nice, red-cheeked man before.

"You don't remember your uncle do you?" Mami asked. "He's *Tant's* husband."

"Tant" was in the concentration camp with us, so I knew her, but not this gentleman.

The next day Onkel sat happily reminiscing with my family and catching up with all the news since we last were together. I just stood and listened, as I often did when old family friends came to visit. Everyone remembered me, but I didn't know them at all.

The more I listened and got to know my Onkel, the more I liked him. Especially after he pulled out his wallet and handed me a 50 pfennig piece (about 12¢). Seldom did I possess this much money. Now I could buy more than a piece of hard caramel. Why, I could even buy *Schokolat.*

Much later, I got to know Onkel very well, for he and Tant also came to America a year after we did. I never called my uncle and aunt by any other name except Onkel and Tant. We spent almost all important family events together. Tant was there along with my mother when I picked out my wedding gown, and I danced with Onkel on their 50th wedding anniversary.

In 1946 my father met a man who was at Hansi's side when he was shot in battle. Although my father knew that his nephew had been killed during the war, he never had the heart to tell his brother or sister-in-law. Both my uncle and aunt died hoping that their only child was still alive.

In a corner of our bedroom behind the door, was a place where I was the ruler. In an area no bigger than two feet wide by one foot deep was my *Puppen Haus*. This doll house with no walls, roof or doors, had only furniture: beautiful wooden chairs, a table, and a bed, all made as if they were for real people.

The day I received the doll house furniture, I came home from school calling out my usual greeting to Mami. She answered from behind the closed kitchen door. I opened the door and walked in.

"Mach die Tier zu," Mami told me. So I turned around and grabbed hold of the door latch to close the door behind me. As I did so, out jumped a beautiful young lady with dark brown, wavy, hair that tumbled over her shoulders. At first I was so startled, I did not know what to say.

"Kennscht' mich net?" said the young woman. "Don't you know me?"

"It's Katili," Mami told me.

"Katili" — the name became clear in my head and I recognized her as one of my *Tanz Lehrerinnen im Lager*. She, along with Marie, was our so-called dance teacher. She had taught us to waltz in the camp yard.

Katili, my second cousin, had changed a lot since I saw her last. She was beautiful. As she stood there in front of me I remember thinking that she was the loveliest girl I had ever seen. Now eighteen, ten years older than I, she had a smile that beamed like a ray of sunshine.

She had a present for me from her father, Niklos Schüssler, Mami's cousin. She handed me a bag filled with small paper-wrapped parcels. I took them out one by one and unwrapped them. I had never seen anything like this: chairs, a table and a bed. Small enough to fit into my hand. The wooden furniture would have been perfect for *Daumelanger Hans* – Tom Thumb.

I spent many hours behind our bedroom door in my make-believe world. I owned no dolls, but that was OK. I was good at make-believe and I made a whole family out of cardboard.

Like my father, my mothers' cousin worked with wood. He was a *Drechsler*, working with a lathe to carve wood into rounded objects; furniture, spindles for staircases, doors, or windows.

Kathi, as we call her now, lives in upper Wisconsin and still is as lovely as she was then. Her smile is what makes her so.

School was still not my favorite thing in life. Our large classroom had a high ceiling that did not let a single whisper go unheard. If the teacher or a pupil spoke, the walls echoed every syllable.

I was a quiet student and hardly ever talked to my neighbor for fear of receiving a *Bratzl*, a crack of the ruler over the back of the hand. I outgrew that fear and at the end of the school year, I got my first and only one because of talking in class.

Five rows of double desks occupied most of the room. We sat two on one bench seat. Each desk had two ink wells. In first grade we used our *Tafel und Griffel* to write most of the time. But once in a while we used pen and ink instead of slate and slate pencil. I was an expert at making *Tinten Klecks* on almost every piece of paper I handed in. Try as I might I always blemished the blue-lined paper with an ink spot and got the ink all over my fingers.

In the front of the room, on a raised wooden platform, was the teacher's desk. To one side was a blackboard and a row of high, curtainless windows. On the other side was a high narrow door, it's varnish cracked with age and next to it was a pendulum clock that told me how much longer until I was free to go home.

My first grade teacher seldom let a smile cross her face. Her sullen black eyebrows were stern over her dark unsmiling eyes, and her lips were a straight line.

Because we had come to Germany late in the school year, everyone in my class was much better at reading and writing. I was never going to close the gap. In my young, naive mind I had decided that I was *dumm*. And when the school year ended and the teacher told my parents it would be best for me to repeat first grade, I had proof. I *was* stupid, never saying out loud how inadequate I felt deep inside, I kept it to myself.

At first I ran right home after school. I was not happy during the school day, and I missed being at home. I was so painfully shy and afraid that someone might laugh when I spoke because I didn't have that Bavarian twang. I hardly spoke to anyone. Everyone thought I was different. But little by little I began to speak like a native born Münchner.

Soon I would speak the correct dialect needed for my surroundings, automatically. Wherever my body was, that's how I talked—*In der Schule: Hochdeutsch. Aus der Schule: Bayrisch. Derhahm: Schowisch.* – In school: High German. Out of school: Bavarian. At home: our Swabian dialect.

Tati and Mami decided that Seppi and I should go *zum Hort* – to a day care center, not because we needed watching, but because of the food. It was government run and for that reason they got extra food supplies from the *Ami's* – short for American.

My brother and I fought against going to the day care center but at the end we lost. Seppi and I now had to go down to the school basement every day after school.

I had worried unnecessarily. There was nothing to fear. I was welcomed and became part of the after-school group in no time.

There we did our homework, played games, did crafts and had books to read. They even had comic books like Mickey Mouse and Donald Duck. The pictures were easier to read than regular books, you could guess by the picture what was being said or what went on.

Fräulein Ascherl was the youngest, prettiest and nicest teacher I had ever seen. She had a soft voice which she hardly ever raised. But Fräulein Ascherl was not always the teacher; she traded days with an old teacher who was very stern when it came to eating your food.

Every Friday we had the same menu:

Powdered Scrambled Eggs
Boiled Leaf Spinach
Rice Pudding

The eggs were rubbery and dry, but the least of the three evils. I managed to get them down first. The spinach was soggy and tasteless. It was like eating cooked grass. The *reiskoch* or rice pudding reminded me of the barley that swam in the *Grauplsupp* in concentration camp. The thought of having to swallow it closed up my throat.

Every Friday I sat at the table with the square of rice pudding on my plate staring back at me. Slowly I'd break the grains apart, with my fork pick them up one at a time and put them in my mouth. Like it or not I had to eat it. I hated Fridays.

Ferienzeit was here, summer vacation, the best time of the year for me. School ended in the middle of July, after my birthday, which was on the tenth. I was free for six weeks. That is, almost free: we still had to go to *Hort*, but that wasn't so bad. Every day we went on an outing. Fräulein Ascherl took us swimming at the *Schwimmbad*, the swimming pools, located in a park not far from the Isar river.

There were two pools, one shallow and the other deep. I always went in the shallow pool. Although I could not swim, I loved the water and I was not afraid to venture in as far as my short legs took me. Sometimes I stood at the edge of the deeper pool and watched as people swam or jumped in.

One day after lunch, as I stood watching everyone, two hands reached out in back of me and gave me a shove, the next thing I knew I was under water. I was suspended in liquid, my feet did not touch the bottom of the pool. Frantically I thrashed around in the blurry blueness. Muffled, gurgling sounds rang in my ears as I kicked and clawed, trying to surface. I tried to hold my breath but water entered my nose and mouth. It seemed an eternity until a hand reached out from above and plucked me out of the water.

A man, grabbed me and sat me on the cement edge of pool. I coughed up the water and continued to cough. "Are you all right?" he asked. I nodded "You shouldn't be near the deep pool if you can't swim, *Kleine,*" he said. Fearful that I might be yelled at if I told anyone, I scurried into the wading pool as if nothing had happened and I played in there for the rest of the afternoon. Fräulein Ascherl never knew and neither did anyone else. From that day on, I never stood at the edge of the deep pool again.

This episode didn't make me fear the water. I still loved it, and when I was twelve, I even taught myself to swim in a small lake in Macy, Indiana.

Along one side of the Isar river was a pathway. Located on one side was a park with trails snaking between trees and bushes. On the other side of the walkway was a stony bank that sloped gently down toward the river. Tufts of tall grass grew sparsely here and there between the rocks. Across the river, on the other side, was a high, grey, cement blocked retaining wall. On that high bank one saw a city street with its local traffic of bicycles, horse drawn carts and, once in a great while, an auto.

I sometimes went swimming in the river if my brother took me along. The water was very cold and the part where we swam was quite shallow. Actually, I waded and my brother swam. Our day care group never swam in the Isar.

We usually went hiking through the wooded area. When we came to a grassy clearing we stopped to play ball, pick berries or just tumble in the grass, practicing our somersaults and handstands. I was getting quite good at standing and walking on my hands. This was something I could do better than Seppi. He couldn't even get his feet off the ground. We also looked for *Dickkoep* – tadpoles – in small pools of water. They intrigued me. It was hard to believe that they'd turn into frogs one day.

In a large clearing stood a round, short-trunked tree we called *Mehlkirsche* in our Karlsdorfer dialect. I don't know what it was called in proper German. *Mehlkirsche*, literally translated, means flour cherries. The fruit was mealy and sweet-tart. It looked a lot like a very tiny crab apple and tasted somewhat like one.

The first time I stood under that tree and sank my teeth into its fruit, the flavor awoke a memory deep within me. I remembered a time long ago when I was two or three years old...Tati opening the kitchen door, carrying a branch loaded with *Mehlkirsche*. Handing it to me he said, *"Des is for mei Madl.* – This is for my girl," and as small as I was, I knew that could have been no one else but me.

We went on outings every week but most of the time we spent in a make-shift playground that was really nothing more than a construction yard storage area. This was the closest I had ever come to playing in a playground.

In the middle of the fenced-in yard stood a large old pear tree; it's fruit was big, sweet and bountiful, and all you had to do was climb up and pluck as much as you could carry. Seppi climbed out on a large limb, picked a few pears, and stuffed them in his shirt. I'd wait impatiently for him to descend and share his treasure with me.

The taste of the green, crisp, juicy, sweet pears from that tree is almost impossible to describe. No fruit of its kind has ever come close to the luscious flavor of the pears my brother took down from those branches. It was also here in the play yard that I perfected my hand stands.

Frau was in charge of our group as we once more played at the play lot. I didn't like her as much as Fräulein Ascherl. She was older and didn't put up with much nonsense. She never yelled at me, but I watched my step around her.

I played in the sand box and helped build a large *Schloss*. But I got tired of having someone always get in my way as I tried to build up my side of the castle, so I decided to join the others at the slide. Our slide was nothing more than a stack of corrugated sheet metal. With so many little behinds skidding down, the metal had become extremely slick. We were always careful to sit in the center, the edge was very sharp. This time, I sat down hastily, with my leg hanging over the side. I landed hard on my seat and was ready to get up when someone yelled, *"Schau! Ihr Bein, Sie hat sich geschnitten.* – Look at her leg, she cut herself." My right leg had a gash so deep that I could see my raw flesh. I screamed, even though the gash didn't hurt.

Everyone crowded around. Frau rushed over and knelt at my side. As soon as she saw the wound she covered it with her clean handkerchief. She picked me up and rushed out the gate and hurried to the hospital. The next thing I remember is lying on a hard, cold table with two or three people around me. On the ceiling was a large round mirror in which everything looked tiny and far away and upside down. Trembling, I tried very hard not to cry but fear got the best of me. Someone wiped my forehead and told me *"Keine Angst, Kleine, bald ist's wieder gut."* I began to calm down. "Don't be afraid, little one, soon everything will be all right." I felt them rub or wash my knee and shin. I remember thinking that my legs were all dirty from playing in the sand. Then I felt something tugging just below my knee. I tried to watch in the mirror, but the image was too small.

After a few days at home I went back to day camp. Everyone was happy to see me, Frau gave me a little present, a small porcelain animal. She said she was sorry I got hurt and was happy to see I was better.

The scar is still visible below my right knee, a permanent souvenir of my summer days in Munich.

In Europe, little girls wore a *Schürzel* or a smock like apron, over their dresses. My mothers magic touch made mine especially pretty, with ruffles and big roomy pockets. The one I liked the best was white cotton with small blue polka dots.

I wore it that morning to day camp. We were going on our weekly outing, but before we left we received a special treat. The minute I saw the teacher take out the brown wrapped, rectangular shaped object I knew what was in store. I had only had a Hershey Bar once before. The first time I received this prize was when we went to visit Michl Batshi.

He was the uncle of my father's half brother, Franz. Although I had never met him before I knew instantly that Michl Haag was a nice man when he greeted us at the door with a big smile. He had only one room in a narrow, three-story apartment building across from the park, but in this room were many mysterious boxes. I didn't think anything unusual was hidden in these containers until he offered me something I had never had before. He asked if I'd like some *Schokolat.*

I didn't know what to say. I didn't know what chocolate was. Not waiting for me to say yes or no, he held out a brown, paper wrapped rectangle with silver writing on it. I took it and thanked him.

I read the silver letters: they spelled Hershey. I pulled off the outside wrapper. Then I opened the white paper that was folded over the chocolate bar. A delicious aroma rose to my nostrils. I had never smelled anything so good in my life. I took a small bite. The sweetness melted in my mouth. I savored every bite, as I slowly ate the whole thing. There must have been magic in all those boxes, I have been hooked on this chocolate taste ever since.

I have asked my father how this nice man acquired all these Hershey Bars. His answer was that Michl Haag "dabbled a little in the black market." This was not unusual after the war.

Now for the second time I held heaven in my hand.

"You may eat it before we leave," Fräulein Ascherl informed us. Everyone opened theirs. I wanted to look forward to the moment of sheer enjoyment for a little longer, so I tucked my Hershey Bar safely in my *Schürzel Sack* for lunch.

We walked two by two to the woods by the Isar river. Marching next to my partner I thought of nothing else but the chocolate bar in my apron pocket.

The hot, sticky morning seemed to drag on and on. When lunch time came, I gulped down my drink and wolfed down my sandwich faster than ever.

Now I was ready to retrieve my Hershey Bar. Full of anticipation I stuck my hand in my pocket, but instead of a candy bar I had a handful of chocolate sauce. What a trick the summer sun had played on me! I took my apron off, turned my pocket inside out and licked off what I could. I couldn't let a treasure like that go to waste.

The best part of our *Sommer Ferien* was finally here. I had waited for this day since summer vactation started. Seppi and I were going on a day's excursion *zum Sternbergersee.* The Sternberger Lake was located in the mountains, just outside of Munich. This was the first time that I had ever been out of the city without my mother or father.

The train whizzed by the city houses and soon we were out in the country. Fields gave way to mountainsides, our train entered a small village. The houses were different from the ones in the city, with little wooden shutters that had small heart cut outs and other decorations.

We came to our stop, and we walked to the *See*. The lake looked like a shiny mirror. After swimming we walked up a hill were we ate our lunch under a cluster of pine trees. I ate slowly as I looked around and enjoyed the smell of the trees and the cool breeze dancing all around us. I loved being in the country.

After lunch we hiked up a winding footpath that led to a small church. Fräulein Ascherl told us to be very quiet as we looked at the beautiful things inside.

I had thought our *Kapuziner Kirche* was magnificent but this little church in the mountain was more beautiful. Gold decorated the ceiling and walls. The statues were rich in color. I thought to myself, this is what heaven must look like.

The summer of 1949 was the last summer that we spent in Europe. It was also the best one I ever had. Next year's summer was still far off. I had no idea that I was going to be thousands of miles away, struggling to become an American while still keeping part of my European heritage.

CHAPTER
18

Friends

Our apartment was on the main floor and across from us lived the two widowed sisters of Tersep's Kathi, the neighbor my father met that first day in Munich.

One of the sisters had pre-school twin girls and the other had a fifteen year old boy named Heinrich. I still remembered the twin girls from concentration camp when they were only babies. My mother always said she was amazed that they lived through that ordeal, for most infants died like my father's cousin Baltasar's infant son, who was born in the summer of 1945. I remembered how his mother held him and walked the floor as he cried constantly. He was so tiny and thin. He only lived four months until he died in his mother's arms from diarrhea and malnutrition.

Above us lived Tersep's Kathi Tant's daughter Kathi, and her husband Ignatz Hefferle, who had been recently married. Because of the housing shortage his single brother Josef lived with them. I called them Kathi Tant and Naatz Onkel, but Josef I just called Sepp. In late 1948 Kathi Tant had a baby girl. They named her Theresia – Terri for short. Next to them lived Herr und Frau Ziessler, with their children, eight-year old Käthe, and her brothers Otto seven, and Richard six. Käthe Ziessler, my first best friend that I can remember, lived upstairs from me. She was a whole year older – eight going on nine – stronger, hardier and a whole head taller. Compared to her, I looked more than just one year younger. I was small and skinny as a bean pole.

One of the neighbors from the front building asked my mother if there was something wrong with me. I was much too "thin" for a normal child and she should feed me better. My mother was very upset that anyone would even think that she was not giving me as much as she could.

Although my family's food supply was meager, I can't recall ever going to bed hungry, as I had in concentration camp. My father did his best to keep us fed. Money was a big obstacle, but even if one had money, food was rationed. For example, one egg per family was all that was allowed weekly. If the egg was used up the first day, no more were available for the next six days. Bread was also a commodity that one could not get enough of. One loaf had to go a long way. If a homemaker didn't know how to make do, hunger always waited at the door.

Once when Frau Ziessler wasn't at home and Käthe, her little brother Richard, and I were alone in their kitchen, Käthe said, "Elsa, I want to show you something special." She headed for the pantry. "We have a *Zitrone.*"

"What's that?" I asked, following her. She opened the pantry and plucked something yellow and oval from the shelf, holding it up for me to see.

"This," she exclaimed. Lemon in hand she went back to the kitchen, with me and Richard right behind.

Käthe got out a knife. "You're not going to cut it, are you?" I asked.

"Of course I am!" she said. "You want to try it, don't you?" And she cut the lemon in half.

With a small spoon she scooped *Zucker* out of a bowl, she sprinkled the sugar on the lemon and bit into it. She slurped the juice, smacked her lips and pronounced it delicious. "Now you try." She handed it to me. I hesitated, but then I, too, took a bite.

The sweet-sour liquid was like honey on my tongue. I had never tasted anything like it before. "Have another bite," she said. So I did.

"Hey let me, I want a taste too," Richard started to whine. *"Ja, ja du kannst ah.* – Yes, you can have some too," His big sister reassured him. I gave him the rest of the lemon half and he finished it all.

Then my friend took the other half of lemon, sugared it, and shared it, fair and square, between the three of us.

A few days later, Frau Ziessler was getting ready to use her precious lemon in a recipe, but it was nowhere to be found. With a little deduction she discovered who had made the rare fruit disappear. And we found out it was not all right to have eaten it all by ourselves.

Food was not something you ate by yourself. Everything was shared with each member of the family, whether it was a small or a large portion. All was equally divided.

For the first time in four years, Mami had enough *Mehl* to prepare her family's favorite recipe: *Strudl*. Flour was hard to come by but Mami had managed to save enough to make this special Sunday meal. I watched in amazement as Mami started to pull the strudl dough over the cloth-covered table top.

"How do you do that?" I asked her.

"Don't you remember?" she said. "Come on, help me like you did back home." I started to pull and stretch the dough as I was instructed, trying hard not to make a hole. I loved the cool feel of it, as I slipped the palm of my hands underneath the dough, coaxing it to the end of the table top.

"It's so thin that I can see through it." I said in wonderment.

"That's what makes a good *Strudlteig.*" Mami said. "If the dough isn't transparent it won't be flaky."

The aroma rose from the baking *Strudl* in the oven, making my mouth water with anticipation. Finally the treasure was brought to the table. I poked my fork into the crisp, thin crust and raised the flaky morsel to my lips. It seamed to melt in my mouth. I could not remember tasting anything this good ever. After the meal we even had leftovers for another time.

We were expecting Sunday guests that afternoon. Mami told me not to mention anything about the *Strudl*, we didn't have enough for everyone.

Because our kitchen was so small, we often used our bedroom as a sitting room. I sat next to Mami on the edge of the bed, listening quietly as everyone talked. All afternoon, all I could think about was that *Strudl* in the cupboard. It seemed to be calling me.

"Mami, ich hab Hunger," I whispered. Mami didn't seem to hear me. "Mami, I'm hungry." I whispered again, a little louder. "I want some *Strudl*. My mother leaned towards me and told me "not now." That wasn't what I wanted to hear. "But I'm s-o-o-o hungry." I whined louder. "What does she want?" one of our guests inquired.

"Oh, it's nothing," Mami said. I had picked up on my mother's irritation, but being a pesty child, I ignored it. I repeated my request a few minutes later. I wanted a piece of that *Strudl* right then and now.

Mami glared at me when the company once more asked what I wanted. She said that it was nothing and continued with the conversation. By her tone of voice I could tell that I had pressed my luck too far.

After good-byes were said and everyone had left, Mami gave me *Strudl*. My bottom was warmed up for quite a while.

We have often laughed over this incident. Since then, we have had *Strudl* many times. In fact, it has become a family tradition to make *Strudl* every Valentine's Day and on my father's birthday. We usually make more *Strudl* than for just one meal. Now we would have enough leftover *Strudl* to serve all of our former guests and then some.

What a delicious aroma came from the frying pan. The smell of Sunday dinner was so good I could hardly wait till Mami brought it to the table. *Schweinekarmanadl* was on the *Speisekarte* today. Meat was seldom on the menu and to have Mami place one whole crisp, flour-coated pork chop on my plate was heaven.

Sundays were special. Tati or Seppi made a trip down the street to the small *Paulaner Brauerei* at the corner of Heberl and Tumblinger Strassen to buy beer. Most of the time it came from the *Fass* or keg. You had to bring your own *Krug* – pitcher – to the brewery to be filled. Bottled beer was more costly than from the tap. Rarely did it find its way to our table, but today a bottle stood in the middle of the table cloth, waiting to have someone flip its white ceramic top and pour its frothy contents into our glass tumblers. Tati poured a little into my glass. I sipped the foamy cold beer. It tasted good with the meal.

The best part of the pork chop was the fat. I cannot describe in words how delicious this pork fat tasted. It was better than candy. Our bodies were in such need of fat that our taste buds craved it. Craving must have been nature's way of getting the substance most lacking in our diet into our bodies.

I can remember having meat only three times during our two and a half years in Munich. Besides the pork chops we also had meat that my father's uncle, Balsvetter gave us. And once Tante Mitzi shared some meat with us when Onkel Michel went hunting.

I enjoyed both of those meals until I found out that the meat I had eaten had once been a horse and an antelope.

Cooking was a big problem, for not only were the meat, vegetables and bread hard to come by, but so were the staples needed to prepare them. Cooking oil or shortening was one of those items almost impossible to acquire.

I remember how excited Mami was when Tati brought home a small, paper-wrapped bottle he had obtained through a friend. This friend had "connections" with people who knew how to get things not available without ration stamps, better known as a *Schwartzhändler.* Tati told Mami that his friend had gotten this bottle of *Koch Öl* through the Black Market. I listened quietly and conjured up this vision of a dark place where people dressed in black and sold things in secret. Mami created all kinds of dishes with her cooking oil, but after a couple of days something strange began to happen. I remember how my underwear showed strange greasy stains. On wash day Mami discovered that all four of us had this same problem. She told Tati that this must be from the *Koch Öl* he had brought home.

Our stomachs and intestines could not digest this so-called cooking oil. Instead of digesting it, our bodies just let it run through from one end to the other. Nature never intended for man or beast to digest mineral oil.

On the black market, selling is what counted – not the quality of the product.

When my mother reached the end of our food supply, she would send me to the green grocer stand for *Rabarber* – Rhubarb, the cheapest thing one could buy. *Rabarber und Kuche* would be on the menu that night. Stewed rhubarb and dry oatmeal cake had plenty of roughage and no cholesterol, very healthy but no taste. The ideal diet. We never had to worry about too much fat.

Nine of us children lived in the rear building and we were the only ones who played in the courtyard. Loud laughter echoed throughout the canyon-like walls of the buildings as we amused ourselves happily. In the summertime Laura, also joined us, sunning herself and screeching constantly, *"Scheenes Madl, Scheenes Madl,"* boisterous and clear. "Pretty girl, pretty girl." Then she'd laugh, and in the same breath she'd string together a slew of swear words, followed by a clamoring for someone to feed her. She was a beautiful, *Papagei.* Laura was owned by Tersep's Kathi Tant. The parrot had been given to her by the American GI family for whom she was a housekeeper.

One family in the front building had two girls about my age, but their parents wouldn't let them come down into the courtyard to play with us.

Afraid that we *Flüchtlinge* – refugees – might have a bad influence on them.

Although we considered ourselves Deutsche, we were not regarded as true Germans by a lot of people in Germany. They could tell we were Volksdeutsche – ethnic Germans – by our dialect, which was different from any of the dialects in Germany or Austria.

On the other hand, not everyone was biased against us. Herr and Frau Wackebauer were the kindest people anyone could have for neighbors. Frau Wackebauer always greeted us with a *"Guten Morgen"* or *"Guten Tag."* She was plump, with red cheeks. She wore her long hair high on her head. Combs held her curls like a crown. Herr Wackebauer owned a *Dreiradler,* a three-wheeler truck that always stood in front of our curb, the only motor vehicle on the whole street. The only other times trucks were parked on the street was when they delivered goods to the stores. Very few motor vehicles drove through the city streets, bicycles dominated the traffic with an occasional motorbike roaring through.

Käthe and I often wondered what it would be like to ride in Herr Wackebauer's little three wheeler truck. One day as we stood admiring it, Herr Wackebauer came out of the building and asked us if we'd like to go for a ride.

Except for the military truck ride in Austria, I had never been in an auto or truck. We got in and the little truck whisked us around the block. It was a short ride but to Käthe and me it was like no other. Since then I have been in all kinds of motor vehicles. I also have been driving for a long time. But I don't think any other ride can compare to the one with Herr Wackebauer.

Wet, cold water jolted me out of my dreams. There above me stood Käthe's kid brother, still holding the dripping glass over my head. He guffawed loudly, chanting *"Pfingscht-lümmel⁹, Pfingscht-Pfingscht-lümmel"* over and over again. I jumped up from under my wet bed covers and started to swing at him. But before my hand could connect he was out the door and up the stairs. Instead of coming to my aid everyone in my family was just standing there and laughing at Richard's prank.

---

[9] *Pfingscht-Lümmel* translates: *Pfingsten* is Pentecost in German and *Lümmel* is someone lazy, who just lounges around.

"Warum lacht Ihr? – Why are you laughing?" I asked my family angrily, as I stood with my hair and nightgown all wet.

Mami, with towel in hand, started to dry me off and told me that this was an old custom back home in Kernei where Ziesslers came from. If a girl was still asleep late in the morning on "Pentecost Sunday" the boys could sprinkle her with water to wake her up. And I shouldn't be mad, Richard just wanted to perform this ritual to see what it was like back home in his home town.

By then I had calmed down and laughed along with the rest of my family.

No one since has ever awakened me in this fashion again and I'm sure no one ever will. I wonder if Richard still remembers his *"Pfingst Montag"* prank he pulled on his neighbor as well as she does.

Now when I think back I realize how many of our customs have ceased to exist. I'm sure that not very many boys have performed this ritual since we *"Schwowe"* have been scattered all over the world. Even our *Muttersproch* – mother tongue – is slowly dying out. Very few of our children born in the 90's will speak our dialect.

When my family and I were visiting relatives in Germany in 1987, all were amused that our children still spoke the *"Schwowischer"* dialect that they recall their parents and grandparents speaking. Most speak high German or dialects of the people in their "hometown."

On the way back to America our oldest daughter, then twenty one, spoke a truth that is so timely.

"I feel like a walking museum," our daughter said "So many relatives have remarked that they had not heard our dialect spoken in years," Heidi commented.

This same daughter is now a mother. She and her husband Nick, who also happens to be a "walking museum" like his wife, have carried on our language by teaching their sons and daughter to communicate in *"Schwowisch"* as their parents taught them.

I looked back over my shoulder to see who was behind me, but there was only darkness. I didn't see the man who was pursuing me, but I knew he was coming closer and closer. As I ran over the barren, stony field, I had to struggle to lift my feet. It was as if they were in quicksand. I battled to move forward, to get away from the two arms ready to seize me. Panting breathlessly, I tried to move faster, but my legs did not cooperate. They moved as if in slow-motion, and my heart raced wildly.

He was getting nearer, I could feel him just a few inches from my back. Desperately I pushed on.

I came to the curb of a highway. I knew if I crossed over, I would be safe. I tried to cross, but my legs would not move. They became a part of the ground, as if roots had sprouted, anchoring me to the edge of the road.

Now I felt the man's hands on my skin. His fingers arched, grabbing me by the shoulders. I screamed in terror ... and then I woke up.

This dream was so real that it always took me a while to pull myself together. I can't tell you when I first started to dream this nightmare. It must have been after we escaped. The nightmare finally stopped when I was in my thirties.

The fear of the Partisaner coming after me took a long time for me to overcome.

The sun was bright outside as Käthe and I hid behind the entrance doors to the archway. We peeked from behind the dark doorway and waited for an unsuspecting passerby to pick up the candy decoy we had placed on the sidewalk. For the past few days we had been fooling people with our little joke. We took used hard candy wrappers, placed a small stone in the center, re-twisted the paper, and tossed it out on the sidewalk.

Peeking through the archway doors, we watched and waited for the *Zuckerl* bait to hook the first catch. Käthe was the instigator in this game so she had the opening act. In no time someone walked up to the piece of candy, bent down, picked up the "treasure" and rushed off. The unsuspecting victim had no idea that behind the entrance gate two little girls giggled with glee at his expense.

Now it was my turn. I tossed the candy out on the sidewalk and waited behind the doors in the darkened gangway. It seemed to take forever for someone to come along. It was hard to see if anyone was coming from behind my hiding place, so I opened the door and stepped out onto the sidewalk. As I looked up, two piercing dark eyes looked straight into mine. With its dark complexion and black mustache, the face looked just like a Partisaner, and for a moment I thought I was back in camp. Heart pounding, I screamed, turned and ran as fast as I could, past Käthe, through the courtyard, up the three steps and into the safety of our apartment. I cowered behind the open door in the corner of our bedroom for a long time. Listening for his footsteps. It seemed like an eternity until I finally got up the courage to come out from behind the door and venture outside again.

Käthe and I loved to go climbing on the top of the ruins in our neighborhood. Each ruin had its own personality. Those that were on the way to the Theresien Wiese must once have been single family houses, the brick piles were not as high as the ones around our street.

All kinds of things grew out along the sidewalks next to the heaps of rubble. One had grapevines growing along a half fallen-down wall. We always stopped there and pinched off the green tentacle-like tips growing at the end of the plants. We were told that back home they called these *Sauerrambl*. We'd chew them for their sour juice and then spit them out.

Inside one ruin was a patch of ground littered with pieces of broken cement. Struggling out between the concrete were a few scrawny plants called *Rühr-mich-net-an* or touch-me-not. When we ran our fingertips along their middle, they reacted as if they were being tickled, folding their leaves like children pulling in their arms and necks, quivering with soundless laughter. When the leaves relaxed and went back to their original shape, we'd do it again.

The ruin I liked the most was the one with the flowers. They grew in a small clearing five or six feet wide, as if someone had taken the bricks and flung them away from the rest of the rubble to give the colorful flowers a chance to grow. Pansies, petunias and others flowers I didn't even know the names of grew there. They were not wild flowers, wild flowers grew all over the park and the lawns of the houses surrounding it. No, these were garden flowers.

Although no one had ever told me, I knew a garden had been here before the war, because the flowers looked like the kind I remembered growing in Mami's flower beds back home.

Across the big intersection next to the *Postamt* was a *Bunker* which was still intact from the war. It looked like the entrance to an underground garage about three cars wide. At the bottom was a dead end. Only darkness was to be seen when you looked in.

Not once did we go down to the bottom of its darkness. Fear always stopped us and I would not go down more than a few feet. I remembered the dark hole back home during the air raids. I could imagine how people must have hovered here in the dark corners, waiting for the bombs to strike. I didn't know if Käthe was ever in an air raid, we never discussed it. But I was reminded every time I walked passed the post office.

I looked for the bunker when we went back to Munich in 1977. It was no longer there. In its place was the entrance to the *Untergrundbahn* or subway. It was all lit up with bright lights, no trace of what had been before, just like the rest of Göthe Platz. The buildings around it were standing straight and tall, with stores inside them instead of booths outside. And on the opposite corner of the post office stood a new symbol of my adopted country. Tucked between the buildings was a McDonald's just like those in America.

Käthe and I always had fun when the *Frühlingsfest* or *Oktoberfest* was in session. Although our pockets were empty, it cost nothing to wander the fair grounds, but it was even more fun to return when the tents and rides where taken down, then we'd hunt for treasures.

Eyes to the ground, we looked for anything colorful or shiny, pieces of bright balloons, ribbons, even a Pfennig or two. We always hoped we'd find a Mark, but this never happened.

We had been searching for some time and only had found a few pieces of latex, none big enough to make even a small bubble of a balloon, when something sparkling in the grass caught my friend's eye. She bent down and picked it up and let out a screech of joy. *"Ah Uhr, ich hab a Uhr g'fun! –* A watch, I found a watch!" This was too good to be true. The small object in her hand was a square gold watch with only one black strap. The other strap must have broken; that's how the owner lost this prized possession. Although the timepiece didn't tick when Käthe wound it up, and the glass part was cracked and dirty, it was still a watch, the best object we ever found.

A block or so into the middle of Göthe Strasse was a large, three story building. This was the *Spital* where Mami took me to see the *Doktor*. Shortly after coming to Germany, we all had to go to the hospital to see the doctor. Different doctors listened to my chest and poked here and there. Then I was taken to a room with a strange machine to have a *Röntgen* taken. I had no idea what an x-ray was. It didn't hurt; that was good enough for me.

A few days later, we were told that I had a spot on my lungs. Mami told me it was because I had come in contact with people who had tuberculosis in concentration camp. I remember being taken by Mami to the hospital many times to get my lungs checked until the spot was gone.

I was quite familiar with the building for we went to visit Hechele's Kathi Tant there when her Terri was born. I was completely confused as to why she was sick in bed. Mami had told me a day or so before that Kathi Tant had gone to Berlin. And now, a few days later, we were visiting her in the hospital. When I asked Mami why she wasn't in Berlin, my mother ignored my question.

I guess that's what happens when parents make something up instead of explaining where babies come from. Of course, back then, that subject was avoided at all costs in front of children.

I thought I knew everything that went on inside that hospital, so when Käthe said that down in the basement they cut up people, I told her I didn't believe it.

"It's true," she insisted.

"Then show me," I said.

We walked down Göthe Strasse until we got to the hospital. The windows of the basement were ground level. We walked from one to the other but didn't see anything.

Since the window frames contained thick, patterned glass it was impossible to see through them. "How could you see them cut up people?" I asked. "You can't even see in."

"The window was open," Käthe claimed. Still trying to convince me of what she saw, we kept going to every window until we came to the last one. "This one is open," she called back to me; I was lagging behind. "Come on, hurry." Käthe said.

Now I was not so sure that she wasn't right. I didn't know if I wanted to see bodies being cut up. But bravely I walked up to her. The window was open only a few inches. Käthe lay down on the grass. "Look I can see in. I think they're getting ready to cut one up." she said. Just hearing that was enough for me. I had no intention of seeing anyone hacked apart. My imagination was real enough. I told her I believed her and ran home.

Schikago! What a funny name for a *Stadt*. I laughed when Käthe told me where her uncle lived. München sounded much better, I told her.

"It's in *Amerika*; that's why it sounds strange," Käthe said. "Chicago is big, it's bigger than here. It has lots of tall houses, autos and many people."

I had never heard of the place. But my friend's uncle sent her nice things from there – like this big book she and I were coloring in. And the many different colors of *Farbstiften* – colored crayons – that came in this mammoth size box. They all came from Chicago.

I found it strange that the name of a *Malbuch* was *Blondie*. Blondie was German, not English. Why did the book have such a title? Not only was Blond a strange name but how would anyone know if the people were blond or not? There was no color in the book. I told all this to my friend as we continued with our work, stretched out on our stomachs here on the floor. I also found the man strange, with his three hairs sticking out on each side of his head. Maybe people actually looked like that in America.

As you probably guessed by now, the coloring book was from the comic strip characters Blondie and Dagwood.

I wonder if Käthe could tell from my snide remarks that I was just a wee bit jealous of her, since I owned only three or four stubby little colored pencils and no coloring book.

In back of the Theresien Wiese, behind the Bavaria, was a beautiful park with many kinds of bushes and shrubs. One late spring day we discovered a bush that had clusters of berries growing on it, like small black grapes. My friend and I knew that this was Holler. "People use these elderberries to make jams," Käthe informed me. I told her I knew that and I had heard Tante Mitzi talk about how she made the jam. "Let's eat some," she said. We ate until our fingers and lips became purple and went home when we had our fill. On the way back to Göthe Platz we started to feel sick. "Do you think maybe the berries have to be cooked before you can eat them?" Käthe said. "I don't know," I replied. "What if they're poison when they're raw?" we asked at the same time. We rushed through the gates and into our yard.

"You know we might die," Käthe said, as we sat on the ground, leaning against the building. "If we're going to die let's stay out here. Our mothers are going to be angry."

An hour passed and we were still alive. We decided that maybe it would be better to go home to our mothers. Our stomachs still ached, but we probably weren't going to die.

The funny thing was, we didn't particularly like the taste of the little dark berries. Most of the fruit was seeds and its taste was blah. I guess we ate them because they looked good and were there for the taking.

In my present home, I have an elderberry bush growing next to my bedroom window. Every spring when the berries ripen I think of Käthe and our little adventure so long ago.

Friendship was very important to us after the war. That's what gave us a place in the new worlds we had to live in. It was hard to start over again, because there was no turning back to where we were driven from.

Although my family was poor when it came to worldly goods, we possessed something that is worth more than gold – friendship. Our family extended beyond the four of us, we had many adopted brothers, sisters, aunts, uncles and grandparents.

My family's home was always open to our friends. And many people came and spent time with us. I loved it when we had company, but I loved it even more when we went to visit.

I sat patiently at the edge of the bed, waiting for everyone to get ready. This time I had been ready for ages, dressed in my crisp clean dress. We were going to see Starke Lis Basl and Franz Vetter. Sometimes I stayed overnight in their one room barrack. They lived in a refugee camp just outside of Munich, surrounded by a large meadow. Blocks and blocks of connected brownish-grey wooden barracks made up the D.P. camp. Most people had small window boxes to brighten up their drab surroundings.

No fence encircled the camp like *"im Lager"* back home. And every family lived in just one room. If you wanted to use the bathroom you had to go outside. You'd walk along the wooden sidewalk that ran next to the barracks, down to the end of the long wooden buildings, where a separate small barrack stood. A row of sinks and toilets in stalls ran along each side of the room.

I hoped that Franz Vetter would let me listen to his radio. No one else could hear it except for the person who had the earphones on. The earphones made it much more fun to listen to than our radio at home. I could sit with all the adults and not hear one word they were saying, this was grand. That they couldn't hear what was being said into my ears was even finer. It was as if the radio and I shared secrets.

What amazed me most was that Franz Vetter had "made" the radio out of all those funny looking wires and metal pieces.

One other reason I enjoyed going to visit Starke was because of Lis Basl and their daughter Resi. Resi was so pretty with her long, light brown hair flowing down her back, all curled and held back with two combs. She sometimes took me along when she went on errands. Resi always talked to me as if I was much older, asking me what I thought and what I preferred, as if I were twenty years old like her and not just a little girl.

Lis Basl was my favorite person. She always had a smile and a little something sweet for me, even if it was just a hard candy. She loved children. Although she was my mother's older second cousin, she and her husband treated Seppi and me as if we were their *Enkelkinder.* They could not have treated their own grandchildren any better. Whatever they had they were willing to share with us.

When were Mami and Tati going to be ready? Why did they take so long? "Can't you hurry?" I thought.

Finally we were walking out the door, through the courtyard and through the dim archway. But, as we came to the street door, someone opened it from the other side. The bright sunshine streamed in as two people walked through. Smiling down on me was Lis Basl and Franz Vetter's happy face with a warm *"Grüss Gott."* Everyone was happy to see each other. Except me. All day I had waited to go to Franz Vetter and Lis Basl's home, and now they had come to us! I did want to be with them, but not here. Not in our house, but in theirs, by the radio and green grass. I started to cry and complain. I even had a small temper tantrum. Mami and Tati were not too happy with me. They scolded me to be quiet. I would not – and did not – stop.

So like all good grandparents, Lis Basl and Franz Vetter talked my parents into returning with them, to come and visit at their place. Not wanting to continue the debate, my parents reluctantly agreed to head for our visitors' home.

So off we went, all six of us. We walked out the gate to Goethe Platz, got on the streetcar and headed outside the city limits. To visit at Lis Basl and Franz Vetter's Haus, all for *"Dem Klan zulieb,"* Lis Basl said, "Just for the little one's sake." But before we walked out the gate, Tati promised that "little one" something special under his breath: When we returned, I was going to get it. This vow I knew he was sure to keep. Regardless of the consequence waiting for me when we got back to Heberl Strasse #8, I still enjoyed the afternoon.

In Munich, cars were not a common means of transportation during the late forties. Most people either walked or took the *"Trambahn"* to reach their destinations. Practically every main street had a street car line.

I enjoyed standing on the corner and watching people get in and out of the linked cars, sometimes as many as four cars together. The entrance was at the rear of each car and the exit at the front. You would get on, sit down, and wait for the *Schaffner* to come around to collect money for your ticket. The conductor's job was easy when it wasn't rush hour. But when the cars were teeming with passengers, he had his hands full.

During rush hours a street car was a sight to behold. So many people crowded onto the cars that bodies spilled out the back. Like bunches of grapes they dangled on the poles, everyone hanging on for dear life. I never rode the streetcar when it was that packed. I bet many people ended up riding for free.

We rode the streetcar to visit our friends who lived at the edge of the city or past the city limits. Tante Mitzi, my father's former landlady was one of those.

We'd ride until we reached the end of the line at *Waldfriedhof* which was named after the a large cemetery nearby. At the corner was a flower shop, the only flower shop I can recall seeing in Munich, that also sold bushes and small evergreen trees. I found it interesting that one could buy such things in a store. We'd cross the street and walk down a row of large grey stucco buildings until we got to Tante Mitzi's, a three-story high rise apartment building that occupied the entire length of the street. We'd climb the high stairway. Tante Mitzi usually stood at the open door waiting for us with something special on the kitchen table. Sometimes Onkel Michel, Tante Mitzi's *Mann*, was at home, but most of the time she was alone.

Tante Mitzi's apartment also housed an elderly couple who were *Untermieter.* Tante Ina and Onkel Merzl were boarders who rented two small rooms from Tante Mitzi, like my father had before. Tante Ina, like Tante Mitzi, always had a plate of something good waiting for us when we came to visit. I enjoyed being fussed over, pampered and treated special. I spent many an afternoon in the presence of both couples.

One fine spring day Tante Mitzi met us at the door with a surprise. She and Onkel Michel had added a new member to their family, a small black roly-poly puppy.

They were very happy with this small bundle of fur, but I didn't know what to make of him. I was not used to being around animals, especially puppy dogs. Not as many people owned pets then as they do today. After all, food was scarce for people, so one didn't rush out to get one more mouth to feed. Tati had often told me about his dog, Bimbo, back home in Karlsdorf. I didn't remember Bimbo, although we still had him when I was going on four. Here in Munich I sometimes watched as a woman in our neighborhood went for a walk with her two large *Russische Windhunde* on a leash. She more or less ran behind the sleek, long haired, Russian Wolfhounds as they trotted across Göthe Platz.

But this was the first time I had been close to a dog. I pretended indifference, but still kept tabs on him from the corner of my eye.

We went for a walk on this fine sunny day with the little puppy dog on the leash. Tati had his small *Fotoapparat* along. Tante Mitzi thought it would be a good idea if we took a picture of me holding the pup. Everyone coaxed me to do it, telling me that it was only a small dog. Reluctantly I took the dog in my arms.

He wiggled back and forth, twisting his round little pot bellied body around, full of ecstatic energy, as I held on for dear life. He was so joyful to be near me that he slurped a wet kiss on my unsuspecting face. Surprised, I dropped him like a hot potato. Or should I say threw him from me out of sheer fright. The little fellow landed on his tail with a yelp. Tante Mitzi was not too happy with what I did. I was sorry that I displeased her. I didn't mean to throw him, she just didn't understand. I was not as thrilled with his wet rough kiss as he was in giving it to me.

My parents still have the picture of me holding this fuzzy blur of a puppy. And Tante Mitzi forgave me for being so rough with her baby.

Looking down from Tante Mitzi's balcony, you saw a cluster of connected barracks, a few blocks away. These were the living quarters for some of the workers in the *Fabrik* that made furniture. The company that my father worked for owned the barracks, which housed a lot of the refugee cabinet makers employed by them. This company also employed many of my father's friends, including his uncle, Balsvetter, and Heffeles Naatz and Sepp who lived upstairs from us.

Many of our friends lived in these one room *"Flüchtlingslager"* – refugee camps. It was lucky for us that Tati helped rebuild the house we lived in or else we'd have been living in just such a room.

Throughout Austria and West Germany many of these camps housed ethnic Germans who were driven out of Poland, Czechoslovakia, Hungary, Rumania and, of course, Yugoslavia. As I have stated before, around fourteen million were displaced and persecuted.

During the fifties, the camps were replaced with family houses and apartment complexes. Sometimes entire new towns were created.

Tersep's Kathi Tant, worked as a live-in housekeeper for an American soldier. She got the job because she spoke English.

My father spent many a Sunday afternoon visiting Kathi Tant and her family at the Private First Class's family home, as did a lot of people from our home town. The soldier's name was Peter, or Pete as he liked to be called. Pete's family was very friendly. Kathi Tant's friends became their friends. My father and Pete got along quite well. Tati had spend hours at his house before we came to Munich. I've asked my father how they spoke together. He said Pete knew a few words in German, then both guessed some of the others, and used their hands for the rest.

We had to walk a few blocks to get to the beautiful house that Kathi Tant lived in. I loved to go visiting the "Ami's," as we called the American family. Nowhere had I ever seen houses like these. Grass grew in the front and in the backyard. Around our neighborhood there was no space between the houses for grass to grow. Tati said the houses were called Villas. This is where rich people used to live before the war. Pete and his family lived there, as did many other American soldier's families.

The building had two stories. Inside were many rooms. It even had a staircase that led to the bedrooms upstairs. One room had a large door that looked like a window. Walking out that door was so different. It was not like any door that I had ever seen: the whole door was a window. It opened onto a patio with a wrought iron table and chairs.

The room which contained this door had nothing in it except *Spielzeug*, toys of all kinds: balls, toy autos, coloring books, picture books and one special toy that I recall, a whistling *Kreisel*. The spinning top was the best thing in the whole room. I only had seen little wooden tops that you wound up with a string. But this metal one was big and colorful, with a stick in the center that you pumped up and down. It made the top spin so fast that the colors became a blur. The faster it spun, the louder it whistled.

I played with this for the longest time, and every time we went for a visit I headed right for this great toy.

They also had many, many comic books. Here I got to know "Mutt and Jeff," and the *"Katzenjammer Kids."* I thought this was strange – that an English book had a German title – *Katzenjammer* is German. It means caterwauling. I had no idea what a "Kid" was. But that didn't matter I could only read the pictures anyway.

Pete's house was like living in a different world.

I don't know Pete's last name but he introduced me to the American way. He was kindhearted, which is how I've found most Americans to be.

Peter and Lissi Eiser were two of my mother and father's closest friends. They often came to visit us, and we them. We also went to different places together to visit mutual friends, as well as to places of interest in the city, such as the park and the zoo.

In 1945 Peter and Lissi had been taken by the Russians to work in the coal mines as slave laborers. With God's help, they had survived and managed to escape.

The most painful aspect of their lives was that they had a daughter who was still in Yugoslavia. Tito's government would not let her go. The daughter was three years old when her parents left her with her grandmother. Both grandmother and child were put into a concentration camp in April, 1945 like all of us in Karlsdorf. A year later, the child's grandmother died and the little girl was left alone. Somehow news reached the grandmother's sister, who was married to a Serbian, and therefore hadn't been put into concentration camp.

The great aunt asked for and got permission to take the little girl in. Years later she received a letter from the Eiser's telling her that they were well and living in Germany. Both the great aunt and the parents began the procedure to bring the little girl to Germany. The Yugoslavian government threw all kinds of roadblocks in their path.

Years went by. When we left for America in 1950, they still had no news. Two years later, their daughter was finally permitted to join her family, but because she was only three when her parents left, they had a hard time becoming a family again. My mother has told me about the painful hurdles that they had to overcome until she began to accept them as her parents.

Because our people were scattered throughout Austria, Germany as well as other European countries, many of our young Karlsdorfer men and women, now in their late teens and early twenties, had no idea where their families were. My father had become a surrogate father to many of them in Russia. They were mere children of fifteen and sixteen when Tati took them under his wing. Now young adults, they still came to him for advice. Our home was always open and all were welcome. They came to seek new jobs or a place to stay for a few days or just to talk.

Although we had only one bedroom we always managed to make room for one more, like Jakob, who came to stay with us for a while until he found a job and a place to live. He had come to Munich hoping for a better future. His blonde hair was always neatly combed, his blue eyes were always shining, and his smile was warm and wide, a perfect older brother. He joked a lot and made me laugh. I enjoyed the short time we spent together.

Hechele's Sepp was also almost a member of our family because of his frequent visits. He lived upstairs with his brother and sister in-law. He must have been in his late twenties. His dark blond hair was always held down by hair cream. Sepp had only one eye, which was a nice grey color. The other eye lost during the war, was hidden under an eye patch. I used to wonder what it looked like. I was tempted to ask, but I had enough sense to know that a question of that kind wouldn't have been polite. He held me on his lap when he visited and actually included me in the conversations that went on between the grown-ups – that was one of the reasons I liked him so much.

Gurjaks Hans came to visit often. He lived only a few streets from our apartment. I knew him best because we were together *"Im Lager"*, as my family refers to the concentration camp. He was only fifteen or so back then and he was Tant's nephew. Hans was always good for a piggy back ride. His dark brown wavy hair, which always hung over his eye, bounced as he galloped me around the hangar. And his red cheeked face and dark eyes had a constant smile to offer. Many an evening he sat at our small table playing games with Seppi and me or sharing a meager meal.

The last memory I have of him is Christmas 1949. He gave me a colorful painted ball with a picture of a little girl feeding chicks, running in a never ending circle. Every time I played with the toy when we came to the U.S. I thought of him and missed him.

CHAPTER
19

Growing Up

S ummer came to an end and school started. Seppi, who had gone to third grade when we started school in December of 1947 now skipped the fourth grade and entered grade five in September, 1948. I, however, had to start from square one. With a heavy heart I went back to school as a first grader again.

Tati always joked, *"Du und ich sein die Dummie in unser Familie un Mami un Seppi sein die Gscheidi.* – You and I are the dumb ones in the family and Mami and Seppi are the smart ones."* I laughed with him. I knew my Tati wasn't dumb. But I wasn't so sure about myself – maybe I was stupid. Deep down I wanted to be one of the smart ones in our family.

I sat in the third, row left side of the double seat, four seats from the front. My teacher had been my brother's teacher the year before. And if that wasn't bad enough he was also the husband of last year's first grade teacher, whose sour disposition had done so little to inspire me.

He looked almost like his wife, with less hair. When he looked at me, his eyes went right through me.

From the beginning I was afraid he knew I was dumb. What I dreaded most was spelling. Every week we had a test. Sometimes he'd call on a person and she had to stand in front of the whole class and spell the words he gave her out loud. My heart would race wildly. I knew if he called on me I would fail. I knew that my turn was going to come, although I hoped he'd forget me. One day my luck ran out.

It was a wet, drizzly day. The sky through the high bare windows was dark with clouds. He called my name. Slowly I walked to the front, stepped up on the platform, to the left of the teacher's desk, and faced the class.

I felt him get up and stand behind me. Looking down at the scrubbed, raw, wooden floor boards, I waited for the word that I knew would proclaim my inability to every girl in my classroom. I didn't raise my eyes.

"Bitte buchstabiere – Garten," he said.

I sounded the word out in my head.

"Please spell garden," he repeated, a little louder.

I started to spell the word. "G-A-R..." Then I panicked. I started again "G-A-R..." I always mixed up the letters T and D. Which was it? *Harter T oder ein weicher D?* The question raced in my head. "Hard T or soft D?" Silence screamed in my ears. I couldn't remember.

It must be D. That's what I heard in my head. "D -E -N," I blurted out quickly. *"Falsch!"* he said in his loud voice. "Wrong, you spelled it wrong. It's a T. How could such a smart brother have such a dumb sister?" The words burned into my brain. I wanted to disappear. I felt all eyes on me. Never had I felt so ashamed as I did those few minutes. Even today as I think about it, I still can feel the silence of the room and the red burning humiliation on my face. The truth was out. I was the stupidest girl in this whole room. The teacher had said so.

If that teacher had known what damage he caused when he spoke those words to me, he would never have let that sentence leave his lips.

It took years to erase the word "Dumb" and replace it with "I'm just as bright as the next person."

One day, the teacher brought an artist to our class. She sat on a chair by the window. The sun streamed in, making her appear as if she were in a spotlight. The blond young woman smiled at us as he introduced her to our class. She was presented as a *Malerin,* an artist who was special. A mouth painter who had to use her mouth because her arms were paralyzed.

In front of her stood an easel like the one I had seen the painter use on the Theresien Wiese. The young lady was going to demonstrate how she used her mouth instead of her hands to paint an oil painting.

Standing next to her was a long legged stool with brushes and paints. She picked up a long brush with her mouth, dipped it into the paint and in a short time turned the white flat canvas into a realistic snow capped mountain scene.

I watched her every action. Each stroke of the brush wove another touch of enchanting color into the picture right in front of my eyes, as though a *Zauberer* was casting his spell of colors onto the canvas before him. She was a magician who knew her skillful artwork like a master.

In our class was a girl with hair that grew in sparse tufts all over her scalp. Her body was skin and bones and made her head look even bigger than it was.

She must have been recovering from an illness. Disease was common because of the lack of medicine and bad living conditions.

She hardly ever spoke. I had never seen her smile. What bothered me most were her big round eyes. They expressed the loneliness that she must have felt as she stood by herself in the corner of the school yard. She was like a shadow at the edge of the bright, circle of children frolicking in the sunshine of friendship. She was dismissed by the others because of her looks, and I was as unfriendly as the rest of my classmates. But I felt sorry for her and remembered how I had felt when I first came here. One day at recess time I made up my mind to talk to her. I can still recall how her face lit up when I greeted her.

I felt good for being the one that made her smile. After that, we became friends.

I rushed home, eager to get started on my homework. The assignment was to bring a blown out egg to school in the morning.

The teacher had explained how to blow out the egg and still have a whole eggshell left. And now I could hardly wait to try it.

"Mami, ich brauch a Ei," I blurted out as soon as I opened the door. "I need an egg."

Mami was busy in the kitchen. "What do you need an egg for?" she asked.

"I don't need the whole egg, just the shell." "I don't have an egg or a shell to give you," she told me. "I used this week's egg already."

"But I need it, Mami," I whined. "We're going to decorate it during art for Easter."

This was a big dilemma for me. Anything to do with art was the best part of school. And now I might have to miss out.

"I'm sorry," Mami said. "You know we only get one egg a week. Why don't you go to everyone in the building and ask if they still have their egg left. I'm sure they'll let you blow out the egg and give you the shell."

With a lighter heart I ran out our hallway. I had to try all three apartments before I was successful. Hechele's Kathi Tant still had her egg, and she was happy to help me out.

I followed the teacher's instructions to the letter. With a long darning needle I poked a hole on each end, stuck the needle through the hole to break the yoke and blew it out. Luck was with me; I did it perfectly. The next morning I went back to school, my egg wrapped securely in a paper bag, ready to make the best egg in the room.

Although many parts of Munich were destroyed, everywhere we went was an adventure. During the summer, box car races were held at the *Theresien Weise*. A few blocks from our apartment was the *"Münchener Marionetten Puppen Theater,"* where weekly fairy tales were performed with puppets almost as tall as I was, dressed in velvet and satin costumes.

But the most magic place in the city was *Zirkus Krone*, – the Krone Circus – which had its winter headquarters in Munich, not too far from our house. The circular building stood on a big cement-covered lot. We had the cheapest tickets in the house, in the standing room only section, at the very top of the amphitheater, and the performers below looked as if they were in miniature.

All kinds of acts stepped out from behind the red velvet curtain, tightrope walkers, acrobats, clowns, animals. The best part of the show was the clowns with their antics and nuttiness.

Walking on my hands, Theresien Wiese, 1949.

Not only adults but children also performed. These little entertainers were given an extraordinary ovation and hurrah: people tossed oranges at their feet. The children scrambled to collect their "thanks," and carried arms full of the fragrant fruit back to their quarters.

When I saw this, I knew what I wanted to become – a *Zirkus Akrobat*. I could walk on my hands already! In no time I would be able to carry off armfuls of oranges and eat my fill.

From then on I worked especially

hard perfecting my hand stand. I became so good that I could walk around on my hands quite freely. After each performance I'd curtsy before my imaginary audience and catch my imaginary oranges. Yes, soon I'd be the world's greatest "Acrobat" and eat oranges every day.

Not all my adventures were fun. The day came when Mami and I walked into the *Zahnarzt's* office. My first visit to the dentist. I knew what they did in that place. I remembered how, back in Karlsdorf Lager, my mothers uncle, Paul Batschi, pulled an old man's tooth. Paul Batschi was only a barber, but people came to him when they had a toothache. I had walked in when he was working on a man's tooth with a pair of pliers. The man was making painful noises, as if he was in agony. Then Paul Batschi gave a yank. I heard the man scream and I saw the bloody tooth in Paul Batschi's hand. I ran from the barn, scared out of my wits.

Now it was my turn to sit in a dentist chair.

The white coated gentleman leaned over me. He held a sharp instrument in one hand and a small mirror on a stick in the other.

"Bitte den Mund aufmachen," he requested.

I pinched my lips together. Not on your life was I going to open my mouth for this stranger. No one was going to pull a tooth from me.

The dentist and Mami tried everything to get me to cooperate. They became angry. But my lips stayed sealed and after ten minutes they gave up, and Mami took my place in the chair.

To see a dentist in those days, you had to go to the health department a few weeks ahead of time to make an appointment. The health department payed for the visit, therefore, the date had to be kept. If it wasn't, it was hard to reschedule another.

I also had a few firsts in Munich. My first Coca Cola. My first banana and my first cigarette.

"Elsa, willscht rauche?" Seppi had asked me as he started to take the scissors and cut a rectangular piece out of the newspaper. "Do you want to smoke?"

"We can't smoke," I quickly reacted. "Tati will find out that we took his *Tabak*.

"Who needs tobacco? We'll just use rolled up newspaper," my knowledgeable brother informed me.

We rolled the newspaper tightly and licked the edge just as we had watched Tati do many times. It was stiff and dry but with enough spit, it held together.

I held the *Zigarette* between my fingers and waved it around feeling quite grown up. Seppi got the box of matches by the stove. "Are you ready to light up?"

With the rolled newspapers between our lips, we put our heads together, dragging to light our cigarettes on the burning match. The newsprint lit easily and we both got a good amount of smoke in our lungs. We coughed like crazy, but that didn't stop us. After a couple of puffs, our *Zigarette* lit up like a torch. I dropped mine quickly and stepped on it, marking my mother's clean wooden floor with a black and brown spot that didn't come out no matter how we rubbed.

"Look what you did." Seppi yelled. "Your in BIG trouble."

"NO I'M NOT — IT WAS YOUR IDEA."

"BUT YOU SCORCHED THE FLOOR."

"YOU MADE ME."

"NO I DIDN'T."

"DID TOO"

We continued rubbing and yelling. But in the end the spot stayed and we had to face the music a few hours later when mother did her normal housecleaning. We both had our bottoms warmed, no time-out back then.

"Ahlan ins Kino gehn." To go alone to the movie show, that was my dream. I had gone with Seppi twice. We sat in the cheapest seat in the house, *Erste Rei* or first row. The film was called "Black Narcissus." It was in English with subtitles, and because I could hardly read, I didn't know what was going on.

The second movie was a half an hour news reel. After seeing it three times, I got bored and wanted to leave. Seppi didn't, and we stayed for three hours.

Finally the day came when I was going to go all by myself. I held the money tightly in my hand as I walked to the newly rebuilt Roxy Kino on a winter Sunday afternoon.

The Roxy was next to the post office on Göthe Platz. I had watched as the broken mortar and stone walls were cleaned away, and then workmen made new walls grow, brick by brick. Now the glass front entrance was clean and shiny. A large billboard, located above the entrance, showed what films played inside.

I walked up to the *Schalter. "Eine Karte, Bitte, erste Reihe."* I asked the lady sitting in the glass ticket booth. I pushed my money through the small glass hole. She handed me my ticket with a smile. *"Dankeschön."*

When I stepped into the theater I was surprised at the vast rows of seats. The movie houses that Seppi and I had attended were only half this size.

I sat down in the first row and soon the lights went out and the film began. One part of the movie is still sharp in my mind: A small boy wandering through a snowstorm. He was lost and couldn't find his way home. The freezing wind tore at his clothes as he pressed onward through the blizzard. He cried out, *"Mama hilfe!"* again and again "Help! Mama, help me!" Soon it was dark and the white icy fangs of sleet bit into his flesh, bringing him to his knees. Too tired to continue, the boy fell asleep on the side of the mountain, covered with snow.

The impact of this moment is still vivid in my memory. I can see every detail. The small, snow covered body lying in the cold whiteness, lost forever – never to return home again. At this time in my life – to be alone and separated from my family – was still one of my biggest fears.

Fasching was one of my favorite times of the year. There was the *Karnevalumzug* – the Mardi Gras parade with music, floats and costumes. Everyone dressed up during Mardi Gras. In my class I had the best costume. Mami had out done herself when she made my Hungarian girl costume for this years celebration.

Because Mami was such a good seamstress, I was one of the best dressed girls in my class. One of my favorite outfits was my *Skianzug* – ski suit – that Mami had made for me that winter. I felt so grown up each time I wore it to school.

Mami also made a sunday suit for Seppi out of an army blanket that she dyed navy blue and a dress for me from two cast-off dresses from America. We wore our new clothes the day we went to the zoo.

Giraffe, Affe, Zebras, Elefante – all kinds of animals were displayed in a natural setting in *Münchner Tier Park*, animals I had never seen before or heard of. Tati, Mami, Seppi and I walked from one display to the other. I was fascinated with all the animals especially the *Affe* – monkeys.

When we got to the elephants, Tati asked if I'd like to ride on one. "Ja!" was my instant answer. I got a prickly surprise when I was placed on the animal's leathery back. The hair went through my clothing as if I had nothing on. But it was a small price to pay for such a great adventure, which was over much too quickly.

As we walked away from the elephants I looked back longingly. Just one more ride, I wished silently. But knowing what the answer would be, I kept still.

We came to a clump of trees where a man had set up a camera. For a small fee, he would take our picture.

"*Jani, los mer Bilder holle,*" Mami said.

"Good idea! We'll have two pictures taken," Tati agreed, "one of the children and one with all four of us".

The man re-arranged us a few times until we suited his professional eye. Finally he snapped our picture, our first family portrait since we were together again.

Our first family portrait after the war,
Spring 1948 at the zoo.

CHAPTER
20

Parting

Iremember the letter that Basl sent with a postcard-size picture of Andres. Straight and tall, dressed in a dark suit, with his hair neatly combed to the side, Andres stood proudly holding his foot- high *Erste Kommunion Kerze.* Only once in a lifetime was one able to carry a beautiful "First Holy Communion Candle." I studied the picture for some time, admiring the artistic wax decorations on the large candle and the long, silk ribbon that hung down over my cousin's hand.

For Andres' first communion, Basl had taken him to the photographer, as was the custom back home. Because this was such a solemn occasion, Basl wanted to share it with us.

I dreamed of the day when I would make my *Heilige Kommunion.* I would carry a candle just like my cousin's or maybe an even prettier one.

A year had gone by since we

Marie and I in 1948.

219

came to Germany. My cousin Andres, Marie and Basl still lived in the *Flühtlingslager* – refugee camp – near Hof. They came to see us, and Marie even stayed for a week. She tried so hard to be a good housekeeper and took upon herself the responsibility of keeping the apartment warm. Every day she fed wood into our tile stove. At the end of the week she had used up most of our monthly allotment of wood, so my father ended up having to scrounge around for more.

In our family album is a picture of a smiling young girl. Her thick, sun-streaked hair, although braided, is arranged in such a manner as to make her look grown-up and as modern as possible. She is wearing a skirt, blouse and open white cardigan. The bareness of her knees and the dark oxford shoes with white bobby socks tell us that the picture was taken in the nineteen forties.

Her hand is resting on the shoulder of a knobby kneed, little girl, grinning from ear to ear. This picture of Marie and me was taken on a sunny afternoon at the zoo in 1948.

A year later we went down to the train station to say good-bye to Marie. She, Andres and Basl were leaving to go back to Yugoslavia.

Vetter, my uncle, had sent a letter informing Basl that he was back in Karlsdorf. Under no circumstances would he come to Germany. His home was in Karlsdorf and he was going to reside there and nowhere else and he insisted that his family return home.

"*Er is der Vater und Mann, und unser Platz is bei sei Seit,*" Basl stated. "He is the father and husband, and our place is by his side." And they had to go back to be a family once more. She told my mother that it was easy for her to say "stay here." She had her husband by her side.

I saw the sadness in Basl and my cousins eyes. Andres stood next to Basl and didn't say a word. I just couldn't understand. Why did they have to go back to Karlsdorf? We had just run away from that horrible place.

Marie was crying bitterly as she hung on to my Mami.

"*Bitte, loss mich do bleiwe bei dir, Lis Tant. Ich will net zuruck, ich will do bleiwe.*" Tears streamed down her frantic face, as she implored my mother with her entire being, "Please, let me stay with you, Lis Tant. I don't want to go back, I want to stay here."

"*Kind, du kannscht net bei mir bleiwe. Dei Elder wolle dass mit ihne lebscht. Du bist dei Mutter ihre Kind und des is was sie will.*" Mami told Marie as she put her arms around her and wept along with her.

"Child, you can't stay with us. Your parents want you to live with them. You are your mother's child, and this is what she wants."

By now we were all crying. Marie slowly let go of my mother. I will never forget the heart-wrenching look on her face. She had given up and had accepted the fact that it was no use; she had to go back to the hell from where we had fled. No one else was in the train compartment, just the seven of us. We hugged and kissed each other for the last time. Then we turned and disembarked the train, leaving Basl and my cousins behind. But the pain that was in all of our hearts was to follow us throughout our lives.

I never saw Marie and Basl again. Letters became our only way of being together. Every time we received a letter from Basl we all gathered around as my mother, the official reader, read it out loud.

Basl wrote that not many Germans returned to our town. There were now only a handful of families there. Life was much harder than in Germany. Food was scarce, but at least her family was together.

A letter came from Marie. I was so excited as Mami opened it and a picture of Marie and a young man in a suit fell out. He seemed tall and slender. His hair was combed back in a pompadour.

The young man was Marie's *Verlobter* – her fiáncee. My cousin was going to be married. He was also a Schwob, from another town, but now he lived in Karlsdorf.

Mami and Tati were surprised at this news. They thought Marie was quite young to be married, not even eighteen. I didn't think she was so young. This I kept to myself. But I did mention that I liked the young man's smiling face.

Six months later we received a letter from Basl telling us that Marie had married a Partisaner. My aunt said nothing more about it in the entire letter. This was hard to understand.

Why would Marie, who was deathly afraid of the communist guards, marry one?

My mother wrote and asked what happened to the young man Marie was engaged to and why she married the Partisaner? But her questions were never answered. Although Basl continued to write, at no time did she mention anything about the marriage or her daughter.

Mutter, my father's mother, was alive. We received a letter from her saying that she, as well as Oma Schüssler, my mother's mother, had been released from the death camp in Rudolfsgnad. Ota Schüssler had died of starvation a few months after they were sent to the death camp.

At the end of 1948, Tito's communist government dissolved the German concentration camps. There were not many of us left. Many had died, and the rest had managed to escape. Now the few remaining were released back to where they had lived before.

Only a handful of our people were scattered throughout the town. No one got their old houses back. My relatives as well as the other Germans now lived in one room quarters allotted to them by the new inhabitants of the town. Not only were the Karlsdorfers now tenants of the new Nationals, they worked under them as hired hands. Life was only slightly better than in the concentration camp.

I can still see Mami sitting at the kitchen table as she read the letter from her brother. Mami said, "Your Oma Schüssler is no more – she died a few weeks after they set her free. She lived only long enough to go back home."

I heard this as a matter of fact statement, because the meaning behind the word "died" didn't quite register. Not having known my Oma for too long, I felt little sorrow. I had a hard time even remembering Mutter. It was a long time since she and I crossed that street to get a glass of milk for me.

Not until I was older did it enter my mind what my mother had felt at the time. At the age of twelve my mother had lost her nineteen year old brother Konrad – Kuni for short. Mami had often talked about him and how he was her favorite brother because he always laughed, joked around and played games with her.

Kuni was a carpenter who often worked in different towns. He was working on a building in Belgrade when he fell off the roof and died instantly. The families sudden loss of their young son and brother took many years to heal. It was especially hard on my mother because she and her brother had been so close. Now her mother and brother both were resting in the small *Karlsdorfer Friedhof*.

She was no one's child anymore, she had no father or mother. She would never be able to go to their graves to say goodbye or place a flower there. She didn't even know where her father's body was at rest. He was dropped in a large hole with hundreds of men, women and children naked, stripped of dignity, covered with dirt and buried without marker or stone.

In 1951 Marie wrote that she had given birth to a little girl, Zoritza. By this time we were in America and I was fast headed towards my teenage years. I didn't give too much thought to my far away relative as I was occupied adjusting to my new way of life.

In July 1953 I was in Grant Hospital where I was recovering from a nose operation. I had broken my nose in summer of 1944. I remember that grave moment in my life as if it had just happened. Hella, our neighbor, played with me in our courtyard, she tossed me up and retrieved me in mid-air as I screeched with delight. Our laughter echoed in the sunny yard as we continued our game of "toss and catch." Up I went again and again, and as I came down for the last time I slipped through Hella's hands, and slammed down on the cobblestones – face first. Blood gushed from my nose as she picked me up.

I don't recall the accident itself but I do recall the aftermath. Red blood was all over. I was frightened when I saw all that blood. The wash basin was full of bloody water. I screamed as Mami held me over the vessel, trying to stop the bleeding from my nose with a wet washcloth. Nothing could be done to repair the fracture until that summer almost ten years later.

I was so worried that my broken nose was never going to be straight. All bandaged up, I sat in my bed, feeling sorry for myself. I was in a room with three other patients, old women who must have been over sixty. I could hardly wait to get out of there.

My mother entered the room, her face solemn: she came and sat down on the side of my bed. After our usual small talk, she looked at me and said, "I have some bad news. We received a letter from Basl. Marie has died."

At first I didn't quite understand. "How could she die. Was she sick?"

"No, she took her own life."

I didn't say anything. I could not believe Marie was dead.

"Marie is dead." Like an echo, those three words bounced around in the cavern of my mind. Gone forever was my cousin, my sister. Never would we be able to see each other again.

Many years have passed since that news from Karlsdorf was made known to me. As an adult I have often thought about my poor cousin's end.

My aunt and uncle are no longer living and Andres cannot talk about it. Why did she not marry her fiánce instead of the Partisaner. I have told myself that maybe she was threatened if she married her sweetheart instead of the Partisaner. Maybe the young man's life had been in danger.

We were told that her husband beat her daily and that she swallowed rat poison because she wanted to end her torture. No other explanation was ever given.

In August of 1995 I met a man who lived in Karlsdorf at the time of my cousin's death. He told me that not only did he know Marie he also was the brother of her best girlfriend. I had a hard time trying to put into words the question that was burning inside me.

When I finally brought forth my question and told him that my family had really never been told exactly what had happened. All we could do was speculate to reach a plausible explanation for my cousin's death.

"Marie was very unhappy," he told me. "Her husband not only beat her but he also was a womanizer. It was said he slipped rat poison in her meals until it finally killed her, freeing him to marry another woman."

I thanked him for sharing his recollections with me and that his explanation brought me some peace. It had always been hard for me to believe that Marie would choose to die and leave her daughter motherless. She who had so much love for others certainly would have found this hard to do.

Being murdered is a harrowing thing but committing suicide is much worse for a family to bear.

With all my heart I hope that Marie is now at peace. For the twenty years she spent on this earth, her young life was mostly pain and sorrow. She was a sweet and loving cousin that gave so much to me, her younger cousin. Sometimes more than any older sister could have given.

CHAPTER
21

Books, God and I, and Christmas 1949

I held the "*Kinderlieder Buch*" in my hands and I opened it as if it were a holy object. The clean, white pages of the "Children's Song Book" smelled of fresh ink. Never had I owned a book before, especially not one like this, filled with pictures on almost every page, pictures with every color of the rainbow. It was a school book, but I was to own it forever and never have to give it back. The clerk wrapped it for me. I held it close and rushed home.

I couldn't read the musical notes printed next to the pictures, but I knew many of the songs by heart. My favorite was "*Dornröschen*," because we had just learned to sing it in school. I liked the words to "Sleeping Beauty" and the picture of the lovely princess. Even the rose-covered castle was depicted. It looked so real that when I touched it with my fingertips, I almost expected to feel a prick from the thorns.

This was my first love affair with a book. That same school year, in late 1949, I received my second-grade, "*Bayrisches Lesebuch – Zweite Klasse.*" Now I owned two books. I spent hours copying the pictures in my second grade reader. To me they were like a special place that I wanted to be a part of. Although I possessed only a few colored pencils I tried my best to "pick the pictures out of the book" like flowers out of a garden.

The reader had many short stories and poems. One *Gedicht* – poem – in particular fascinated me, it was called "*Die Schuhe*" or "The Shoes." Ever since Fräulein Ott told our class that her best friend was the author of this *Gedicht*, it became my favorite.

I was so proud to be Fräulein Ott's student. "Imagine, she actually knows a person whose words are printed in a book," I thought happily to myself.

I remember sitting on my father's lap as he ceremoniously took his pen in hand and printed my name and address on the inside cover of the reader. Tati had a special way of printing fancy letters on important papers and now he did the same for my book. He wrote: Elise Hugery, (Elise, which was short for Elisabeth, is what I was called by most everyone in school) on the left side of the inside cover and followed with our address below. I felt so important. Now I owned an item of such importance that it needed the special touch of my father's printing.

Second grade was a new beginning for me. My teacher, Fräulein Ott, was a white haired lady who loved children. One day she invited me to visit her at home. Although she was a lay woman, she lived among the nuns at the convent by Kapuziner Kirche. We chatted over tea, and afterward, Fräulein Ott asked, "Would you like to see my garden and help me harvest the green beans? I replied with a happy, "Ja," since I was delighted to do whatever she asked me.

We walked out the back door to a large garden next to the high fence that separated the yard from the street. I had often wondered what was behind the white stucco wall when I walked past it. The bean patch was in the middle of the yard. I had not been in a garden since I was four, when I accompanied my grandmother back home in our garden.

"*Mutter, Bitte loss mich ah Erbse roppe.*" I used to beg my grandmother. "Please, let me help pick peas." Mutter smiled and told me, "Ja, but don't eat too many or you'll get a stomach ache."

This garden was different from our garden back home. It had no fruit trees, only vegetables. The beans were planted in two rows and each plant was coiled around a string that led up to a long suspended pole in the middle of the row. The green plants looked like a high, long tent in the middle of the garden. Hanging from the plants were slender bean pods waiting to be picked. The two of us finished the job in no time. I liked being with Fräulein Ott a lot, it was more like being with my "Oma" than my teacher.

Since we had received letters from Mutter, she began to become more real to me. Especially since I could now communicate myself with her on paper. I had written a letter to Mutter, and Mami made me copy it over.

"Mami, warum muss ich den Brief wieder schreiwe?" I wanted to know why I had to rewrite the letter to Mutter. It looked good to me. Mami said that it needed to look as perfect as possible, so Mutter could see how I had grown up, and was capable of writing a neat and correct letter to her.

Determined to do my best I sat with my feet curled around the chair legs, head down, with the tip of my tongue slightly protruding out of the corner of my lips. I was intent on the work before me. I formed each letter of each word with great care. At the end of my effort the one page letter was crisp and clean. I wondered if Mutter would be able to see how grown-up I had become.

I'm sure my grandmother loved receiving the few letters she got from me. I still recall the first lines of each letter. This, I was told, was how you began a letter. *"Wie geht es Dir? Mir geht es gut. Ich hoffe Dir auch. –* How are you? By me everything is going well. I hope by you also." A little stiff, but very grown up.

Slowly, as I grew older and began to understand a little of what religion was about, the meaning of faith and God became a part of my life.

We went to church at St. Antonius, but we only called it *"Die Kapuziner Kirche* – The Capuchin Church" because it was part of the Capuchin Monastery located there.

In my daily surroundings of the broken and battered city, no other place was as whole, unblemished and beautiful as this structure. Raw wood, stone and metal had been turned into magnificent carvings, altars and statues. The house glorifying God was a kind of prayer. I considered this church a piece of heaven.

Very clear in my memory is the carved mahogany pulpit attached to one of the large pillars to one side of the church and the spiral stairs leading up to it.

Once the priest spoke to us from the top of this platform. He looked as if he was on a cloud descended from up high. The other objects that I can recall were the large banners that hung on a high gold pole in front of the first pew. Each was made of white satin, fringed with gold, with a brilliantly colored picture depicting the church seasons at the center. The silk threads were so finely stitched they looked like paint on paper.

The priest said the mass in Latin. The people followed along by silently reading in their missals and responded in the same tongue that linked them to Christians who had worshiped a thousand years before. I knew all the responses by heart and replied along with the rest of the congregation even though I had no missal of my own.

Most children received their first *Messbuch* on the day of their *Erste Kommunion*. And since I had not passed that milestone, I could hardly wait to own a massbook like those around me.

Old songs of praise and glory rang out throughout the mass, different songs for every season. *Weihnachtslieder* – Christmas songs – are what I enjoyed the most. The sound of hundreds of voices singing as one made the church walls echo as if they, too, were singing along. I sang with enthusiasm because it was the best part of the mass.

The first time I went to church in America I was so surprised that no one sang except the choir. And what amazed me even more was that they sang in Latin and not in English. I can not recall singing anything but German songs in Munich, although I'm sure Latin was sung at certain masses.

Next to the church was a small *Kapelle*. Inside the small Chapel was a man-made Grotto. There in the miniature cave, carved wooden figures depicted the stories from the new testament. This was a favorite part of the church for most children.

The chapel was located right next to the church with no connecting door between the two. You had to go outside and walk through two iron gates and across the tiny courtyard, where a small door led into the chapel. A few feet from the entrance was the Grotto. The Kapelle was always darkened, so that the scene appeared realistic as the man-made sunlight or moonlight shone on the foot high statues. The figures looked as if they were frozen in time. Beautifully crafted faces and hands expressed their humanity, down to the drape of their robes and sandal-clad feet.

Every month or two a new story was told in three dimensions. This motionless theater was much easier to understand than if the story had been read to me. Each time I went back to the Grotto, I saw something new in the silent scene before me.

At Christmas time *Jesukind* smiled at you with his tiny hands reaching up to you. And Maria und Josef knelt down in front of our Lord with eyes only for the babe in the *Krippe* – manger. At Easter I recall the *Auferstehung* – Resurrection, the realistic looking landscape and the mountainside tomb with the stone rolled away at the entrance; Jesus pointing up to heaven dressed all in white, glowing from the sunrise of the fiery sky in the background.

I can also remember the *Christihimmelfahrt* – Ascension. This must surely have been how it really was, Christ rising up into the heavens to join his father. It was almost as good as being there.

The life of Christ, told through the clever hands of an artisan, was a wordless bible. I'm sure this little grotto in the chapel had been in the same spot for more than a hundred years. And perhaps it had been a way to re-enact the stories of the new testament for people who could not read or write back in the years when schooling was provided only to the privileged few.

The Grotto was an important part of my religious education. It was like an Advent Calendar for all the holy days of the year, not just at Christmas-time in December.

The church was packed with people this day. Mami and I were seated in the fourth row from the front, my father and brother stood up on the alter steps. This was Seppi's big day, his *Firmungstag*. Being confirmed meant that one was considered an adult in the church's eyes. I was proud of my brother. He looked handsome in his new suit that Mami made for the occasion.

When the *Bischof* stood in front of Seppi and annointed his forehead with oil he was considered an adult. But standing in front of Tati, he didn't look very grown up to me. He didn't even reach to my father's chin. Tati was a "stand in" for his brother, Onkel Franz. Seppi had written to him and asked him if he would be his *Firmpate*. Onkel had written that he would be happy to become Seppi's confirmation sponsor, but was sorry that he was not able to come in person because of his work. Onkel lived in Austria and worked as a farmhand on a large *Bauernhof* and this was their busy season on the farm. So arrangements had been made for my father to represent Onkel. I remember being a little bewildered. "How can Onkel be a sponsor to my brother if he isn't even in the church?"

Now that he had become an adult he also received the traditional *Handuhr* from Onkel. It was the custom back home, as well as in some parts of Germany and Austria, that the *Firmpate* presents his sponsored boy or girl with his or her first wristwatch.

During Holy Week, we learned about the suffering of Jesus in the Olive Garden. I listened intently as the monk told us how Christ agonized about what was going to happen to him. He told us that Jesus sweated blood. For the rest of the day I could not get the religion lesson out of my mind. At home I kept on thinking about it. At bedtime, as I was lying in the dark, I had a silent talk with God as I often did about what troubled me. *"Bitte Herr – net loss mich Blut schwitze."* I pleaded. "Lord, don't ever let me sweat blood." Soon I fell fast asleep, covered up to my ears in the warmth of the featherbed, as a result I began to perspire.

Half awake, I wiped my forehead with the back of my hand. My hand was wet. Suddenly, like a bolt of lighting, it hit me – my forehead was wet! I held my hand in front of my eyes, trying to see better, but it was too dark.

My heart raced. I got up and rushed to the bathroom. Now I felt wet and cold all over. I fumbled for the light switch and flicked on the light.

Again I touched my fingers to my forehead and examined them quickly. I breathed a sigh of relief when I saw not one speck of blood on my finger tips.

I watched Mami as she cut out the large circle from the piece of snow white, satin material. It was hard to believe that this flat fabric was to be my first *Handtasch* – my very own purse – just like a grown lady. I would be able to wear it over my arm as I walked along in my first *Fronleichnam Prozession* on Sunday. Corpus Christi was a big holy day in Catholic Munich. I had never been in a procession before. For that matter, I had never even seen one.

The sidewalk in front of the church was filled with people. I could see a cream and gold canopy being held up by four altar boys at the entrance of the church, waiting for the procession to begin. "This must be what is called the *Himmel* – Heaven, I thought to myself. It was called Himmel because the Host was carried under it.

Soon three priests came out of the church dressed in gold and silver embroidered church vestments. One carried the *Hostie*. The white Host was in the center of a gold sunburst shaped receptacle, used only for this purpose. As soon as the priests were under the canopy, the Host was held high and the procession began.

Everyone followed the priests as they walked across the street, through the two high wrought iron gates and into the cemetery, singing and praying in unison.

I participated proudly; I was proud not because I was participating but because of the new purse hanging from my arm. No one had a shiny purse like mine. It made me feel so grown up and elegant.

I'm afraid I was more vain than pious that day.

Advent and *Weihnachten,* 1949 was the last year that I believed totally and fully in the magic of *Sankt Nikolaus* and *Christkindl. Sankt Nikolaus* is the saintly bishop whose name day is December 6th. Traditionally, we put out our shoes on the doorstep the evening before so that St. Nick could leave apples, oranges, nuts and the like in them.

Christkindl comes on Christmas Eve. It is literally translated "Christchild," but it means Christmas spirit, or Christmas Angel. The person representing *Christkindl,* is always dressed in a long white gown, and the face is covered with a veil.

1949 was the year that *Sankt Nikolaus* came to our house in person. But I am getting ahead of myself. Let me begin at the beginning.

Kapuziner Mönche – Capuchin Monks – with their *Kaputz* pulled over their head and their hands tucked into their wide sleeves of their dark brown, coarse robes tied at the waist with a black knotted cord, were always present in Munich.

In fact, the city's seal is a small monk holding a large white radish in one hand and a stein of beer in the other. Since the *Kapuziner* church was just a few blocks up the street, many of the brothers walked on our street.

Whenever we saw a brown clad, hooded figure walking down the street, we children ran to greet him, whether we knew the person or not. We'd hope he'd pull something from his large wide sleeves. Usually it was a *Heilichs Buidl,* which is Bavarian dialect for holy picture. Once in a while the good monk had something better up his sleeve – a small hard candy.

It was late afternoon and I was on my way home from school when I saw the tall brown attired figure across the street from our doorway. I ran across *Heberlstrasse* and stopped directly in front of him. Stretching out my hand I gave him a big smile and said in a loud sure voice *"Grüss Di Gott, Pater."* I curtsied, as we shook hands. This was the manner in which young girls greeted adults.

"Grüss Di Gott, mein Kind. – God's greetings to you, my child," he replied. I watched as he pulled out two round objects from beneath his sleeve. *"Hier mein Kind, für dich. –* Here my child, for you," he said, smiling, as he stretched out his hand and gave me two oranges.

I was so surprised that I didn't know for a moment what to say. I stammered a thank you and just stood there, holding the large fragrant fruits in both hands. He smiled down at me, walked around me and continued on his way.

It took awhile to register that the oranges were just for me. An orange was not something one received every day. An orange was up there with chocolate and walnuts! They were a rarity reserved for special occasions and from special people like *St. Nikolaus* or *Christkindl* who, in fact, weren't always able to produce them.

Still stunned, I ran back across the street, through the gangway, across the yard, into our house, and breathlessly banged on the door. Mami let me in and when I showed her excitedly what the monk had given me she was just as happy as I was.

"Let me put these away for later," she told me. Giving her my valued present, I babbled on and on. Didn't she think they were truly the biggest oranges she had ever seen? And weren't they grand? Mami agreed with me that they were. But now it was time to do my homework, it was nearly evening. I washed up and went about my business. After all it was St. Nikolaus Eve and it was smart to be especially good tonight.

At supper, I was at the far side of the kitchen table next to the window and Seppi was at the other end. There was a loud knock on the door. The door opened and a dark, heavily cloaked figure walked through the kitchen door. A scarf covered the bottom half of his face, and a large hat was pulled over his eyes, making it impossible to see who he was. His deep voice gave a loud greeting.

"*Ich bin der Sankt Nikolaus*," he stated. "*Für die brave Kinder hab ich was Gutes und für die Böse hab ich die Rute.* – I'm St. Nikolaus. For the obedient children I have something good, and for the bad ones I have a switch."

He stepped through the door and started to hit my brother with the switch. My brother ducked and covered his head. I said not one word. My eyes grew bigger and bigger each time the switch landed on my brother. For each bad deed my brother committed during the year, the switch landed on his back. Seppi was given four or five raps and then St. Nikolaus stopped and pulled out a large orange from his pocket. "Here, this is for all the times you were good," he said and handed it to Seppi.

Now it was my turn. He walked over to me and asked me if I was a good girl all year. "Yes, I think so." I said, hoping that I had given him the right answer. I knew that this wasn't always so, but I didn't want to feel the *Rut* on any part of my body.

"I suppose you were most of the time," he agreed in his deep voice. "Here, this is for you for being good." He handed me the orange from his other pocket. "*Brav sein, bis zum nächste Jahr,*" he said as he turned around and walked out the door. "Be good till next year," he had told us. I wasn't just going to be good till next year, I was going to be good forever. I was so happy that the switch didn't dance around on my back.

I never asked my mother what happened to the two oranges the monk had given me. Deep down I knew. But I wanted to hold on to my childhood so badly that I was afraid to admit there was no Nikolaus. I figured it out the minute we each got an orange. But not until the following Christmas in 1950, did I allow myself to think it. I wanted that magic to last just a little longer. I had to hold on as long as I could to my new found childhood. Three Christmases wasn't enough for a child of nine.

Like dainty frolicking dancers, snowflakes swirled around us. I held out my hand and captured a few ballerinas as they floated down. The flakes that stuck to my dark, woolen mitten looked like tiny six pointed stars. Each one was shaped like small crystal lace doillies, all different and yet the same. I had just discovered this fact and was enthralled with my find.

I slowed almost to a halt under each luminous street light and examined my hand. "*Elsa, kum doch schun. Es wert kalt. Net bleib immer stehn.* – Come on. It's getting cold. Don't always stop under each light," our upstairs neighbor Heffele's Kathi Tant urged.

"I'm coming" I replied. When I caught up to her, I held on to Kathi Tant's hand. I clasped the bag that I held in my other hand tightly to my chest . "It's getting late," she said. We walked faster down Göthe Strasse and turned down our street. "Yes," I thought, "I can hardly wait to get home so I can show everyone my present." Heffeles Kathi Tant, had taken me along to the *Christkindlmarkt*. The Christmas market was one of my favorite places on earth. And any time I was able to go I happily went.

We walked from booth to booth and admired all the beautiful things for sale. The ground was covered with fluffy snow, and thick flakes were still coming down. The snow muffled all the noise around us, as if you held your hands over both ears. Every sound was hushed as the snow covered the marketplace and all of Munich.

The snow crunched as we walked from place to place. I watched with amusement as the man behind the *Spielwaren Standl* – toy booth – demonstrated two small cars that ran all by themselves. He rubbed them on the counter a few times and then let them go. Quick as a mouse they raced to the other end. No key to wind or string to pull. "They run on friction," he explained. I didn't know what friction was, but whatever it was, it enchanted me.

Once more the *Puppen Standl* captivated me. I stood in front of the dolls as I had the year before. More than anything I wanted one on Christmas Eve. Again I wished with all my might that *Christkindl* would bring me my doll on *Heiliger Abend*.

On the counter was a paper dolls display. Colorful sheets of paper had different dresses printed on them. "I'd love to have one of those," I thought. I became so engrossed in what was in front of me, that I didn't hear Kathi Tant the first time when she asked me, *"Elsa, willscht so a Pop zum spiele?* – Would you like one of those dolls to play with?" I spun around and looked her straight in her face to make sure I heard correctly. *"Such dir ahni raus.* – Pick one out." "To take home?" I asked. "Ja" she said "Go ahead and pick one."

I couldn't make up my mind. Finally I chose one, which the man put in a bag for me. I reached up over the counter and retrieved my doll from his outstretched hand.

The only thing I had ever carried away from the *Christkindlmarkt* were empty handed wishes. But this time I was actually carrying a small treasure home.

If I got my wish on Christmas Eve, even if it was just a small doll, I'd never want anything else again. A doll with moving eyes and real hair. There was never a doubt in my mind that I would one day get such a present. Every time I didn't get my doll I always told myself "next year." Christmas 1949 was the year that my dream came true.

We were going to have guests for *Heiliger Abend*. Our good friends Peter and Lissi Eiser and Gurjaks Hans. It seemed forever until they arrived. I was so excited I could hardly wait to go into the bedroom. I just knew that this year *Christkindl* would bring my doll.

Finally everyone was here, dressed in their best clothes. We stood around the tree and sang *"Stille Nacht."* Hans had given me a present and so had the Eisers. By coincidence I received two identical colorful balls, with a picture of a girl feeding chicks.

"Did you hear that bell?" someone asked. We all listened. I heard a high tinkling sound coming from the hall. The door opened and there stood a figure dressed in white from head to toe. It was *Christkindl*, her face covered with a veil.

Christkindl greeted Seppi and me. In a high voice she asked us to recite our prayers and a Christmas poem we learned in school. I tried to see her face but failed. Except for 1943, when I was three years old, I had never seen *Christkindl* in person. I was so taken aback that I recall only a white blur who was gone as fast as she came.

She had given me a long rectangular box. I opened the cover and there was my wish. Just like *Dornröschen* asleep in her bed, my Sleeping Beauty had her eyes closed in her box. She was over a foot tall, dressed in blue silk, with beautiful golden hair, and dark eyelashes caressing her pink cheeks.. I carefully picked her up and slowly rocked her in my arms. It was hard to believe that I had gotten my heart's desire. I held her up for all to see.

But something was wrong. She remained asleep. "She won't open her eyes," I said to Tati as I handed her over for him to see. Tati took her and shook her a little, then under his breath he said to Mami: *"Ka wuner Sie hat net viel Geld gekoscht, Ihre Aue sein zugepickt.* – No wonder she cost so little, her eyes are glued shut."

Looking back at me he smiled and told me he'd fix it. Tati was good at things like that, he could always fix everything. With a screwdriver and a little patience on my father's part, the eyes soon opened to reveal their glassy blueness. Although her lashes were to remain forever damaged, I loved my new baby just as she was. To me, she was perfect.

Years later my parents told me how they had been searching for a doll for me, but were never able to pay for such an extravagant present. They already had accepted the fact that Christmas 1949 would go by, just like the previous year. A doll was out of the question.

A few days before Christmas Eve my parents happened to pass a toy vendor. They stopped to glance over his wares. A beautiful doll caught my father's eye. Not so much the doll as the unbelievable price tag attached to the box. Never thinking to take her out of the box, my parents bought her at once, and hurried on home, happy to have found this unexpected windfall.

The next year my doll crossed the ocean as my prized possession. I loved her dearly. But her ordeal with bodily injuries was not over. When we came to Barrington, U.S.A. near Chicago, we lived with my father's brother and his wife, Peter Onkel and Frieda Tant, who owned a big German shepherd. He was a watchdog that was on a long chain outside their house. Only when he was fed was he allowed in the house.

Not thinking of the dog, I left my doll lying on a kitchen chair. Apparently the dog was still hungry. When he finished the food in his dish he decided to chew off my dolls hair. I walked into the room in time to see him snatch the last lock off her head.

My tears flowed like a fountain but that didn't bring back my baby's hair. In time I came to accept her misfortune like the good doll mother that I was. She still was pretty in my eyes, although now she had to live out the rest of her days with a bonnet secured around her bald head.

On *Silvesterabend*, Mami and Tati went upstairs by the Ziessler's, who were having a New Year's Eve party. Seppi and I were all alone for the evening.

It was a cold and windy night that last eve of 1949. Seppi was thirteen years old and still up to his old tricks of having a good laugh at my expense. We had been allowed to stay up a little later than usual. And because it was New Year's Eve we decided to remain awake in our beds until midnight.

The wind and our voices were the only sound in the dark room. The two of us were in deep discussion, as we often were when we were alone in our bedroom. I remember hugging the corner of my feather bed coverlet, as I had a habit of doing since I was very small. Seppi's voice came from his corner of the room where his bed stood.

"You know that at midnight ghosts wander the earth," my brother stated. "They come and try to get into people's houses through the windows."

"That's not true, I don't believe you," I replied half-heartedly. I wasn't so sure.

"It is. I sometimes hear them as they try to come into the window." Not knowing what to say next, I simply kept quiet. Seppi also held his tongue, waiting for my next comment. Since I didn't jump at his bait he decided to try a different approach.

"Do you hear that howling?" he asked.

"I don't hear anything except the wind," I said.

"That's not the wind, that's the ghosts."

"It is not," I yelled.

"It is, they're getting ready to come through the window," he insisted. The sound got louder and louder as the wind whistled down and around in our small yard.

A gust of wind took hold of the window frames and shook them mightily. "They're trying to open the window!" my brother yelled out in a mock fearful voice. I screamed and covered my head with the coverlet.

He laughed loudly, "I thought you didn't believe me."

I stayed under the covers all night and didn't go to sleep until my parents came home.

Thus ended the year 1949 and the world stepped into the fifties. I, who wanted nothing to change, had no idea what great changes the next few years held in store for all of my family.

CHAPTER
22

A New Beginning

My family started to talk about going to "Amerika" at the beginning of 1950, and specific plans soon took shape. Amerika was a place I associated with my father's brother, Peter Onkel, a far-away land where packages with good things came from. It existed only in objects for me.

Käthe and I had all kinds of notions of what this fabulous land was all about. The subject often came up when we played with her *Amerikanische Malbücher* – American coloring books.

Käthe, who had more relatives living there than I did, told me that in Amerika everyone had more food than they could eat and everyone had money. And in the streets, gold bricks were used for pavement instead of gray cobblestones.

I had a hard time imagining such a place. I fancied shiny, gold strips of roads leading to the cities. Amerika was in the same league as *Schlaraffenland*, the fairy tale place that Tati often told us about. In *Schlaraffenland*, food was in profusion and part of the landscape.

America was known all over the world as the land of plenty. From every country on the globe, people emigrated to the U.S.A. and wrote back to their relatives of all the riches one could obtain there. A lot was exaggeration on the part of the new "*Amerikaners*," but many tales were also true. America, the land of abundance, was there for anyone who was willing to work hard.

When I first heard about my family's plans, I was not happy. I wanted to stay here, where I finally was beginning to belong. I even started to like going to school. Fräulein Ott had helped me become interested in learning.

In May, I was going to make my *Erste Heilige Kommunion*. I could hardly wait. I had this vision of my First Holy Communion ever since my brother made his. I would walk down the church aisle dressed in a long white dress. A circle of white flowers would crown my long *Stopslocken* – banana curls – with a *Schleier* down my back. Only brides and girls who made their First Communion had long white veils. I'd be able to carry a *Kommunionkerze*. Ivory colored wax flowers would wind all around the Communion candle like a vine growing up a white tower. A long satin ribbon would be tied to its base, cascading past my gloved hands. I'd have white shoes with straps and buckles, unlike my *Schnierschuh* that came up past my ankles and tied at the top.

I knew that the clothing was not the most important part of the Sacrament but it certainly made the ceremony beautiful. I had dreamed about this moment.

But then my worst fears came true. We were leaving for Amerika at the end of April. Arrangements were made so I could make my *Kommunion* alone, before we left Munich. I was very unhappy. I wanted to make the sacrament in May with the other girls. But by May, we would no longer be here. The lady who tutored me lived on Lindwurmstrasse. Her apartment was on the third floor, two blocks from our house. There we'd sit at her table and study for my Communion day. These one on one lessons were dull compared to the religion classes Pater Pazifikus taught with his colorful felt pictures.

Once or twice, my second grade teacher, Fräulein Ott, also taught me at her home. I found all the special attention that she gave me flattering, but what I really wanted was to make my Communion with the rest of my classmates.

At the end of March, a month before we were to leave, my tutor informed me that I couldn't make my First Communion. *"Es tut mir leid."* she said. "I'm sorry but I misunderstood, I prepared you for your first Confession and not your first Communion."

I walked home from my lessons, heartbroken. Now I had to wait until we came to America before I could make my first Communion. I didn't understand English. How would I be able to understand what was going on? Again I'd be considered "different." I didn't want to be that again. More than anything in my life I wanted to be the same – a nine year old girl who belonged.

Seppi asked me to go along with him *zum Kino* to see a cowboy film, which we pronounced covboi film. The show was packed with people, which was usually the case when a Western movie was shown. As I stared up at the black and white screen and watched the giant people I felt as if I was up there with them.

The landscape was different from anything I had ever seen before. As the cowboys rode their horses through the town, clouds of dust rose up and covered everything. The houses were not at all like those here in Munich. Every one wore a gun and a big hat. In one scene a handsome man dressed in a shiny black suit, with a white shirt and tie, announced to all the others that he was a gentleman.

Seppi and I discussed the movie, as we walked home. My big brother explained that when we got to Amerika he was going to be *ein Gen-T-le-mann* too. I agreed that this was certainly a good person to be.

"*Ein Gen-T-le-mann* must be a very important person in America," I said.

But to myself I thought, "I'm a girl — I can't be a cowboy. What will I be in America?"

Everyone had to pass the medical test before entering the United States of America. Seppi, who was soon to be fourteen, was giving my father a hard time.

He kept insisting that since this was the month of March, he was to be considered fourteen already. Tati told him this was not so and if he insisted that he was fourteen, he might not pass the physical and be made to take it all over again, which would take extra time that we might not have.

Our tickets had to be booked before a certain date. Children under ten were half price. We had to book our *Schiff* tickets before I officially turned ten in July. But first we had to pass the medical tests.

The American consulate was located near the edge of the city. We boarded a streetcar that rambled to the end of the line, then walked for quite a way until we got to our destination. We climbed the five steps and entered the building.

In a large, brightly lit room people stood in lines waiting their turn to be checked by doctors and nurses. We went from one station to the next. Each time we had to hand over a piece of paper to the person in charge. For the blood test, children over the age of fourteen were to line up with the adults on one side of the room. Those under fourteen were to stand in the other line.

I went right and Seppi went left. As I moved up in my line, I could see what the nurse in Seppi's line was doing. She had a long needle with a vial behind it. She pushed the needle into a vein in the crook of the elbow and drew out blood. In my line they just pricked your index finger and extracted a small amount of blood with a thin tube.

Now it was my brother's turn. I watched to see what he would do. Before the nurse even had a chance to take his arm, my brother spoke up: "Wait, I made a mistake," he stammered, "I'm only thirteen. I won't be fourteen until the end of this month." The nurse stopped and checked his papers.

"That's right, you still have a few days," she smiled.

"Please move over to the children's line." Seppi quickly stepped to the back of my line. The long needle had convinced him Tati was right.

Everything was going forward as planned, and our paperwork for emigrating to Chicago was almost completed. Peter Onkel had purchased our boat tickets and on the twenty-second of April we were leaving from Le Havre, France on the SS America.

Tati had told me this was such a big *Schiff* that it was almost as long as the whole length of our street and even higher than the buildings. Our street was long and the buildings were three and four stories high. I had a hard time trying to imagine such a big ship.

Arrangements had been made for the Doctor to come to our house *um uns zu impfen* – to vaccinate us. Everyone who entered the USA had to be re-vaccinated for smallpox.

My brother informed me that the doctor would cut off my arm. Why did I still believe everything he told me? I should have known better by then. When the doctor walked into our house, I stayed as far away from him as possible. We were in the kitchen when the doctor opened his bag. As he withdrew his hand from the satchel, my fears were confirmed. He had a small knife. I stared at the silver weapon that rested in his hand. He motioned to me, I was to be first. I started to cry, as he took my arm, I pulled away. Tati took hold of me. "Don't be such a baby," he demanded.

Both my parents now held me tight, but still I wiggled free. No way would I let the doctor do this terrible thing to me.

By now, all the adults were struggling to pin me down. Even Seppi was called to assist. Six hands held me. By this point, even the doctor was furious.

I watched helplessly as the knife point touched the skin on my upper arm. I screamed and closed my eyes. Two sharp cuts and it was over. Hands released me and – behold! – I still had my arm, with a *Pflaster* – band-aid – that the doctor had put on the cut. Now I felt foolish for having carried on like this. After all, I was already nine years old.

As soon as the doctor vaccinated the rest of my family, he rushed out of the house as if it were on fire. He must have thought I was the most spoiled child he had ever seen.

The next night I stayed with Franzvetter and Lisbasl Stark and I became so sick because of the vaccination that they had to bring me home early in the morning, I remember how disappointed I was.

I ended up with deep pock marks on my left arm. I believe it's because the doctor had lost his cool and wasn't too gentle with the procedure. I wonder if Seppi ever was sorry about the lie he told me.

I was to get a new pair of shoes, a pretty pair of dress shoes. Up until now I'd always gotten brown *Hochschuh*. They were very practical: laced to the top and tied securely at the ankle. There was nothing pretty about them. But now I was going to get a fancy pair of shoes for Easter and for when we left for America. Käthe's mother, Frau Ziesler, took both of us to the shoe store.

The store was located not far from *Waldfriedhofstrasse*, the end of the streetcar line. There were a few small shops in a single story building. This area was so different from the *Innenstadt* – inner city – where we lived. Between each building was an open space. The streets were wide, and most of the buildings were only one story high. There were no ruins, since the area had been newly built after the war.

In front of the store, a few feet from the curb, stood a small glass showcase all by itself. Displayed in the four-sided stand, resting on a white silk scarf next to a pair of shoes, was a fire red, patent leather *Schultertasche*.

"*Oh, is die scheen!*" I exclaimed. Käthe agreed with me. This was the prettiest purse she, too, had ever seen. It definitely was a purse you carried when you were all dressed up. I thought of the fine young ladies, dressed in their most elegant Sunday clothes, walking down our street. Their shoulder bags swayed in step with the clicking of their high heels.

Frau Ziesler interrupted our dreams. "Come along. We are to buy shoes, not purses." Reluctantly we turned from the display case and walked to the shoe store window.

All kinds of shoes were placed in different groupings and in the middle of the window, stood a pair of dainty, white slippers, with a thin strap across and silver buckles on each side.

"Die Schuh will ich!" I said. "I want those shoes!"

We went inside. Frau Ziesler explained to the salesman which shoes we wanted. He brought out the box and showed them to me. Then he put them on my small foot. Before he even had the buckles fastened, I could see they were much too wide. I stood up, hoping they might somehow fit if I walked in them. But my feet slipped in and out, as if feet and shoes wanted to move in different directions.

"I think the young lady would be better off with a pair of *Schnür-schuhe*," the salesman said.

"Ja," Frau Ziesler agreed.

I kept still, but inside I protested. "No, not shoes with laces. I want pretty dress shoes." If Mami had been with us I would have objected loud and clear. Since she wasn't, I kept my lips sealed.

Sadly I watched him walk away and come back with a few shoe boxes. He took out a pair of white *Halbschuh* and showed them to me. *"Wie gefallen dir diese?"* he asked. "How do you like these?" Small, patterned perforations covered the sides and tops of the shoes, making them look dainty and girlish. I nodded in approval. They didn't look that bad even if they did have laces. And they ended just under my ankles.

The man put the shoes on my feet. I walked back and forth. I liked them more and more. At least both feet and shoes moved in unison.

I have always wondered why I went with Frau Ziesler instead of my mother to buy the shoes. I recently found out it was because Herr Ziesler and my father had done some work for the shopkeeper. And Frau Ziesler was in charge of collecting the fee: two pairs of shoes.

New shoes were a big deal. In fact this was my first pair of fancy shoes since I was three years old, when Onkel's skilled hands had made my *Lackschuh* back home in Karlsdorf – they were shiny, black patented leather with a strap across.

The first thing I saw that Easter morning in 1950 was the *roti Schultertasch*, the same red purse Kaethe and I had admired in the showcase by the shoe store. It rested on the nightstand next to my nest that I had prepared for the *Osterhas*. I had not told anyone in my family about the purse. How did the Easter rabbit know I wanted it? I picked it up and hung it on my shoulder. Just the right length, I thought. Now I look like a real lady.

With all the excitement of the purse I had not even really looked at the contents of the Nest. There in the center, encircled by a few colorful eggs, was a *Zuckerhas*. The crystal red candy rabbit sat up on its hind legs, with a basket of eggs perched on its back. This was also a total surprise to me. All I had expected the night before when I prepared the Easter nest was a few eggs. I held the rabbit up to the light. It looked like a large red jewel. I thought the *Zuckerhas* was too pretty to be eaten, and set him back in the grass. But since he was made of candy, my taste buds won out, and a few days later, he was gone.

My red rabbit was the first and only one I have ever seen made of candy. I wonder how thrilled my kids would have been with an Easter bunny made of hard candy instead of chocolate. He might not even have been eaten, just like the Christmas candy canes that always stay in the bottom of the cookie jar, year in and year out.

The red purse was made only of plastic but to me it was priceless.

Mami braided my hair neatly and looped the braids on each side of my head. Then she tied two wide, plaid ribbons at the top of each loop, as was the fashion. We were going to get our picture taken at the *Fotograf*. This was my first time at a photographer's studio. We were going for our passport pictures.

Mami had made me a new dress. It was dark blue with a large sailor-type collar and a red tie knotted in the middle. Seppi got a store bought suit for the first time in his life. All dressed up in our Sunday best, we walked to the studio which was not far from the train station. The studio was a small room with lots of lights and a camera, a large square box stood on long spindly legs. Mami straightened my ribbons and made sure every hair was in place.

The photographer told me to sit on top of the high stool that stood in front of the camera. Bright lights shone from all directions. I sat quietly as I watched the man adjust his camera.

"Bitte still halten," he said as he snapped the picture. "Please hold still, I need to take a few more." I sat as motionless as a statue. In a few minutes it was all over and my image was frozen in time.

A skinny, large-eyed little girl with two big bows behind each ear and a faint smile looks out of that passport picture. The picture of the young boy with his hair slicked back show him to be just as thin as the girl. The pictures of the man and woman, in their thirties, don't reveal for one moment their hopes and fears of the future that must certainly have been on their minds.

At first glance, all that the pictures show are the faces of a happy family. No one would suspect what had gone on in our lives in the past six years. This could be said about most families during and after the war in all of Europe. Everyone had suffered.

After it was over, people had to pick up the broken pieces that were in the wake of the ugly monster called war. This is the nature of the beast. There is nothing romantic about war, except to people who have not lived through it.

My school days at *Tumblingerschule* were numbered. We had just a few more things to pack in the two large wooden boxes that Tati had made to hold our belongings. I couldn't understand why my doll furniture and my song book had to be left behind. Mami said there was not

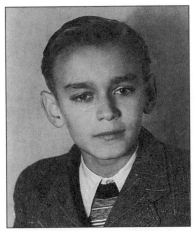

My brother Seppi's passport picture, 1950.   *My passport picture, 1950.*

enough room in the trunks. I was especially unhappy about leaving my song book, it was one of my most treasured possessions.

The day before, I had been called down to *Herr Rektor's* office. Never before had I been summoned there. I walked slowly, figuring I was in some kind of trouble. I couldn't imagine what I had done. When I opened the door, my eyes met a friendly face.

"*Grüss Gott, mein Kind,*" the smiling principal greeted me.

"Please sit down." I breathed a sigh of relief when I detected no hint of displeasure in his voice. "I have been informed that your family will sail for America. Won't you please tell me about it."

I told him my family's plans and where we were going, in very short sentences, I still was not so sure I wasn't in some kind of difficulty.

Then he opened his top drawer and pulled out a Hershey bar. My eyes almost popped out of my head. He handed me the chocolate and told me, "Elise, please take this small farewell present to remember us by and to wish you good luck.

"*Danke Schön, Herr Rektor!*" I curtsied and returned to my classroom. But I was baffled. Why would the principal give me such a prize? I was going to the land of plenty. Didn't he know that in America Hershey bars were everywhere? Why didn't he give it to one of the children who was staying here where *Schokolat* was a scarce commodity?

Winter was ending as spring pried loose the last frosty days. Lukewarm rays of early April sunshine streamed down on Käthe and me as we played outside, bouncing the colorful balls I had received for *Weihnachten* from Hans and the Eisers. We were not used to the luxury of playing with two of the same toy, since we usually had to share.

"*Du werscht immer mei beschti Freindin sein,*" I told her.

"You will always be my best friend. Even if we're miles apart."

"*Mir were uns immer Briefe schreiwe,*" Käthe reassured me.

"We'll always write letters to each other."

"And we'll visit each other when we're grown up."

"It will be so much fun." We made all kinds of plans and speculation the last days we were together. It was almost fun to guess what was going to happen in America. But inside I was already missing my best friend. Who would be my friend in Chicago? Would I even have one?

Jetz war's so weit. – The time was here for us to go. I wore my new two tone dress that Mami had made for our trip. She fashioned part of the bodice and skirt from a discarded beigy-rose plaid dress. But the material she used to make the sleeves and shoulders was new. To make sure it matched, she had taken me along to the store to help her pick it out. It was *schick und modern* – a chic, modern frock, perfect for a young lady.

I also wore my new white dress shoes with a nice patterned pair of matching knee socks. I felt pretty all the way to the ends of my looped pigtails tied with bows.

It was with mixed emotions that I walked out of our home for the last time and into the courtyard. All the excitement of the last few days had given our home a party atmosphere. But underneath the bustling of last minute preparations and the animated chatter about all the good things and great places we were going to experience in the new world, I felt a hard knot in the middle of my stomach.

All I had come to know and love would be changed. Every person place or thing, except for the objects in the two wooden trunks and the three people in my family, was going to be new. Even the language would be new.

The Sunday before we left, we paid a final visit to Tante Mitzi, Onkel Merzel and Tante Minna. As we said our tearful good byes, Tante Mitzi handed Mami a big box and told her this was a farewell present for us.

Inside the huge box were many different kinds of home baked cookies. Baking was not an easy task back then, for most of the ingredients were still under ration and it took some doing to make one kind of cookie, let alone so many. We deeply appreciated Tante Mitzies present.

This was the last time we were to see our adopted grandparents. It was also the last time we would see the families from our building as well as Familie Wackebauer. All had come outside to say their farewells and wish us luck. Little Terry looked so cute in her coat and bonnet. I had watched her grow from a tiny baby to a toddler. I had been her babysitter sometimes. She was like a little sister to me.

Tati took a picture of Käthe, Terry and me. And someone took a few family pictures of the four of us as well as some with our friends. The hardest was saying good-bye to Käthe. Again we promised to write and visit each other.

We walked to the train station, where many of our other friends had come to say good-bye, people who had been a part of our lives since we had come to Munich. Old friends and new: Starke, Eiser's, Bals Vetter,

Käthe, Terry and I on the day of our departure, April, 1950.

Ziesler's, Heffele's and many more. We hugged and kissed, our hearts were heavy, tears of joy as well as tears of sorrow flowing freely as we exchanged goodbyes. Everyone wished us luck and happiness as we boarded the train.

I remember standing by the open train window, my head outside the window, an arm outstretched. I waved as the train rolled away, more than a dozen arms waved back. Some we would never see again. Others, like Lisbasl, Franz Vetter and Resi Stark joined us in America. Many years later they babysat my children. A few handkerchiefs fluttered like flags of farewell, getting smaller as the train picked up speed, soon disappearing into the distance.

Our train rolled on through the Bavarian spring countryside, taking us to the city of Paris and then to the port of LeHavre where the steam ship "SS America" was waiting. Like the red poppy field waving in the breeze back home, I remember how the ocean waves rippled in the wind. In America there would be no barbed wire. In America, the land of many dreams and opportunities, there would be room for us all.

A year later, in Chicago at St. Vincent De Paul Church, I finally made my First Holy Communion. I wore a beautiful dress and veil. The dress was short, but still pretty. And as for the candle, it was not customary for a Communicant to receive and carry one to the altar here in America, but I got over that disappointment.

I had worried needlessly. My First Holy Communion was one of the happiest occasions in the first ten years of my life.

I lost touch with my best friend Käthe. I can't even form a mental picture of what she might look like as a grown woman. To me Käthe remains a warm smiling ten year old with dark eyes and pigtails. And she will forever remain my very first best friend. We helped each other grow up in a special way.

Our last family picture on the day we left Munich, April 1950.

On board the SS America, Mami, Seppi and I, April 1950.

CHAPTER
23

Summer 1977

I got off the train and looked around the terminal. Nothing had changed. The black, steel beams and glass roof were as sooty and gray as they were the day we left, though none of the beams or window panes were broken. And as the train pulled away, the same silvery tracks, running in every direction, greeted me, just as they had bid me farewell. A strange, quivering feeling passed over me. I stood on the same spot that I had left twenty-seven years before. This time I was not a child, but the wife and mother of the small group surrounding me.

"Mami, are we there now?" Michael, our five year old, asked. I gave him the same answer that I had given him many times before. "No, not yet."

"When?" asked his two sisters, Heidi, twelve, and Linda, nine.

"Soon, it won't be long now." Mike, my husband, reassured our three impatient children.

For many years I had dreamed of this day. How often had I told my children about Basl, Andres and Marie, and my childhood adventures in Munich, our home on Heberlstrasse, *Zirkus Krone, Christkindlmarkt,* and of course *Oktoberfest.* Now they would finally get to see the places I had loved.

What I wanted more than anything was to show my children Karlsdorf. To show them where there roots were. But this was impossible – for our Karlsdorf was only a place in our memory. It doesn't exist anymore; the new town of *Banatski Karlovac* is not Karlsdorf. It now belonged to citizens of Tito's Yugoslavia, who didn't even know that the houses they occupy had once belonged to Germans that had lived there for almost a hundred and fifty years.

A few weeks before, on the last day of May, we landed at Luxemburg Airport. As the plane came to a halt, I looked out the window and saw before me a welcoming field of poppies. I was traveling back to my childhood. Was this going to be a dream come true or a disappointment? Similar emotions would surface often during the next few weeks.

The next day as we drove through the Black Forest countryside on our way to my cousin Andres home, I thought of my mother's ancestors who had emigrated from this beautiful region down the Danube river. What had possessed them to leave this beautiful land and embark on a new and dangerous way of life in the swampy wilderness of *Banat*?

We drove down the narrow country roads, through small towns and hamlets, until we found ourselves in the village where Andres lived.

"This is the address," Heidi called out excitedly as we pulled up in front of the small white house. Susanne, Andres' daughter, and Heidi had become pen pals four years before.

As we stood in front of my cousins house I became a little nervous. I hoped he hadn't changed too much. Twenty eight years was a long time, and many things had happened since the last time we saw each other. The door swung open and there was Andres, looking just as I had pictured him – more mature but still the same.

"Elsa!" he cried.

"*Theres', Susanne, sie sein do,*" he called to his wife and daughter. "They're finally here." The two came rushing to greet us.

Seventeen year old Susanne greeted us in her best classroom English. "How do you do."

"*Mir kenne Deitsch,*" our nine year old spoke-up. "We know German, you don't have to speak English." Everyone burst out laughing and started to speak at once, hugging and talking, as if they had known each other all their lives.

After supper we adults sat in the living room deep in conversation, my cousin and I had a lot of catching up to do.

"What was it like when you got back to Karlsdorf?" I asked. "I know it was hard from your mother's letters."

"Every day I wished I was back in Germany," Andres said sadly.

"In Karlsdorf there remained about a hundred Germans. Not all were

Karlsdorfer. Many came from different towns after Tito abolished the camps in 1948. Although we lived among the Serbians, we were still considered less than the rest of the townspeople. In school we 'Schwabo' children were presumed to be inferior to the rest of the students. This provoked me to be even prouder of who I was. At the beginning I spoke only a few words of Serbian, but soon I overcame that barrier and became one of the best students in school."

"Were you able to return to your old house?"

"No. All four of us lived in a room that we rented from a family," Andres answered. "To get any kind of food, you had to stand in line for hours, and for meat a whole day. A few times we managed to buy two piglets. When the hogs were ready for butchering, we could keep one and the other we had to give to the government, not getting one Dinar in return.

"In 1951 Germans were allowed to leave Yugoslavia for a price. That's when most of our people left. They managed to scrape the money together somehow. Most sold everything they had, some leaving with only the clothes on their backs. I told myself, 'One way or another I'm going to be one of them.'"

"What did Vetter and Basl say about you leaving?" I asked him.

"I never really talked about it to them," he said. "In the fifties, Tito's government gave permission to own houses. To get a house you had to put up a bid for the houses available. The highest bidder got the house. At the time, I was only seventeen years old and a minor. But because I had a trade as a *Schuster* I made more money than my father, who was a laborer working at odd jobs. After my apprenticeship as a shoemaker, I scrimped and saved every bit of money I could get together to carry out my plan.

"I went to the *Gemeindehaus* – town hall – and went to the office of the clerk in charge, who knew me well. 'I'd like to put up a bid for a house!' I told him.

"He gave me a list of houses available and a form to fill out. When I handed it back to him with my bid, he looked at the signature and said, 'Andres, since when is your name Josef Pletitsch?'

"Of course my name is Josef. Don't you remember? Just take it and be quiet."

"A few days later I got the house which was now in my father's name. I kept up the payments until I left for Germany in 1956 at the age of twenty, with my wife and son. Before leaving I handed my mother and father the papers and told them it was all theirs. Now I could leave knowing my mother, father and my niece Zori (Marie's daughter Zoriza nicknamed Zori) had a roof over their heads."

The whole time I was listening to my cousin, one question burned in my mind: "What happened to Marie?" Finally I had the courage to ask. Andres became still, and looked away. The silence hung between us like a heavy curtain. I heard my heart pound in my ears as I waited for his answer. He must have been as afraid of this moment as I was.

He let out a sigh and looked down at his hands. Finally in a broken voice he said; "I'm sorry... I can't talk about it."

Andres' twenty-one year old son Josef, nicknamed Sepp, no longer lived at home but in the next town. When we met him the next day I had a hard time keeping my eyes off him. He was a carbon-copy of Andres, and both looked like their mother and grandmother, Basl.

That day our relatives gave us a guided tour of the region they called home. We drove through the mountainous Schwarzwald where we visited a *Bauernhof* Museum. The house and farm building had been restored as they had originally been built a few hundred years ago with thatched straw roofs, sloped gables and white washed walls criss crossed with dark wood beams. Inside were hand made furniture and farm implements of long ago. As we walked from building to building, I felt as if I had been here before.

The rest of the day we spent looking at a miniature storybook garden, a church located next to the small mansion of the then-world-famous Diana von Furstenburg, a princess, turned model. Our last stop was at a small, bubbling spring in *Donaueschingen*. It was hard to believe that this tiny well leaping out of the ground turned into the mighty *Donau*, the same Danube River that I waded in as a child and that also flowed in and out of my family's history.

The nine of us returned home in the evening tired and happy. I was especially grateful to have my second *Bruder* – brother – back. It was as if I had found a piece of myself that I didn't know I was missing. A piece of my broken childhood that I was trying to mend.

It was fun to watch our children getting to know each other. I noticed that our three started to lose their shyness and become more chatty with everyone, especially Susanne.

Susanne kept trying out her English, but since she had learned the "Queen's English" with a German accent, her American cousins could not always understand her. After a while they became impatient trying to decipher what she was saying, so they asked her, "Please, speak Deutsch so we can understand you better."

That evening we sat around once more, sipping wine and reminiscing and filling in our missing years.

"Wie lang hat's g'hol bis ihr eng einglebt hat in Amerika?" Andres asked.

"Oh, it took quite a while until we liked our new homeland," I replied.

Mami often said if someone would have given us the money to buy a one-way ticket back to Europe, we'd have taken the next boat.

My American Peter Onkel and Frieda Tante had no I idea what we had been through or that so many changes had taken place since they had left their homeland. They had come to America by choice, leaving everything and everyone behind, still associating with how things had been. Our family had been torn apart and ripped from our way of life. We had to leave to survive. Our two families were no more alike than aliens from different planets. We did not get along well because we didn't understand each other.

Our long time American relatives considered us to be less worldly. After all they had lived in the U.S.A. for over thirty years and we were only greenhorns from a small backward town with no plumbing – what did we know? They wanted us to live their way, dependent on them. But we wanted to live our way, independent and on our own. After four months, we parted company and came to live in Chicago," I continued.

"It wasn't as easy for my parents to learn English as it was for Seppi and me," I said. "But with time, patience and hard work, our family managed to get by."

I told him that the first years were the hardest. We had to pay off our boat tickets which were three thousand dollars. My father got a job as a cabinet maker, for eighty dollars a week. My mother was a piece-worker in a baby shirt factory. She sewed sleeves onto the shirts and received 14 cents per dozen. At the beginning she was slow, so her paychecks were small. As she got better her paycheck got bigger, and soon she was making thirty dollars a week.

At ten years old, it was hard for me to understand why my mother couldn't work at home as she had in Munich. I hated to come home to an empty house every day. I'd look under the bed to make sure no one was hiding there.

I missed Munich. At first when I went to school in the small town of Barrington, all the children were nice to me; but after we moved to Chicago I was called names. I was often called "Nazi" and many times the third grade teacher referred to me as "the foreigner".

"Mami, hawe mir bal' genuch Geld das du nimmer arweide gehn muscht?" Every night I'd ask the same question. "Do we have enough money now so you won't have to work anymore?" But her answer was always the same. "Not yet." After a year we finally paid off our debt, but Mami still had to work because we needed the money.

And in the winter of 1951 Mutter, who was seventy two years old came to America. I remember waiting at Midway Airport for her plane to land. What excitement! My brother Joe, as Seppi was now called, was just as eager as I was. I had never seen an airplane on the ground before. I watched all the people get off the plane, but I didn't see Mutter.

"Look, there she is," Tati said pointing. I saw only a small, old woman hobbling towards the waiting room.

That can't be Mutter, I thought. She's so small. She's only as tall as I am.

"Elsa, mei Kind," she cried as she hugged and kissed me. "My child how you have grown."

I wasn't the only one that had changed. Gone was her dark, grey-streaked hair – it was white as snow. And all her teeth were missing, making her face small and wrinkled. The eyes behind wire-rimmed glasses held together with string, sparkled as she smiled. Although her face was worn and tired, Mutter's smile was still the same.

Mutter and I became closer than ever. For four years until I was fourteen, we slept together on the living room couch. She was my link to our family's history. Every night she'd tell me about her childhood, and how at the age of ten she became a *Dienschtmagd* – maidservant – for the Rumanian priest in our neighboring town of Nikolenz. About her first husband and children and my grandfather and Tati. And of course of the pain and suffering she and my Oma and Ota Schüssler experienced in Rudolfsgnad.

Since she was the only grandparent I had left – she and I were the oldest and youngest members in our family – we experienced a special bond.

"I remember when your grandmother left Karlsdorf," Andres said, "I was fifteen at the time, and I wished I could have gone with her. I thought of America as the land of plenty because of your packages. You know that if it had not been for the packages you sent us, life would have been almost impossible in Karlsdorf.

"People used to knock at our door to see if we got anything new. Once you sent us a bathing suit. Items like that were a scarce commodity for miles around. We got more Dinars for it than what we could earn in a week."

"I remember that bathing suit," I said. "I always helped mother decide what to put in the _Packet_ because we were allowed to send only so many pounds.

"And when we received it, the package usually weighed half as much, for the Yugoslav customs officers helped themselves."

"I'm sure life was much harder in Yugolsavia than by us in America," I said. "Even during hard times when money was in short supply, we always had enough to eat. Although at the beginning not all was a bed of roses."

In the spring of 1952 Tati got sick and had to stay in the hospital for six weeks. We ended up owing $3000 in hospital bills. The insurance company claimed that his illness was a pre-existing condition: therefore they didn't have to pay a penny.

This made my mother the sole breadwinner in our family. But feeding five people on thirty dollars a week was impossible. She quit her job at Rubens Baby Shirt Co. and went to work in a rubber factory for fifty dollars a week, which still barely covered our living expenses.

The heat and the smell from the melted rubber were sometimes unbearable. In the summertime, the only breeze moving through the ancient building was from a few open windows. The workers were mostly greenhorns – women like my mother, willing to put up with the sweat and hard labor to earn a few dollars more. The majority of them were _Donauschwaben._

Six months went by until my father got well and could return to work and after a year we managed to pay off our bills. In the summer of 1954 we bought our first house and three years later my father started his own business. For the last twenty years Tati ran his cabinet shop and Mami was his secretary. And on the weekends they spend their time with their five grandchildren, who adore them.

"And how has life treated my 'Bruder Sepp'?" Andres asked.

"Seppi is happily married, has two beautiful children, owns his own home and works for a good company as a CPA." I told him. "We've come a long way since we arrived in America with only our two wooden trunks and the clothing on our backs.

"Yes! I believe we're all happy. Mike and I have a good family life, we own a house and have our own business. We belong there. How about you? Are you happy here?" I asked.

"Oh yes!" Andres nodded, smiling. "We're glad to live here."

"At first Theres and I had a hard time starting out. We had left both of our families behind and found ourselves totally alone and with almost nothing to our name. I was only twenty years old with a wife and baby. We had to start building a new life and had no one to lend a hand. The trade of shoemaker was not such a good one as it had been in Karlsdorf. I ended up with a low paying job in a shoe factory. It took many years until we were on our feet again. We wanted more out of life than just making ends meet. We wanted a house and a good future for our children. So I looked around and worked in different factories trying to find a new line of work.

"After a few years I found a place that paid well and I liked what I was doing. Soon I even had a few men working under me and life looked much brighter. After both children were in school, Theres also went to work. Soon we were able to save enough money to buy a lot.

"I slowly began to build our new house with my own two hands. It took a few years until it was finished – progress is slow when money is in short supply and the builder can only work in the evenings and on weekends. But eventually our small dream house was complete."

"You certainly did a professional job. You can be proud of your work." I told him.

"Thank you," he said, as he grinned proudly. "Times are getting better all the time. We now can even enjoy a few luxuries in life."

We spent four days with Andres and his family. During that time our families grew closer, especially Andres, Theres, Mike and I. In the evenings we reminisced about back home.

"You know Andres, every time we received a letter from Basl, the four of us would gather around Mami and listen as she read out loud. For a few minutes we would be together again."

"Life was hard for my mother and father." Andres said.

"Near the end of the fifties only two *Schwowe* families remained in Karlsdorf. Everyone else had left."

"She used to write us about their dilemma," I said. "How Zori's father wouldn't let them take her to Germany."

"He was heartless. He didn't want his daughter but he wasn't going to let her go. He made hell on earth for my parents," Andres said.

"Not until Zori was fourteen did he finally sign the papers for her to leave Yugoslavia."

I remembered the letters Basl sent us. Life was nothing but heartaches for her. Not only did she lose her daughter, she was powerless to remove her grandchild from this land of poverty. She also developed cancer. Because medical facilities in Yugoslavia were so bad, the cancer was never properly taken care of. She finally did join her son and his family in Germany. Basl died in 1969 at the age of fifty nine after only three years of life in the free world.

All those years my mother and her sister remained close, even if only on paper. It must have been hard for both of them not to speak or embrace during their time of pain. But both were strong and so was their love and friendship.

Five years before, in 1972, Vetter, Basl's husband, had come to visit us in America. The month that he stayed with my parents helped us get re-acquainted, since I had no memory of him from back home. To me he was only a person who I knew through Basl's letters and through my parent's stories. He was an old, old man next to my parents. Life had also chipped away at him. He was soft-spoken and I somehow felt less angry with him for taking my Basl and cousins back to Karlsdorf. Times were hard, and who knows why things happened the way they did. When he left, I felt sorry that we had so little time together.

In 1974 Vetter also developed cancer, cancer of the mouth, and to save his life his lower jaw was amputated. His face was disfigured and it was hard for him to talk and eat. He died in his eighties in 1987.

All visits must come to an end. When we left Andres and his family, we knew this was not the last time we would see each other.

"Don't you wait twenty eight years until you come to see us." I told Andres.

"We'll come to see you in a few years. I'd like to see how my American relatives live," he said jokingly.

We hugged and said our farewells cheerfully. The world was shrinking. We could visit by phone or by plane.

Before we left, Theres gave each of our children a *Tafel Schokolat* to snack on. Giving visiting children chocolate bars, to our offsprings' delight, was a common custom in Europe. By the end of our trip they had eaten quite a few and still had about ten left when we boarded our flight back home. What a change from when I lived in Germany.

"It sure is different here than back home," my son Michael said. "They don't only speak German in the *Märchenbuch* – storybooks. They speak German all over." Every night or before nap time I had made a ritual of reading books to my children. Michael's favorite was his thick German fairy tale book that had to be read daily.

Yes, everything was different from back home. The mountaintops covered with snow made for some excitement. We had to stop and have a snowball fight. Old churches with ancient art work created before a white man ever set foot in the Americas – this impressed us more than it did our children. What left the biggest impression on them were the castles, especially on our girls. Once we ate in a small castle, high on a mountain overlooking Salzburg.

"Do you think the princess might have sat at this same table?" Heidi asked Linda in a hushed tone.

"Of course – this *is* the royal dining room. Where else would she have had her lunch?"

When we got to Augsburg we stayed with my mother's cousins Marie Tant and Schüsslers Kathi Tant. Both spoiled our children by making all their wishes a command.

Augsburg was only a short train ride from Munich so we decided to take the train and spend the day exploring all the places I had told my family about.

We were almost at the end of our vacation. I had hoped to spend more time in my beloved München. But we could stay only for the day.

"Come on, lead the way, Mami," my family commanded, pulling toward the waiting room of the station. "Show us your old home."

As we entered the waiting room I was expecting to see a large cavernous building, but it was much smaller than I had remembered. Small shops were on both sides, with a few small booths in the center. People rushed in every direction, their footsteps echoed through the place. No trace of shrapnel was to be seen anywhere; all the signs of war had been erased.

We walked through the high doorway and out to the streets. I found myself in a foreign place. I knew that there would be no more ruins, but I expected at least some buildings that I would recognize.

As we stood on the steps of the *Bahnhof*, I looked down the streets that lead to our old apartment, trying to figure out which one we should follow.

"Let's go Mom. Which way?" Linda clamored.

"Don't rush me. It's been a long time and everything has totally changed," I said. "Including me."

I chose one of the streets and led the way, with the others right behind me. I started to get nervous when nothing looked familiar. I was looking for the large intersection with the high platform in the middle. As I child I used to watch the policeman stationed on top, directing traffic, his arms and hands performing a dance of their own to the tune of his shrill whistle.

We came to the Sendlinger Tor intersection. The name was correct but everything else looked unfamiliar.

"Are we lost, Mami?" a small voice piped up behind me.

"Of course not," I answered. "Everything is just not the same."

"Maybe we should ask someone where Heberlstrasse is," my husband suggested.

"No. I'll find it."

We continued down the busy street. Cars were parked on both sides. One bicycle after the other whizzed past us on the small path allotted them on the sidewalk. Things sure had changed since 1950. "In the next ten years Munich will be rebuilt, and no more trace of *Ruine* will remain," my brother had told me. He was right. We saw no trace of a ruin or signs that there had ever been a war.

We continued on, everything still looked strange to me. Finally I saw a familiar street sign: "Göthe Strasse."

"We have to go down that street!" I exclaimed as I rushed toward it.

A feeling of relief came over me when I spotted the hospital. It looked the same. The large basement windows with the thick, patterned glass were still there, all closed tight.

"No way to see if there are any cut up bodies down there." I chuckled to myself. A large sign across the entrance proclaimed it to be an Eye Care Hospital now.

We came to Göthe Platz. There were so many cars it was impossible to cross. A sign in front of us stated: pedestrians use underground passage.

Our little group entered the underground tunnel and looked for the Heberlstrasse sign. I felt like a total stranger in a place I thought I knew like the back of my hand.

"You never told us about the tunnel," my children said.

"That's because when I lived here, there was no tunnel."

We found the Heberlstrasse exit and walked up the steps, I expected this also to be totally changed, but to my surprise the street, with the exception of the restored and repaired buildings, looked the same. Heberlstrasse #8 was just as I remembered it!

I opened the heavy, wooden door and stepped into the cavernous gangway and felt the cool air surround us. Our footsteps echoed on the worn cobblestones as we walked through and stepped out into the sunlit courtyard.

Time had stood still. Nothing had changed, with the exception of a few straggly bushes that grew on the side of the neighbor's fence. A strange feeling came over me that is hard to describe. I was here, yet I did not belong. I wanted more than anything to go inside and enter our *Wohnung*. But the apartment was not for me to enter. Others were living there, and I didn't have the nerve to go and knock on the door.

For a minute I felt frozen in time, alone with my feelings and thoughts. This place had been a part of my life. Seeing, touching, feeling, hearing and breathing the very same air as the people who lived there with me in this small world of my childhood. As I looked around I "saw" my family and friends laughing, playing, coming and going. Ghosts of the past, here beside me, coming back to live in the present.

I was jolted back to reality by my son impatiently jerking on the hem of my skirt. "Mami! Mami!" he cried. Pointing to the patch of earth under our old bedroom window. "Where is the grass? This garden has nothing in it but dirt. Our yard is much nicer back home."

The girls complained, too. "Let's go. There is nothing to see here. This is boring."

Disappointment welled up in me. "Just give me a few minutes more," I said. I had expected my family to feel the same way about this place as I did – which of course was impossible. After all, they had no connection to it except through my stories.

Touching me on the shoulder my husband said, "No need to get angry, Schatz. Just take your time."

After a few minutes I turned around and we stepped back into the gangway.

"Let's look for Tersep's Kathi Tant's name on the mail box," I said.

"Tersep, Tersep, I don't see the name. "Are you sure she still lives here?" Mike asked.

"That's what I was told by my mother."

We looked among the many mail boxes that lined the wall. We were about to give up when an older, white-haired woman came walking through the front door.

"*Grüssgott!*" she said, by way of greeting.

"*Gutentag!*" we answered.

"*Suchen Sie Jemand?*" she asked.

"*Ja, Bitte.* We're looking for a Frau Tersep. Do you know if she lives in this building?"

The woman gave us a puzzled look and said, "Why yes. That's my mother. She lives with me, I'm Katherina Muck." I looked into the woman's face. Why, it was Kathi Tant!

"*Kathi Tant! Kenscht mich net?*" I blurted out. Her face showed no recognition. "You still don't who I am, do you?" I laughed. "I'm Elsa, Elsa Hugery."

"*Elsa! Mein gott von wuh kumscht du her?* – My god, Elsa where did you come from?" she cried as we embraced.

I introduced my family to Kathi Tant and asked if she still lived in the back building. "Oh no, I've lived in the front building for years." She invited us to come upstairs, showed us her apartment and offered us something to eat.

Kathi Tant turned to the children and said in perfect English, "I bet you're hungry. I'll make you some good Bologna sandwiches."

All three looked at her in amazement. "You speak American. Where did you learn to speak English?"

"I was born in New York City, where I lived until I was fourteen. I'm American just like you." she told them.

I was just as amazed as the rest of my family. I knew she could speak English, but I never questioned why. Tersep's Kathi Tant was the one person I always was a little afraid of. She was a tall woman with a matter-of-fact way about herself, and when she spoke her re-sounding voice echoed authoritatively throughout the room. When-ever my mother wanted me to do something and I didn't listen, she'd say, "Do you want Kathi Tant to come over to tell you what to do?" I immediately did what I was told.

As we sat eating lunch, I watched as she joked with the children. I thought back to those days in the late forties and smiled to myself. How foolish I was back then to have feared her. She was only about five foot-four, her gray hair had softened her face, and the only thing loud about her was her rollicking laugh, which my children loved. I told her that I had no idea that Tersep was her maiden name.

"No one ever called me by my married name," she said. "To all the Karlsdorfer's I was still Tersep's Kathi."

"Wait till I get back home," I kidded, "I'll let my parents know that they shouldn't expect their daughter to learn things through osmosis. If we hadn't run into you, we would have presumed that you didn't live here anymore."

"We meet again, just as your father and I did when he came back from Russia," she said. "Funny how things happen sometimes."

I asked her about her family and the other neighbors in the building. She told me that all had moved away. They were all well except for Herr und Frau Wackebauer. Herr Wackebauer died many years ago, and Frau Wackebauer had just died the year before.

"Whatever happened to your parrot, Laura?"

"Do you know she just died this year. She was a tough old bird," Kathi Tant said with a smile.

We said our good-byes and invited her to come and see us if she ever came back to America.

Kathi Tant did come to visit us three years later. We had a great time over dinner and talked more about the good old days. Shortly after she returned to Munich, she passed away. I'm happy that I got to know her when I was an adult. She was a good hearted lady.

We walked out of the building and headed towards my old school. We passed the *Metzgerladen* – butcher shop – which also had not changed much from the outside. Crossing over to the other side of the street we came to the *Paulaner Brauerei* at the corner of Heberl and Tumblinger Strassen.

"Do you want to go inside?" Mike asked.

"Yes, for old time's sake."

We entered the small *Bier Stube* and sat down. "This looks just like a restaurant," the children said. "I though you said that it was a beer store."

"You can just buy beer or eat here," I said. "Let's all have something to drink".

We ordered two beers for us and the children each had a Spätzi, which is a popular soft drink in southern Germany – a mixture of lemonade and coke.

"You know this is only the second time that I've actually had something to drink here in the Brauerei," I told my family. "Tante Mitzi brought me here one summer to their beer Fest which was held outside in the small courtyard.

"Tante Mitzi ordered a large *Mass Bier* for me. The stein was so big that I had to hold it with both hands."

"You mean you actually drank a whole stein of beer when you were just nine years old," my children asked.

"I thought it was real beer but in reality it was a large stein of 'near beer'," I laughed.

We left the *Brauerei* and walked up Tumblinger Strasse to show my children were their Onkel Joe and I went to school. We came to the school and I hardly recognized it. It looked so stately with its restored third floor and roof. A fenced in yard with clipped grass and bushes adorned the front. What a far cry from when I was a student there.

"Let's go inside," my family declared. "I don't think so. It's been so long ago, I would not know what to say to anyone." I said.

"Ah, come on it will be fine," Mike said, taking me by the arm and somewhat pulling me. I felt like a child again – too nervous to go to the entrance door.

"No, I don't think so, it's late, we might miss our train."

"Okay," he shrugged. "If you don't want to we can go."

I looked back with mixed feelings as we walked back toward Heberlstrasse. I yearned to go inside but lacked the courage.

We walked past Heberlstrasse #8. I gazed at my old home for a minute and silently said: "Good-bye for now – someday I will be back." We continued past Götheplatz and up towards the park.

Die Bavaria still reigned over her beloved *Theresien Wiese*. The children ran ahead and up the stair leading to the great lady. "Look, you can go inside," Heidi called back to us. "*Bitte* Tati, can we go up and look out, please, please," all three begged.

Of course we let them. Mike took our youngest and marched up the stairs with the kids as I remained outside so that they could wave to me.

"Mami, Mami, we can see real far!" Linda called to me.

"Yes, real, real far!" Michael echoed. "This is fun."

My heart skipped happily as I listened to my children's laughter from the top. This is what I had longed for, to show my three a part of my childhood. Although I don't recall ever going inside the Bavaria I now shared her and my kingdom with my family.

Mike and I walked across the *Wies* and watched our children frolic in the grassy meadow.

"It's time to go," my husband told me.

"Yes," I said, "its time to go back home, where we now belonged."

We walked out of the park, back down towards Heberlstrasse. When we came to my old street I said; "There's one place that we haven't seen, let's stop by the *Milchladen*. Its only a few houses in."

"Okay. We have a little time left," Mike said.

The small milk store was still there and looked just as I had remembered. I reached for the ornate iron door latch – half expecting the tiny store to be the same as it had been in my childhood. It was a disappointment to find that the large milk vat which had spread almost across the entire 12 foot wide store was replaced by a refrigerator. And there were no groups of people, milk cans in hand, waiting to be served.

An older lady behind the counter greeted us cheerfully.

"Can I help you?"

"Well, not really, I'm more or less just re-visiting your store. I used to buy milk here as a child." I said.

"How nice," she said.

"Would you know what ever happened to the lady who we all called *"Milch Anna*?" I asked.

"Why, yes, I'm Anna."

I looked at her more closely and sure enough it was the same lady who served me so many years before.

"We're here on vacation from the U.S.A.," I told her, "and I wanted to show my family were I grew up."

I'm sorry I can't remember you," she said, "but I am happy you came from so far to my small establishment."

Before we left, I pointed to the shelf stocked with sweets and told my children they could each buy a chocolate bar. I did it as a token to my own childhood...when there was far too little chocolate.

About the Author

Elizabeth Walter has been involved in the visual arts for most of her life. Ms. Walter taught oil painting to children for more than nine years; in addition taught the basics of art at St. Anne's Grade School in Barrington for five years. Today, art still plays a major role in her life; she still paints, draws and now has taken up printmaking.

For the past twenty-seven years Ms. Walter has been the director of the "Kindergruppe—children's group" of the Chicago American Aid Society of German Descendants, a cultural group founded to help displaced "Danauschwaben—Danube-Swabiens" after World War II. The group folkdances, sings and performs plays in German.

Ms. Walter was born in Karlsdorf, Yugoslavia. She spent three years in a Yugoslav Communist concentration camp AFTER World War II. Why? Because she was an ethnic German. She and her mother and brother escaped on foot across Hungary and half way across Austria. After scaling a mountain range, they reached the American Zone. Finally they reunited with Ms. Walter's father in bombed out Munich. In 1950, when Elizabeth was nine years old, the family immigrated to the United States and started their new life in Chicago, IL.

Ten years ago, Ms. Walter started writing down her experiences for her children. Since then, she has become "addicted" to writing. She has had some short stories published in a German-language newspaper and a magazine. Her book BAREFOOT IN THE RUBBLE is included in the bibliography of the Holocaust Memorial Foundation of Illinois.

On September 8, 1998, Ms. Walter received the American Legion Auxillary 1998 WOMAN OF THE YEAR award for sharing her personal story of survival in the face of physical and emotional suffering, by writing the book BAREFOOT IN THE RUBBLE, to inform the public about the inhumanity of post-war ethnic cleansing that continues to this day.

On October 12, 1998 to October 16, 1998 BAREFOOT IN THE RUBBLE was displayed in the Senate Russel Rotunda in Washington D.C. entitled "ETHNIC CLEANSING 1944–1950 The expulsion of ethnic Germans".

On October 12, 1999 she spoke at the INTERNATIONAL GERMAN AMERICAN BOOK FAIR at Wayne State University in Michigan.

Elizabeth and her husband, Mike, live in a suburb of Chicago. They have three grown children and three grandchildren.